GENDER $\underline{IN}$ HISTORY

Series editors:
Pam Sharpe, Patricia Skinner and Penny Summerfield

The expansion of research into the history of women and gender since the 1970s has changed the face of history. Using the insights of feminist theory and of historians of women, gender historians have explored the configuration in the past of gender identities and relations between the sexes. They have also investigated the history of sexuality and family relations, and analysed ideas and ideals of masculinity and femininity. Yet gender history has not abandoned the original, inspirational project of women's history: to recover and reveal the lived experience of women in the past and the present.

The series Gender in History provides a forum for these developments. Its historical coverage extends from the medieval to the modern period, and its geographical scope encompasses not only Europe and North America but all corners of the globe. The series aims to investigate the social and cultural constructions of gender in historical sources, as well as the gendering of historical discourse itself. It embraces both detailed case studies of specific regions or periods, and broader treatments of major themes. Gender in History titles are designed to meet the needs of both scholars and students working in this dynamic area of historical research.

Women of the right spirit

MANCHESTER
1824

Manchester University Press

ALSO AVAILABLE
IN THE SERIES

Gender, myth and materiality in an island community:
Shetland, 1800–2000
Lynn Abrams

'The truest form of patriotism':
pacifist feminism in Britain, 1870–1902
Heloise Brown

Masculinities in politics and war: gendering modern history
Stefan Dudink, Karen Hagemann and John Tosh (eds)

Noblewomen, aristocracy and power
in the twelfth-century Anglo-Norman realm
Susan Johns

The business of everyday life:
gender, practice and social politics in England, c. 1600–1700
Beverly Lemire

The independent man:
citizenship and gender politics in Georgian England
Matthew McCormack

WOMEN OF THE RIGHT SPIRIT

PAID ORGANISERS OF THE WOMEN'S SOCIAL AND POLITICAL UNION (WSPU) 1904–18

━━ Krista Cowman ━━

Manchester University Press
Manchester and New York

distributed exclusively in the USA by Palgrave

Copyright © Krista Cowman 2007

The right of Krista Cowman to be identified as the author of this work has been asserted by her in accordance with the Copyright, Designs and Patents Act 1988.

Published by Manchester University Press
Oxford Road, Manchester M13 9NR, UK
and Room 400, 175 Fifth Avenue, New York, NY 10010, USA
www.manchesteruniversitypress.co.uk

Distributed exclusively in the USA by Palgrave
175 Fifth Avenue, New York,
NY 10010, USA

Distributed exclusively in Canada by UBC Press
University of British Columbia, 2029 West Mall,
Vancouver, BC, Canada V6T 1Z2

British Library Cataloguing-in-Publication Data
A catalogue record for this book is available from the British Library

Library of Congress Cataloging-in-Publication Data applied for

ISBN   978 0 7190 7002 0   *hardback*

First published 2007

16 15 14 13 12 11 10 09 08 07   10 9 8 7 6 5 4 3 2 1

Typeset in Minion with Scala Sans display
by Northern Phototypesetting Co Ltd, Bolton
Printed in Great Britain
by Biddles, King's Lynn

To my daughter, Freddie –
some wholly inappropriate role models

Contents

List of figures

Acknowledgements

I wish to acknowledge the financial support of the British Academy, the Arts and Humanities Research Council, the Leeds Philosophical and Literary Society and the School of Cultural Studies, Leeds Metropolitan University, each of which facilitated the research for this book. I am grateful also to the Department of History at the University of York for hosting my visiting fellowship during which the writing was done. Individuals at a number of libraries and record offices helped with research queries, and I express my thanks to Beverley Cook at the Museum of London, Gail Malmgreen at the Tamiment Library, New York, Kate Perry at Trinity College, Cambridge, James Peters at Manchester University, Mary Ann Prior and Lindsay Stainton at Camellia; my thanks go also to the staff at: Birmingham City Art Gallery; the Bodleian Library, Modern Papers room; the British Library; the Fryer Library, University of Queensland; Gloucester Record Office; the National Library of Scotland; Nottinghamshire Record Office; the University of East Anglia; and the Women's Library, London, along with Warwick Taylor Kenney and Betty Miessner. Many colleagues and friends have been generous with both time and critical suggestions, particularly Diane Atkinson, James Chapman, Elizabeth Crawford, Barry Doyle, Mary Eagleton, Simon Gunn, June Hannam, David Howell, Jon Lawrence, June Purvis, Ruth Robbins, Miles Taylor and Susan Watkins. Thanks also to my husband, Jim Sharpe; to Guy and Elfreda Cowman-Sharpe, for living through the whole process with good grace; and to my mum, Joan, for everything.

All efforts have been made to trace the copyright holders of archive material. The publisher apologises for any unintentional omission and will be pleased to insert the appropriate acknowledgement in any subsequent edition of this book.

Introduction

There really is nothing in my life worth writing about. I was born in 1865 ... I did not realise the importance of the women's vote until the militant movement began. I was not in the least opposed to it, but did not see that it mattered. The reaction to militancy opened my eyes ... I left home to work for the vote which I did till war broke out, going to prison twice and being forcibly fed once ... it really does not seem worth while writing this down.[1]

It seems to me now, looking back, that all my previous life had been a preparation for this great experience. While indirectly it caused me much sorrow, it brought me many contacts which have immeasurably enriched my life ... the struggle of women seemed like the quest of the Holy Grail.[2]

THESE OBSERVATIONS WERE MADE by prominent members of the Women's Social and Political Union (WSPU), the militant organisation formed by Emmeline Pankhurst in October 1903 with the aim of obtaining the parliamentary vote for women. The difference between the attitudes expressed by these two ex-suffragettes encapsulates the paradox that has faced historians who have attempted to investigate the WSPU. The first speaker, Lettice Floyd, had not always been so reticent about her involvement in militancy, but had worked as an assistant to Annie Williams, one of the WSPU's longest serving organisers, in Newcastle, Huddersfield and Cardiff. Yet by the time she was approached by ex-colleagues eager to add her own personal version of the suffrage campaign to other memoirs being collected by the Suffragette Fellowship, she had no desire at all to participate. She was living in quiet retirement with Miss Williams, who did not respond at all. Their attitude towards their own suffragette pasts was replicated by hundreds, if not thousands, of other women throughout the country, and has frustrated researchers who seek new perspectives on the militant campaign.

The second speaker's enthusiasm for her WSPU work presents a different problem. Although Hannah Mitchell left the WSPU, after a breakdown in health, in 1908, she returned to political life via the Women's Freedom League (WFL) and remained active in politics, becoming a city councillor after the First World War. She and other activists left more formally crafted memoirs marked by what the historian Sandra Holton has described as a 'golden aura of nostalgia' for 'their participation in the votes-for-women campaigns [which were] a transformative experience or the high point of their lives, or both.'[3] One explanation for the marked differences in perspective from which women who had worked alongside each other viewed their time in the WSPU lies in the divergent trajectories followed by ex-suffragettes after the First World War. Some clearly regarded their time in the WSPU as a closed chapter in their lives once the vote was won. Others felt that creating a suffrage history was an essential task for feminists, and one which was as much part of the overall campaign as their pre-war work had been. By the 1930s, those who tended towards the latter perspective grouped around the Suffragette Fellowship, which formed in 1926 'to perpetuate the memory of the pioneers and outstanding events connected with women's emancipation and especially with the militant suffrage campaign, 1905–14'.[4] To this end, the Fellowship held regular meetings commemorating key events in the militant movement. Initiatives for broader recognition were also pursued, including the erection of a statue to Emmeline Pankhurst in London, an additional tablet at its base commemorating Christabel Pankhurst and a plaque at the Free Trade Hall, Manchester, the site of the first suffragette arrests. The leaders of the Suffragette Fellowship also began to solicit, collect and preserve accounts and memorabilia from as many ex-militants as could be traced.

Building on the friendship networks of its early members, the Suffragette Fellowship was able to shape the narratives of much 'first-wave' suffrage history. A project was begun to compile a 'Book of Suffragette Prisoners', and to that end a questionnaire was sent out to as many as could be traced, requesting details of specific acts of militancy, including arrests and imprisonments. As a result of this initiative, much of the material which came into the Fellowship's London reading room and formed the basis of the Suffragette Fellowship Collection, now preserved in the Museum of London, was thus shaped from the outset by the prison experience. In many ways, this was understandable. Militancy was what distinguished the WSPU (and the WFL, whose members also participated in the Suffragette Fellowship's initiative) as a suffrage society. In the post-vote era, many ex-suffragettes were anxious both to protect the memory of their work and to refute suggestions that militancy had had no part in their victory. Nevertheless, an undue focus on the prison experience – which was shared by only just over 1,000 suffragettes, a small percentage of the overall membership – unwittingly underplayed the other work done by numerous women in pursuit of the vote.[5] The WSPU was a large and autonomous women's organisation, which employed over 150 full-time workers between 1904 and 1914, alongside innumerable part-time volunteers and honorary officials such as branch secretaries, literary secretaries and branch treasurers. The attention on individuals' journeys towards prison within the autobiographical material collected by the Suffragette Fellowship led many historians to emphasise such activity in accounts of the WSPU at the expense of considering or evaluating less obvious or exciting contributions. Consequently, while we have detailed outlines of the chronology of the suffrage campaign and of specific experiences of militancy, very little is known about how the WSPU functioned as an organisation, how it recruited and retained a membership, and what constituted suffragette activism on a day-to-day basis.

While the Suffragette Fellowship was engaged in collecting memorabilia and autobiographical fragments, some suffragettes attempted to construct a narrative of the work of the WSPU on a larger scale. Sylvia Pankhurst published *The Suffragette Movement* in 1931.[6] Although the work is highly autobiographical, Sylvia's proximity to her subject matter offered a wealth of detail on the leaders of the campaign, particularly her mother Emmeline and younger sister Christabel. Sylvia's account was not popular in certain quarters of the Suffragette Fellowship, but Christabel's perspective, *Unshackled*, was not published until after her death in 1958[7] The first attempt by a non-participant to interpret the WSPU proved equally controversial: Roger Fulford's *Votes for Women*, which appeared in 1957, was not overly sympathetic to militancy as a tactic, nor was he wholly approbatory in his assessment of Emmeline Pankhurst's leadership.[8] The furious reaction to his work on the part of many ex-suffragettes, which was augmented when Fulford's liberal sympathies were discovered, did little to inspire others to approach the subject.[9] Neither, more surprisingly, did the emergence in Britain in the 1970s of women's history as a distinct category. Although there were still a number of suffragettes surviving at this time, the close connections between socialist and feminist history led most historians away from the WSPU to the constitutional National Union of Women's Suffrage Societies (NUWSS), which formed an electoral alliance with the Labour Party in 1912.[10] The ironies of this were clearly visible during the 1978 celebrations of the fiftieth anniversary of the 1928 Equal Franchise Act. The life-long socialist suffragette Connie Lewcock, who organised an arson attack on a railway station, listened as Conservative MP Sally Oppenheim informed her that 'suffragettes were noted for their dignity', while contemporary figures from the second-wave feminist movement, excluded from the invitation list, heckled from the sidelines in a parody of the activities of those whom the event purported to celebrate.[11] Meanwhile, Jilly Cooper, sent by *The Sunday Times* to interview Sybil Morrison, reported that the former militant had confounded her expectations by being 'a jolly Junoesque figure ... a kind of Voter Sackville-West [sic]', generous with her servings of whisky and gin.[12]

The 1980s witnessed a revival of interest in the women's suffrage movement among feminist historians working on British history, who sought to 'position the women's suffrage movement within the broader context of women's struggles to achieve justice and freedom'.[13] New organisations, including the WFL, the United Suffragists, the Men's League for Women's Suffrage and the Women Writers' Suffrage League, appeared in histories which broadened understanding of the scope of the movement beyond that of the WSPU.[14] There were also several studies influenced by the attention given to recovering 'lost' figures of women's history, which restored the stories of forgotten or neglected women to the dominant narrative of suffrage – figures such as Jennie Baines, Mary Leigh, Dora Montefiore and Mary Richardson.[15] Local studies formed another important aspect of feminist reappraisals of the suffrage movement, as they challenged impressions drawn from a national perspective while recognising that the majority of suffragettes who engaged with the movement did so in their *local* branch rather than in London.[16] Elizabeth Crawford's impressive study *The Women's Suffrage Movement: A Reference Guide* offers an excellent starting point for researchers, providing chronological and biographical information on hundreds of suffrage activists but the book's status as a work of reference offers little space to comparative discussion of the lives and works it contains.[17] There have been attempts at constructing new overviews that surveyed the WSPU's campaign in the context of a longer series of feminist demands. Yet none of these have really synthesised the findings of new investigations into individuals or localities to reappraise the WSPU as a political organisation. Sophia Van Wingerden used her own legal knowledge to good effect in examining suffragettes' use of the Edwardian justice system, but the breadth of her book, which looks at a variety of organisations between 1866 and 1928, precludes detailed engagement with the WSPU alone.[18] While Martin Pugh's *March of the Women* claimed in its subtitle to provide 'a revisionist analysis of the campaign for women's suffrage 1866–

1914', it barely engaged with recent feminist scholarship, and so did little to alter existing perspectives on the WSPU.[19] Regional studies focused attention on local organisers and suffragettes who lacked national prominence but epitomised the cause in particular areas. Nevertheless, Pugh still concluded that the WSPU began as 'an essentially *family* organization, a quality it retained despite its enormous expansion, down to 1914', thus avoiding the complexity of its structure as both a political body and a large employer.[20] Laura E. Nym Mayhall's *The Militant Suffrage Movement* is wider in approach. She acknowledges the complexity of meanings which attached themselves to suffrage and has much to say about the various aspects of the campaign, but does not interrogate the mechanisms through which these were implemented.[21] The flurry of Pankhurst biographies, by Martin Pugh, June Purvis and Paula Bartley, which accompanied the 2003 WSPU centenary celebrations not only sparked off fresh controversies about the interpretation of its key figures but, against recent historiographical trends, simultaneously redirected the spotlight back onto the Union's more famous leaders.[22]

This book attempts to synthesise new approaches, particularly local studies, with recently discovered sources to interrogate how the WSPU functioned as a political organisation. One obvious starting point was the tranche of activists immediately below the leadership. The WSPU was a significant employer, with over 150 full-time workers during the 10 years of its main activity. Some of these organisers, as they were more commonly called, were based in London; others were deployed throughout Britain for periods ranging from a few days to – in the case of the longest serving district organisers – a number of years. It was they who really made the WSPU's campaigns happen. Metropolitan organisers co-ordinated national events, staffed the WSPU's offices, prepared its propaganda and produced its newspapers. The London offices were in the front line of preparing for the spectacular 'monster' demonstrations, which brought tens of thousands of suffrage supporters onto the city's streets. Workers there took a key role in preparing for the militant acts which characterised the WSPU's more violent demonstrations. They filed lists of provincial volunteers and matched them with London hostesses who saw the offer of board and lodgings as their own participation in 'active service' for the Union. London organisers also synchronised large-scale militancy such as the mass window-smashing raids of 1911 and 1912. When women were arrested, organisers kept a close eye on their treatment in prison, and arranged for legal representation and visits. In the provinces, organisers carried out a variety of duties. They undertook short-term deployments to carry out specific campaigns, but might also be expected to live in their allocated districts for several years. Once in post they were charged with building up branches and running local militant campaigns which could replicate those devised in London or take on different characteristics more suited to a particular area. Either way, for many members throughout the country it was the local organiser rather than the national leadership who represented the WSPU. By focusing on the work of organisers, therefore, this book recovers many of the mechanisms through which the WSPU functioned throughout Britain and aims to recapture a sense of what membership of this organisation meant to the majority of its adherents, most of whom never went to prison.

The Union's main leaders – Emmeline and Christabel Pankhurst, Emmeline Pethick Lawrence and Annie Kenney – are not absent from this study, for they themselves were organisers, and employees of the WSPU as well as its leaders. There was also a degree of movement between the lower ranks of organisers and the upper tier of the leadership, particularly following 1912. After Christabel Pankhurst fled to Paris and the Pethick Lawrences were expelled from the WSPU, Annie Kenney was recalled from her district post and leadership of the Union shifted between a group of experienced organisers, among them Grace Roe, Olive Bartels and Rachel Barrett, with newer workers primed to come forward whenever acting leaders were imprisoned. All of these women are included here, along with their less well-known co-workers. Their experiences have been recreated via numerous disparate sources. The WSPU's own publications, *Votes for Women* and the *Suffragette*, are invaluable in identifying organisers and providing details of their work in provincial centres and outposts. Autobiographical material relating to organisers is less easy to come by. Out of over 150 identified organisers, fewer than 20 have left autobiographies, and in many of them suffrage work forms but a chapter in a larger life.[23] Some organisers were interviewed by Brian Harrison in his investigation into the history of the British women's movement, although the current uncertainty over the copyright of these interviews means that many of them are currently unavailable to researchers.[24] Nevertheless, some sources remain. Organisers' local prominence meant that they were often recalled by name in others' reminiscences. The nature of their work also demanded frequent correspondence with other suffragettes or with headquarters. Most archival collections relating to suffrage thus contain *some* material emanating from or relating to organisers, and these have proved invaluable in mapping the work of organisers throughout Britain. As well as drawing on collections such as those of the Suffragette Fellowship for references to organisers, this study makes use of less familiar archives relating to individual organisers. The papers of Jennie Baines,

Annot Robinson, Nellie Hall, Dora Marsden, Mary Gawthorpe and others have been invaluable in reconstructing how a WSPU organiser's employers expected her to fill her days, as well as suggesting what might happen to her if she failed in these appointed tasks.

This book is broadly thematic, although the complete change in direction that eclipsed the WSPU after August 1914 dictates that this part of its campaign remains separate. The other chapters broadly span the years 1905–14, the period of the WSPU's main activity, although dates of commencement vary slightly depending on the subject described. Chapter 1 defines the function of the organiser, and investigates the backgrounds and experience of women before they came to work as organisers for the WSPU. Chapter 2 explores the characteristics of itinerant campaigning within the WSPU and looks at the effect on organisers of punishing schedules as they spread the campaign throughout Britain. In contrast, the two chapters which follow investigate the work done by organisers in fixed locations: chapter 3 looks at the role of district organiser, and the extent to which post-holders shaped WSPU campaigns in the provinces; and chapter 4 is concerned with the work done by women at the WSPU's London headquarters from its establishment in 1906. In chapter 5, the issue of militancy is addressed. While it is generally accepted that this was what distinguished the WSPU from other suffrage organisations, militancy had specific implications for women who received a salary from the Union, particularly in its more violent manifestations, such as arson. Chapter 6 tests the notion of autocracy within the WSPU by looking at the mechanisms which the its leaders drew on when the relationship between themselves and individual organisers broke down. Chapter 7 describes the reaction of the WSPU's organisers to the outbreak of war, and the extent to which paid workers supported Emmeline and Christabel Pankhurst's new campaign. The concluding chapter sketches the career trajectories of WSPU organisers after the vote was won, and questions the extent to which suffrage work offered a grounding for a future political career.

Finally, a word about the terminology employed in this study. As many other suffrage historians have noted, the disjuncture between modern historical convention and the ways that suffragettes addressed each other is often too great for the writer to bear.[25] What I have done here is to follow the conventions which the suffragettes themselves used in their many communications with each other. 'Mrs' or 'Miss' followed by the surname was the most common form, although the younger suffragettes were often much freer in their use of each other's first names, as I have been here. What is absent from my work is the use of a surname alone when referring to an individual: the only time that a suffragette was addressed by her surname was when she was in prison; there, its use formed part of the treatment which suffragettes of all classes recognised as degrading in its deliberate disrespect. Knowing this, I feel that identification by surname would be incongruous here, and so have avoided it throughout.

Notes

1 Lettice Floyd to Edith How Martyn, 20 April 1932, Suffragette Fellowship Collection, Museum of London (hereafter cited as SFC.).

2 Hannah Mitchell, *The Hard Way Up* (London: Virago, 1977 [1968]), p. 135.

3 Sandra Holton, *Suffrage Days: Stories from the Women's Suffrage Movement* (London: Routledge, 1996), p. 4.

4 Suffragette Fellowship (SF), 'Objects', in Thelma Cazalet Keir, MP, 'I knew Mrs Pankhurst' (London: Suffragette Fellowship, n.d.), p. 8.

5 In the SF's 'Roll of Honour', 1,097 names feature, not all of them accurately: see Martin Pugh, *The March of the Women: A Revisionist Analysis of the Campaign for Women's Suffrage, 1866–1914* (Oxford: Oxford University Press, 2000), p. 212.

6 E. Sylvia Pankhurst, *The Suffragette Movement* (London: Longmans, 1931).

7 Christabel Pankhurst, *Unshackled: The Story of How We Won the Vote* (London: Cresset Women's Voices, 1987 [1959]).

8 Roger Fulford, *Votes for Women* (London: Faber & Faber, 1957).

9 See, for example, Christabel Pankhurst to Frederick Pethick Lawrence, 6 April 1975 and 25 May 1957; Sylvia Pankhurst to Frederick Pethick Lawrence, 2 July 1957, 25 June 1957 and 8 July 1957, Pethick Lawrence Papers, Trinity College Cambridge, reproduced by kind permission of the Master and Fellows of Trinity College, Cambridge.

10 For an overview of the ties between socialist and feminist approaches to women's history in Britain see Selma Leydesdorff, 'Politics, identification and the writing of women's history', in Arina Angerman, Geerte Binneman, Annemicke Keunen, Vefie Poels and Jaqueline Zirkzee (eds), *Current Issues in Women's History* (London: Routledge,1989), pp. 9–20, at p. 11.

11 *Spare Rib*, August 1978.

12 *Sunday Times*, 2 July 1978.

13 Maroula Joannou and June Purvis, 'Introduction: the writing of the women's suffrage movement', in Maroula Joannou and June Purvis (eds), *The Women's Suffrage Movement: New Feminist Perspectives* (Manchester: Manchester University Press, 1998), pp. 1–15, at p. 4

14 See, for example, Hilary Frances, '"Dare to be free!": the Women's Freedom League and its legacy', in June Purvis and Sandra Stanley Holton (eds) *Votes for Women!* (London: Routledge, 2000), pp. 181–202; Claire Eustance, 'Meanings of militancy: the ideas and practice of political resistance in the Women's Freedom League, 1907–14', in Joannou and Purvis (eds), *The Women's Suffrage Movement*, pp. 51–64; Krista Cowman, '"A party between revolution and peaceful persuasion": a fresh look at the United Suffragists', in *ibid.*, pp. 77–88; Claire Eustance and Angela John (eds), *The Men's Share: Masculinities, Male Support and Women's Suffrage in Britain, 1890–1920* (London: Routledge, 1997);

Sowon S. Park, "'Doing justice to the real girl": the Women Writers' Suffrage League',
in Claire Eustance, Joan Ryan and Laura Ugolini (eds), *A Suffrage Reader: Charting
New Directions in British Suffrage History* (London: Leicester University Press, 2000),
pp. 90–104.

15 See for example Krista Cowman, 'A footnote in history? Mary Gawthorpe, Sylvia Pankhurst, *The Suffragette Movement* and the writing of suffragette history', *Women's History Review*, 14: 3–4 (2005), pp. 447–66; Karen Hunt, 'Journeying through suffrage: the
politics of Dora Montefiore', in Eustance, Ryan and Ugolini (eds), *A Suffrage Reader*,
pp. 162–76; Hilda Kean, 'Some problems of constructing and reconstructing a suffragette's life: Mary Richardson, suffragette, socialist and fascist', *Women's History Review*,
7: 4 (1998), pp. 475–93; Michelle Myall, "'No surrender!": the militancy of Mary Leigh,
a working-class suffragette', in Joannou and Purvis (eds), *The Women's Suffrage Movement*, pp. 173–87; Judith Smart, 'Jennie Baines: suffrage and an Australian connection',
in Purvis and Holton (eds), *Votes for Women*, pp. 246–66.

16 There are many local studies available that examine suffrage in varied cities and
regions as well as investigations into the movement in Scotland, Wales and Ireland.
For an overview of this work see Krista Cowman, "'Crossing the great divide": inter-
organizational suffrage relationships on Merseyside, 1895–1914', in Eustance, Ryan
and Ugolini (eds), *A Suffrage Reader*, pp. 37–52; June Hannam, "'I had not been to
London,": women's suffrage – a view from the regions', in Purvis and Holton (eds),
Votes for Women, pp. 226–45.

17 Elizabeth Crawford, *The Women's Suffrage Movement: A Reference Guide 1866–1928*
(London: Routledge, 1999).

18 Sophia Van Wingerden, *The Women's Suffrage Movement in Britain, 1866–1928* (Basingstoke: Macmillan, 1999).

19 Pugh, *The March of the Women*.

20 *Ibid.*, p. 176.

21 Laura E. Nym Mayhall, *The Militant Suffrage Movement: Citizenship and Resistance in
Britain, 1860–1930* (Oxford: Oxford University Press, 2003).

22 Martin Pugh, *The Pankhursts* (London: Penguin, 2001); June Purvis, *Emmeline Pankhurst: A Biography* (London: Routledge, 2002); Paula Bartley, *Emmeline Pankhurst*
(London: Routledge, 2002). For the debate between Purvis and Pugh see, for example,
the exchanges between both authors in *The Times Higher Education Supplement*, 25
January 2002.

23 Published accounts are: Mary S. Allen, *Lady in Blue* (London: Stanley Paul, 1936); Mary
S. Allen and Julie H. Heyneman, *Woman at the Crossroads (Reminiscences of Mary
S. Allen)* (London: Unicorn Press, 1934); Clara Codd, *So Rich a Life* (Pretoria: Insti-
tute for Theosophical Publicity, 1951); Mary Gawthorpe, *Uphill to Holloway* (Penob-
scot, Maine: Traversity Press, 1962); Margaret Haig (Viscountess Rhondda) *This Was
My World* (London: Macmillan, 1933); Cecily B. Hale, *A Good Long Time* (London:
Regency Press, 1973); Annie Kenney, *Memories of a Militant* (London: Edward Arnold,
1924); Constance Lytton with Jane Warton, *Prisons and Prisoners: Some Personal
Experiences* (London: Heinemann, 1913); Hannah Mitchell, *The Hard Way Up*; Helen
Fraser Moyes, *A Woman in a Man's World* (Sydney: Alpha Books, 1971); Molly Murphy,
Molly Murphy: Suffragette and Socialist (Salford: Institute of Social Research, 1998);
Christabel Pankhurst, *Unshackled*; Emmeline Pethick Lawrence, *My Part in a
Changing World* (London: Gollancz, 1938); Frederick Pethick Lawrence, *Fate Has Been*

Kind (London: Hutchinson, 1943); Mary Richardson, *Laugh a Defiance* (London: Wiedenfeld & Nicolson, 1953); Evelyn Sharp, *Unfinished Adventure* (London: John Lane, 1933). Helen Archdale and Gertrude Harding left unpublished autobiographies which have been heavily drawn on in two studies: Gretchen Wilson, *With All Her Might: The Life of Gertrude Harding, Militant Suffragette* (New York: Holmes & Meier, 1998); Deidre Macpherson, *The Suffragette's Daughter: Betty Archdale, Her Life of Feminism, Cricket, War and Education* (Kenthurst, New South Wales: Rosenberg Press, 2002). There is also an unpublished autobiography by S. Jessie Stephenson in the SFC.

24 The Harrison Tapes are held in the Women's Library, but currently only a small proportion of them are accessible for research while the Library ascertains who holds their copyright.

25 See, for example, Ann Morley with Liz Stanley, *The Life and Death of Emily Wilding Davison* (London: Women's Press, 1987), p. 176.

1

Becoming an organiser

I T IS DIFFICULT TO RECOVER the exact numbers of women who were employed as organisers by the WSPU between its first meeting in October 1903 and the outbreak of the First World War in August 1914 when much of its national organisation collapsed. Later autobiographical accounts of the WSPU's earliest work concur that its first paid workers, Annie Kenney and Teresa Billington Grieg, were appointed early in 1905.[1] By the end of 1906 these two original organisers had been joined by another six: Hannah Mitchell, Mary Gawthorpe, Helen Fraser, Minnie Baldock, Nellie Martel and Flora Drummond.[2] The WSPU's Second Annual Report recorded that by February 1907, there were eleven women officially employed by the WSPU. They were not named, but undoubtedly included Christabel Pankhurst and Emmeline Pethick Lawrence. The number rose again to somewhere between 30 and 40 by February 1908. Of these, fourteen were described as 'outside' staff or organisers, while the remaining women worked in the WSPU's offices in London and Manchester. After this point the figures for office staff and organisers were combined in the annual reports which showed that salaried employees rose from 75 in 1909 to 98 in 1910 and 110 in 1911. From 1912, only the salary figures were listed. These suggest that there was a small drop in staff numbers between 1912 and 1913, but that this had levelled out by 1914, when the report also noted that 'with a view to further extension, a number of probationary organisers h[ad] been appointed' who would be taking up new districts shortly.

Further information about the placements and identities of the organisers represented by these numbers can be found in the pages of *Votes for Women*, the WSPU's official newspaper from 1907 to 1912, and of its successor the *Suffragette*. The detailed local reports, which were published at the end of both papers each week make it possible to chart the movement of individual organisers around the country, at least for the last seven years of the WSPU's campaign. Between 1907 and 1914, approximately 104 districts in Britain, from Aberdeen in the north to Falmouth in the south, and from Hull in the east to Belfast in Ireland, had a WSPU organiser at work. Several of these were temporary appointments, created to cover short, intense, propaganda campaigns, particularly during by-elections.[3] There were also 20–30 staff deployed as permanent district organisers at any one time, although the districts themselves varied, as did the patterns of distribution. Some places including Birmingham, Liverpool and Brighton, got their first organiser as soon as the WSPU expanded its regional representation in 1909 and kept full-time appointments up to 1914. Others, such as Huddersfield, had no district organiser in post until 1911.

Altogether, throughout Britain data from these local reports show that about 140 different women worked as WSPU organisers in the regions. As a figure representing the organising staff of the WSPU, however, this is probably slightly conservative as it takes no account of activists who were based at the WSPU's headquarters, including Beatrice Sanders, the financial secretary, and Mrs Pankhurst herself. When they and others such as Evelyn Hambling – a suffragette who appeared in no contemporary list of organisers while she worked at WSPU headquarters, but was described as an organiser in her obituary notice in *Calling All Women* – are added, then the number of organisers rises to over 150 between 1903 and 1914. It has been possible to retrieve some biographical data for all but around twenty-five of these women. Although much of the evidence is patchy in quality, it is sufficient to allow for some consideration of their backgrounds, previous working experience and motivations, and for some broad trends to be identified.[4]

The social backgrounds of WSPU organisers were extremely diverse. Among the WSPU's earliest workers was a group of women drawn from the radical socialist networks which formed around the Independent Labour Party (ILP) in northern Britain. This was the base from which the WSPU itself had emerged and on which it built extensively in its first 2–3 years of existence. These first organisers were not political innocents. All had some previous experience of agitation and propagandising through their time in trade unions, or through the ILP and the network of Labour churches and local socialist societies which surrounded it. Annie Kenney, the very first organiser whom the WSPU appointed in 1905, exemplifies these earliest suffragettes. She had earned her own living from an early age, having started as a half-time worker in a cotton factory in Oldham at the age of 10. By the time that she first met Christabel Pankhurst, in the summer of 1905, 25-year-old Annie was a regular reader of the *Clarion*, with a good amount of trade union work under her belt, including a spell representing her fellow-mill girls on a union district committee.[5] She quickly proved a useful recruit, and persuaded the Pankhurst women to try propagandising at the wakes, the touring fairs which moved between the mill villages surrounding Manchester in the summer months. This initiative was a marked success, and the small group of speakers who were at the WSPU's disposal at this stage became a regular sight and 'soon rivalled in popularity the Salvation Army and even the tooth-drawers and patent-medicine peddlers'.[6] Intense propagandising continued around Manchester for much of 1906, but Annie left the north in January, famously setting off to London with £2 in her pocket and charged with transforming the WSPU into a national organisation.[7] Within two years, 2 of her 10 siblings, Nell and Jessie, were to join her on the WSPU pay-roll. Both of them had also started their working lives in cotton mills, although more recent developments had offered them better preparation for organising. Nell had given up the factory due to problems with her health and had been working in an office. She had just managed to secure a similar position for Jessie, who had been learning typing at night school when she was offered work with the WSPU.[8]

The Kenney sisters were certainly the best-known ex-mill girls among the WSPU's full-time workers, but their transformation from factory workers to political organisers was not unique. Another WSPU worker with first-hand experience of the harsh realities of life for many working-class girls was Jennie Baines, who was an itinerant organiser for several years, specialising in arranging militant protests throughout the country. Jennie had starting working alongside her mother in a Birmingham gun factory at the age of 11. She became involved in the Salvation Army and, like Annie Kenney, the ILP. Her political interests helped her move out of factory work, and she had a spell as a court missionary and on the Stockport Unemployed Committee before joining the WSPU in 1905, inspired by news of Christabel Pankhurst's first arrest.[9] Lucy Minnie Baldock, an early organiser who resigned through ill-health in 1909 but continued to work for the WSPU on an out-of-pocket expenses basis, also fits into this group of radical, working-class, socialist women. She too had been a factory worker, and was married to a fitter. The Baldocks were ILP activists, and he was a local councillor. Mrs Baldock was one of the WSPU's first workers with no connection to Lancashire or the north of England. She lived in West Ham, and was one of the Union's first London supporters. She also stayed loyal to the WSPU for a long time, and only stopped work when her health broke down in 1911.[10] In Leicester, the WSPU branch secretary Alice Hawkins had come into suffrage politics through an identical route. Alice had left school at 13 to work in a local shoe factory, and had joined the ILP on its formation.[11] She was one of a small number of WSPU secretaries who were full-time workers for the cause but were not paid organisers (Alice Milne in Manchester and Edith Rigby in Preston also fit this category). In Alice Hawkins' case this meant that she combined her suffrage work (which continued until at least 1913) with work for the Independent National Union of Women Boot and Shoe Makers which she founded in 1911, a potent combination that allowed her to rest her demand for votes for working women on a most authoritative case.[12]

A number of other organisers from similarly working-class families had also been involved in the socialist movement before coming into the WSPU. Teresa Billington was a young teacher in Manchester when she met the Pankhurst family, not long after the WSPU was set up. Initially quite comfortably off, Teresa had been forced to leave school at 13 'owing to financial difficulties at home, and set to work to learn millinery'.[13] She loathed the work and went to stay with relations in Manchester where she worked as an unqualified supply teacher to support herself while she put herself through the Queen's Scholarship Examination, helped by a benevolent tutor who, in lieu of her fees, accepted her promise of free tuition to another pupil once she was qualified.[14] Although she had been raised a Catholic, Teresa was by then an avowed atheist, and this created conflict with the Manchester education authorities when she refused to teach religious instruction. Emmeline Pankhurst, then a member of the local education authority, took pity on her and helped her to secure a post in a Jewish school. She also introduced her to Christabel, who was of a similar age, and to the ILP. Before long Teresa was a committed socialist, finally abandoning her teaching post in 1905 to work as a full-time ILP organiser, the first woman to be appointed to such a position.[15]

Hannah Mitchell, who became an organiser towards the end of 1906, was also a socialist before she was a suffragette. Hannah had been in service before her marriage in 1895. Thereafter she had done some dressmaking and became involved with her local ILP in Ashton-under-Lyne where she was also the lecture secretary for the Labour church. It was these Manchester socialist connections that introduced her to the WSPU, which she joined soon after its formation, and with which she was actively campaigning by 1905.[16] Another early recruit, Flora Drummond, also came via the Manchester ILP. She had left Scotland on her marriage to an upholsterer in 1898, but the new family was not well off. Mrs Drummond continued working after the birth of her first son, Percival, in 1900 and was employed in the office of the Oliver Typewriting Company in Manchester when she joined the WSPU.[17] For the first year or so of her association with the Union, she flitted between political organising and full-time office work, temporarily taking over the WSPU's Manchester office from the young organising secretary Alice Milne in September 1906 when a by-election called available workers away, then running 'to and fro from her typing office' for the next few weeks.[18] Flora Drummond and Hannah Mitchell would have known each other before joining the WSPU.

Such socialist connections were not restricted to Lancashire. Across the Pennines in Leeds, the younger Mary Gawthorpe had started work for the Women's Labour League (WLL) in June 1906.[19] Mary's political background was identical to those of Hannah Mitchell and Annie Kenney, and her first speeches had been made at the local Labour church. Like Annie, Mary had been a keen trade unionist, campaigning for the National Union of Teachers and representing their interests when the local lord mayor set up a committee for feeding schoolchildren. She too first met her WSPU colleagues while engaged in socialist work, and was finally persuaded to leave the WLL and work for the Union in September 1906. Meanwhile, in Glasgow, the WSPU recruited Annie Rhonda Craig, who later described herself proudly as 'the first militant suffragette in Scotland'.[20] In common with the Manchester recruits, she had broad experience of ILP work, and had represented the ILP on Dumbartonshire School Board prior to taking on the post of WSPU organiser in Glasgow in 1909.

Different aspects of Mary Gawthorpe's background were shared by others among her fellow-organisers who were not necessarily socialists. Mary, the daughter of a Leeds tanner, had lived through an impoverished childhood, but managed to avoid factory work herself by taking advantage of the pupil teacher system. This system, established in 1846, offered bright working-class children the opportunity to stay on at their local elementary schools, and to receive a few years more education while they concurrently studied for the Queen's Scholarship Examination. Pupil teachers would be put in charge of classes, sometimes in the schools that they themselves had attended, for a small wage while they continued studying at the local pupil teacher centre in the evenings and at weekends until fully qualified. Even those who succeeded in the extremely challenging Queen's Scholarship had no guarantee of progressing to full-time study, as Mary herself found when she realised that the award would not leave her enough money to support her mother. She was forced to continue the exhausting pattern of full-time work and part-time study. Being a pupil teacher was extremely demanding, and although she was grateful for the chance to escape Yorkshire's woollen mills, Mary, who entered it at 13 years of age, found echoes of the harsh realities of factory life in the pupil teacher system, which she described as a 'mill of drudgery and grudgery'.[21] Yet the scheme did offer working-class girls the opportunity to continue their education and even to go to college, so many were keen to use it.

The efficiency and self-motivation that good pupil teachers required also made for good organisers, and several more of the WSPU's workers had trodden the same path. Edith New, the organiser who was also the WSPU's first window-smasher, had been a pupil teacher in Swindon, and had taken up her Queen's Scholarship at Stockwell College. She spent a further seven years teaching in poor schools in East Greenwich and London before the WSPU took her on to its staff in January 1908.[22] Fellow-window-smasher Mary Leigh was also a teacher, married to a building labourer. Annot Robinson, also an ex-pupil teacher, had taught in Dundee and Fife before working for the WSPU.[23] Adela Pankhurst, the only one of the Pankhurst sisters to earn her own living before embarking on suffrage work, had also gone through the pupil teacher system in Manchester.[24]

Two more Manchester teachers, Dora Marsden and Rona Robinson, gave up their posts to become WSPU organisers in 1909. Rona's background is uncertain, but she certainly had no family wealth as her first concern on leaving the WSPU at the end of 1910 was to find another job.[25] Dora too had no money to fall back on. Her father had abandoned the family and Dora had been brought up largely by her mother in Yorkshire where she had worked as a pupil teacher in her home village before coming to Manchester to take up her Queen's Scholarship in 1900 at the age of 18. Violet Hughes of Altrincham, who organised in Lancashire in 1911, had a similar background. Her life illustrates some of the barriers which faced bright working-class girls whose ambitions could be controlled by family expectations. Violet was one of the seven children of William Hughes, a fire insurance clerk. The Hughes children were evidently academically minded, but the 1901 Census records how their gender pushed them in very different directions. While two of the boys, Ernest and Thomas, were medical students, the eldest daughter Edith was a teacher, while Violet and her twin-sister Lillian were both pupil teachers and presumably were helping to support their brothers' studies through their own wages. Frustration at such experiences was a common theme when women were asked to discuss what motivated them to become suffragettes.

As the WSPU expanded its number of staff from 1907, different types of women came forward to work as organisers. Some of them were also socialists, but from a very different background to Mary Gawthorpe, Hannah Mitchell or the Kenney sisters. Emmeline Pethick Lawrence and her sister Dorothy Pethick had enjoyed an upbringing that was comfortable, but informed by strong Nonconformist beliefs about equality. Both girls involved themselves in voluntary social work. Emmeline had worked with Mary Neal, running a club for working girls in west London, while Dorothy went to the Women's University Settlement at Blackfriar's Road before becoming superintendent of a girls' club in Nottingham. Emmeline then married Frederick Lawrence, the editor of the *Labour Echo*, and became friendly with Keir Hardie. She was soon penning articles for Frederick's new paper the *Labour Record & Review*, connecting her club work with socialism and reminding socialists of 'the importance of keeping this side of life awake in the Labour movement'.[26]

While Dorothy shared the same adherence to a romantic and independent socialism, her beliefs were less partisan: she was an admirer, on her own admission, of Garibaldi, Mazzini and Joan of Arc.[27] The Pethick sisters had much in common with WSPU worker Louise Eates, who was converted to suffrage by her husband, a doctor in general practice with working-class patients.[28] She too followed a path from radicalism to suffrage, and formed the Kensington WSPU, acting as its secretary between 1906 and 1910 as well as working further afield in two election campaigns as an itinerant WSPU organiser. The social consciousness of other organisers had been shaped in religious rather than political environments. Helen Watts, who became assistant organiser to her home branch of Nottingham was a vicar's daughter, as was Margaret Cameron who was co-organiser in Glasgow in 1909, and then worked at the WSPU's London offices.[29] Maria Violet Aitken, a suffragette prisoner and hunger-striker who was briefly employed as a full-time worker on the *Suffragette*, was the daughter of Canon Hay Aitken of Norwich Cathedral. Elsie Howey, an itinerant organiser between 1908 and 1909 and a frequent suffrage prisoner, was also a minister's daughter and the granddaughter of a canon of York Minster, although both reverend gentlemen were deceased by the time Elsie began her suffragette work.[30]

The WSPU's growth drew into its ranks women whose backgrounds differed markedly from those of its first recruits. Its organisers now included some women who were financially extremely comfortable, from families with no obvious links to radicalism. Some were aristocrats with significant social connections, the best known undoubtedly being Lady Constance Lytton, the second daughter of the Earl of Lytton, who agreed to work full time for the WSPU in 1910. Although she is the most familiar example, Lady Constance was not the only woman of her class to take this step: Mrs Rosamund Massy, an organiser who worked mainly from headquarters on itinerant campaigns and made by-elections her speciality, was the daughter of Lady Knyvett; and Miss Frances Parker, who took over the organisation of the Dundee branch in 1912, was Lord Kitchener's niece.[31] Mildred Mansell, who was in charge of operations in Bath from 1910, was the granddaughter of Lady Charlotte Guest; she was also a cousin of the Liberal Chief Whip Ivor Guest, which proved a useful connection for the WSPU when she took over co-ordinating links between 'safe' organisers and houses and prisoners out on licence in 1913, as she was considered untouchable.[32]

The WSPU also attracted workers who were less obviously aristocratic but who nevertheless had connections to key areas of the British establishment. A surprising number of these, given the questionable legality of much of the WSPU's work, had links to the armed forces. Both Mildred Mansell and Rosamund Massy, mentioned above, were married to colonels, and Helen Archdale who was both an itinerant and a district organiser, was a lieutenant-colonel's wife. Several organisers had fathers in the army: the artist Georgina Brackenbury, who took over as Manchester organiser for a brief period of time in 1910, was the daughter of a general. Georgina and her sister Marie were active suffragette supporters who braved prison themselves and, with their mother's support, opened up their house in Campden Hill Square to suffragette prisoners out on licence. Marie drew on her father's heritage in explaining her actions, and described herself as 'a soldier' in the 'great Cause' of suffrage.[33] Clara Giveen, who organised in Norwich, Bexhill and Hastings between 1912 and 1913, as well as taking on missions involving arson, was the daughter of an army officer, as was Arabella Scott, who worked as organiser in Brighton under the pseudonym of Catherine Reid while on the run from the police in 1913.[34] Gladys Hazel, who held the post of district organiser in Birmingham, Leicester and Bristol between 1911 and 1914, was the daughter of a naval officer. Other areas of the military, too, were represented: Olive Bartels, who first worked as a district organiser in Cambridge and then transferred to the WSPU headquarters where she became the chief organiser during Christabel Pankhurst's exile in France, was the daughter of an army contractor; and the father of the WSPU's national secretary, Mabel Tuke, had been the clerk of works at the Woolwich Arsenal.[35]

Another group of organisers who came forward as the WSPU expanded were from comfortable backgrounds, with connections to the newer mercantile classes who had obtained great wealth but not necessarily full social recognition by the end of the nineteenth century. Janie Allan, who ran the Glasgow branch from 1912, was the daughter of a shipping-line owner. Her fellow-workers Maud Joachim, who worked in Aberdeen, and Lilias Mitchell, who first ran branches just over the border in Newcastle and was then moved to Birmingham, were the children of Scottish wool merchants and timber merchants respectively, while English organisers Olive Walton and Evelyn Sharp were the daughters of fairly well-established merchants. Phyllis Ayrton and Cynthia Maguire, who founded the Clerks' WSPU in January 1911 and continued to be active in the WSPU's campaigning until the end of the First World War, were the daughters in turn of a diplomat and a stockbroker. Dorothy Evans, who worked in Birmingham between 1910 and 1912 and then organised in Belfast, was the daughter of a wealthy and successful London builder. Laura Ainsworth, who held a number of district posts between 1909 and 1911, and Clara Codd, who briefly organised with Annie Kenney in Bristol, were daughters of school inspectors, while the fathers of Nellie Crocker, Katharine Douglas Smith, Mary Phillips and Edith Rigby were doctors, as was Edith's husband.[36]

The WSPU never made any claims to be a class-based movement. Rather, Christabel Pankhurst explained, it was 'a Woman's Movement … We take in everybody – the highest and the lowest the richest and the poorest. The bond is womanhood!'[37] This did not mean that suffragettes took no account of class, and, as well as highlighting the inequality of denying a vote to well-qualified and highly educated women, the Union could often be seen arguing vociferously for the vote for working-class women at by-elections or during events such as the 1913 deputation of working women organised by Flora Drummond. Although membership expanded across social classes, working women continued to be targeted by the WSPU in constituencies where they were numerous. In Jennie Baines's 1910 campaign in Oldham, for instance, she returned to the early tactic of factory-gate meetings in the hope that 'a strong local WSPU [would] be formed' among the local factory workers.[38] Yet despite the Union's own insistence on the importance of gender over class and its consistent attempts to retain the support of women of all classes, many historians have seized on the affluence of certain prominent suffragettes as a means of undermining the political dimension of the WSPU's work, employing a pejorative sense of the term 'middle class' to suggest that the work undertaken by such women in pursuit of their claim to the vote was in some way not quite serious.[39] Full-time workers have attracted the most attention, as they are the easiest to identify and locate, while the composition of the WSPU's provincial branches still remains obscure.

To counter this, it is worth considering that for those organisers who were economically fortunate (who comprised only one group among many different social classes who worked for the WSPU), the social status prescribed by class in the early twentieth century was entwined with conventional notions of respectability. Many of the customary privileges of class (and all of those associated with a classed notion of gender) were consequently removed from the women who publicly associated themselves with the WSPU, with even stronger censures reserved for those who went to work for it full time.

Nor was there any deference offered to suffragettes, on the grounds of either sex or class, by the hostile crowds, which often taunted them and broke up their public meetings. When she was interviewed in the 1970s, Olive Bartels recalled the disgust she felt at some of the treatment meted out to her during her WSPU work, particularly 'one ... rowdy meeting ... [where] they were throwing things ... I got ... a mass of horse, cow dung in my face. I always remember that, the horror ... the smell and the taste'.[40] Many middle-class organisers had experienced extremely restrictive Victorian upbringings, and so had never encountered anything like this behaviour in their lives. Helen Archdale, so innocent that, on her own admission, on her wedding night she knew nothing of the facts of life, found public speaking as a suffragette a revelation. Her worst memory was of 'speaking from a carriage ... in darkness, when I smelt a dreadful smell, put my hand down on the seats to search and it went into something soft, wet and warm. I grabbed it (quite the bravest deed of my life) and flung it back into the crowd'.[41] Other workers recalled being subjected to sexual innuendo. This was a common complaint among paper sellers, but was seen at its worst during the so-called 'Black Friday' demonstration of November 1910 when many women had their breasts twisted and skirts raised by the police.[42]

By 1908, almost every social class in Britain was represented among the ranks of the WSPU's organisers. Mill girls and pupil teachers were to be found working side by side with titled ladies and colonel's wives at the Union's headquarters, in its district offices and on itinerant campaigns. Despite their varied backgrounds, many organisers found that they were inspired by common motivations, which cut across class lines, forging some unexpected links between them. Surprisingly, considering the apparent affluence of some organisers, there was much convergence around the issue of a salary. Paid organisers received around £2 a week.[43] For the WSPU's first workers, this was vital to their ability to undertake the work. Hannah Mitchell, one of the few working-class organisers to have written an autobiography, recalled that she and her husband were struggling to support themselves, their son and an adopted niece on 30 shillings a week and so were 'really glad of the small salary the WSPU paid'.[44]

Although her autobiography is extremely critical of the WSPU, and of the Pankhursts in particular, even hindsight did not persuade Hannah that the salary divorced suffragette organisers from their roots and moved them into the ranks of the middle classes. Rather, she felt that the WSPU's ability to recruit wealthier women into its ranks actually broadened the social composition of its staff, as donations were now coming from 'many wealthy members, who were glad to make it possible for poorer women to serve the cause'.[45]

The testimonies of other working-class organisers agree that it would have been impossible for them to contemplate full-time suffrage work without a WSPU wage. Mary Gawthorpe was an independent single woman before her appointment to the WSPU's staff, and so looked on the salary a little differently from Hannah. It was still essential to her, as she had resigned her hard-won teaching post some months earlier to work for the WLL, 'with no prospects whatever ... a child of this awakening storm which was ... carrying a school of human corks of whom I was one ...'.[46] Mary claimed that it was not until some years later that she realised how concerned her mother had been at her decision to work for the WSPU and turn her back on the 'comparative security of the past few years' as a schoolteacher, but this is unlikely. She had been the family bread-winner for some years, having encouraged her mother to walk out on her father when her parents' marriage broke down, and, despite her mother's constant denials that money was a worry, had sufficient inkling of her concerns to immediately promise that she would 'send half the weekly two pounds to her'.[47] The need of many organisers for a salary did not diminish as the campaign progressed, as recruits continued to emerge from a variety of social backgrounds. The two Manchester teachers, Dora Marsden and Rona Robinson, who gave up their jobs to work for the WSPU, could not have done so without an offer of an alternative wage. Other recruits such as Vera Wentworth, a shop assistant, and Hilda Burkett, Gladys Roberts, Jessie Stephenson and Marguerite Sidley, who were all previously working as secretaries or clerks, also exchanged one salary for another when they became organisers.[48]

Working-class organisers were not alone in needing the salary. Some surprising names emerge among the lists of those organisers who were classed as *paid* rather than honorary – for instance, Lady Constance Lytton took a WSPU wage despite having a considerable private income of her own. Their reasons for doing so reveal how vulnerable many wealthy women were in the early twentieth century if they chose to step beyond the bounds prescribed by their families. Even sympathetic families could balk at the more outrageous undertakings of their wayward suffragette relations. The Lyttons were reasonably supportive of Lady

Constance's suffrage work, although her mother worried about the effect it was having on her health, but some of her female cousins clearly believed that in her first imprisonments, at Newcastle and Liverpool, she had gone too far. One family friend declared to Constance's sister Betty that she found Constance's actions 'quite insane', while another, Margot Asquith, who, through attacks on her husband and her Cavendish Square home, felt that she had suffered more than was necessary on account of the WSPU, demanded of Frances Balfour: '[I]s Connie off her head?'[49]

Another, more forgiving, friend confided to Constance's mother that it would have been much better had her daughter been persuaded to remain content with the good work that she had been doing in the village at Knebworth, the family seat, organising a small WSPU branch among servants and estate workers rather than breaking windows and courting imprisonment.[50] This sort of reaction from her family made Constance value the WSPU salary, not for its fiscal worth, but for the independence it signified, allowing her to rent a small flat in London with no possibility of being called to account for abuse of family funds.

Other organisers were subject to more than mild disapproval. Helen Craggs needed the salary as her father refused to finance her while she was involved in suffrage work. For a while she managed on her dress allowance, but when Helen interrupted a Liberal meeting at the Albert Hall, things came to a head. Unknown to Helen, her mother was in the audience and, when she stood up to see if her daughter had been hurt by the stewards, she was mistaken for a suffragette and thrown out. Sir John and Lady Craggs felt that things could not continue in this vein, but before they could impose a prohibition on further militant activities, Helen was saved by 'the offer from Mrs Pankhurst to become a paid organiser for the WSPU', which she accepted, much to her parents' disgust.[51] Other organisers also found that the salary saved them from some of the less pleasant personal consequences of family disapprobation. Jessie Stephenson, who took over from Mary Gawthorpe as organiser in Manchester, came from a comfortable background but had not been as well educated as her brothers, and, lacking 'independent means', worked in a barrister's office to support herself. When she was imprisoned in Holloway after her participation in the violent demonstrations of Black Friday, she lost both that job and, more painfully, the support of her family. Her memoir recorded how her 'married-to-a-clergyman sister ha[d] never sent me even a line since I was in gaol. She [now] said not only would she never have me in her house again, but several times that she would never speak to me again if I went to Holloway'.[52] The sister kept her word and Jessie was ostracised from her family, which undoubtedly contributed to the depressive illness which finally forced her to give up her WSPU work. In spite of their fortunate backgrounds, many middle-class women were extremely vulnerable, and were wholly dependent on the good will of their families for their income. If they threw in their lot with the WSPU against their families' wishes, they became every bit as reliant on their organiser's wage as the ex-factory girls and ex-pupil teachers alongside whom they now worked.

The importance of a wage to organisers from across the social classes dictated that most of them were paid for their efforts. A small number continued to work for out-of-pocket expenses, although they were nevertheless regarded as employees, fully accountable for their actions. Predictably, these were women from more privileged backgrounds, whose families were wholehearted in their support for their militant daughters. The WSPU relied heavily on unpaid volunteers for its first two years of campaigning, but the practice of taking on voluntary organisers who were expected to work on a full-time basis rather than simply doing what suited them, was initiated by Emmeline Pethick Lawrence in February 1909, when she published an appeal for more workers in *Votes for Women*. Explaining that the current staffing levels were failing to meet 'the enormous growth of the movement', she appealed for more:

> I say to you young women who have private means or whose parents are able and willing to support you while they give you freedom to choose your vocation, come and give one year of your life to bringing the message of deliverance to thousands of your sisters who are still living lives of social and economic and mental and moral bondage because they have never realised their human birthright and dignity.[53]

Elsie Howey and Mary Blathwayt were named in the appeal as examples of young women who had agreed to this scheme, although both went on to work for longer than the proposed year. Local reports in *Votes for Women* identify a few other 'honorary' organisers in their listings over the years, including Bertha Ryland in Birmingham, Edith Rigby in Preston and Miss K. Birnstingl in Southampton. As their families, or private incomes, supported them, these women did not seek financial independence through the WSPU, but their motivations show some interesting commonalities with their more economically precarious colleagues.

The most obvious link between all of the WSPU's organisers was a deep shared sense of frustration at their position as women that was felt equally across class lines. Many organisers had had this sense heightened through their educational experiences. The pupil teachers discussed above were highly motivated women who had seen education as a means of social advancement, only to find themselves thwarted by the realities of unequal pay with their male colleagues and a marriage bar in many local authorities which forced them to choose between husband and career. There was also a group of organisers who had taken advantage of expanding opportunities for university education; several of them were from less-affluent backgrounds, and had benefited from University study through the extension schemes and scholarships available in the late nineteenth century.

Christabel Pankhurst, who gained a law degree at Owens' College, Manchester, but was not allowed to practise, epitomised the frustrations of bright young women from humbler backgrounds who took advantage of the new opportunities available in the 1890s, only to have their ambitions quashed by arcane regulations that continued to privilege men. Rona Robinson was the first woman to achieve a first-class degree in Science at the University of Manchester, where her tuition was paid for by a Dora Muir scholarship worth £25 a year.[54]

Florence Macaulay, an organiser from 1907, was another scholarship winner. She went to Sommerville College, Oxford, but when her father, a bookseller, died the scholarship was insufficient and she was forced to leave. After some time as a school teacher she tried to return on a further scholarship, but again ran out of funds. Florence was a learned young woman, whose reports as a local organiser were strewn with historical references that suggest the frustration she felt at abandoning her education.[55] Other women interrupted their studies to work for the WSPU, convinced that only the vote would allow them to reap the full benefits of university degrees.

Alice Paul and Lucy Burns were two young American graduates who had come to England for postgraduate work, at Birmingham and Oxford respectively, when they encountered the WSPU.[56] Another postgraduate recruit was Rachel Barrett, who took her London B.Sc via extension study at the University of Aberystwyth, then gave up her postgraduate studies at the London School of Economics after being persuaded to offer her 'trained scientific mind' to the cause.[57] Elsie Howey and Helen Archdale had been at the University of St Andrews, while Gladice Keevil and Grace Roe were at art college. For all these young graduates, WSPU organising provided a ready outlet for their talents and the chance to feel that they were doing something to to smooth out the obstacles that they faced, so that other women might have an easier time. Economic and gender inequalities combined to heighten their sense that full reform could come about only when women took a full part in the legislative processes that restricted so much of their lives.

Those organisers who had not spent time at college or university were by no means uneducated. In the mid-nineteenth century, a number of new girls' schools had been established in Britain as part of the attempts, promoted by an earlier generation of feminists, to equalise education, and several of them now sent alumnae into the ranks of WSPU organisers: Dorothy Pethick and Una Dugdale attended Cheltenham Ladies' College; Dorothy Evans went to the North London Collegiate School; Gladice Keevil was from the Frances Buss School; and Olive Bartels from Streatham High School. Camden School for Girls produced Marguerite Sidley and Elsa Gye had attended the Croyden High School. Many of these schools had been founded on a feminist philosophy which still coloured their teaching. Dorothy Evans recalled that at the North London Collegiate School 'Miss Buss' memory made women's enfranchisement a faith' among the pupils, while Helen Craggs had never considered the issue of votes for women until her attention was drawn to its importance by some of her teachers at Rodean.[58] Dorothy and Helen epitomised the paradox of middle-class girls, educated by fathers who saw learning as a means of displaying family

1   Gladys Keevil ascertaining her whereabouts from postmen in Albert Square, Manchester, February 1907

status, but then went on to disapprove furiously of the ideas which it had implanted in their daughters' minds.

Other suffrage organisers were frustrated at not having been so academically fortunate. Olive Walton, a clearly capable young woman who had worked as an untrained social worker before coming into the WSPU, recalled bitterly that her family did not consider her bright enough for university. Aeta Lamb, who worked in the office for many years, was universally remembered as rather bookish and intelligent although she had been denied formal schooling by her father, a botanist, who did not approve of educating girls. Aeta's biographer felt that she 'found her niche in the militant suffrage movement', as a young woman in whom feminism 'burnt ... with an ever-consuming fire'.[59] For her and for many of her co-workers, organising provided the route out of a repressive and limited home life.

Emmeline Pethick Lawrence's appeal for voluntary organisers recognised the position of many young Edwardian girls who had lives 'filled with domestic tasks and social duties and pleasures' but lacking in intellectual fulfilment.[60] Innumerable young women found that the WSPU filled a void of which they were all too aware. Middle-class Edwardian women who often felt more confined and restricted than their working-class contemporaries, discovered a palpable sense of relief in devoting their energies to effecting a reform they hoped would challenge the limitations on their lives. Helen Archdale was just one who recalled how all her feelings of 'boredom, anger ... a variety of incoherent emotions' crystallised around her decision to work for the WSPU. 'All the ... indignation and resentment ... had one cause, the subjection of women, and one cure, the emancipation of women'.[61] Margaret Haig found a similar sense of relief through suffrage work. Reflecting on her reasons for becoming involved with the WSPU, she explained:

> For me and for many other young women like me, the militant suffrage was the very salt of life. The knowledge of it had come like a draught of fresh air into our padded, stifled lives. It gave us release of energy ... the sense of being some use in the scheme of things ... it made us feel that we were part of life and not just outside watching it.[62]

Women in this position made tremendous personal sacrifices to work for suffrage. Nellie Hall, who was associated with the campaign from childhood through her parents' friendship with Emmeline Pankhurst, recalled how 'at least two suffragettes left their husbands, and many more quarrelled bitterly'.[63]

Margaret Haig was one such woman. Her husband was supportive of her suffrage work, but the marriage broke down because of the way she had changed during the campaign. Helen Archdale also found that her WSPU work affected her marriage. Her husband, a lieutenant-colonel, felt that he ought to check with his commanding officer before permitting his wife to embark on suffrage work. His enquiries revealed that '[t]he Colonel ... did not object to the wives of his officers working for votes for women provided that they did not do it in his district', which ought effectively to have ended Helen's plans, as the district 'covered about a quarter of England'.[64] Undaunted, Mrs Archdale left home to work in Scotland, going to organise in Sheffield only later when her husband was posted back to India. Appeasing the colonel was not the only family problem provoked by Helen's activism. When her children were holidaying with their Irish grandmother, the latter forwarded Helen a letter from her other son, Helen's brother-in-law, which said 'that now she had got the two boys in her house she should hold onto them and thus get them away from "that pernicious mamma of theirs"'.[65] Not all married organisers found this, however. Louise Eates was one who remembered that her husband 'supported her throughout and helped her and made possible all her public activities' for the WSPU.[66]

While many organisers were prepared to risk their reputations and the disapproval of their families for the fulfilment that involvement with the cause brought, others had already made similar commitments to political organisations before coming into the WSPU. Alongside the socialist and trade union work of the first organisers were other activities. Louise Eates had worked for the Women's Industrial Council in the early 1900s. Nelly Crocker, the district organiser for Nottingham from 1909, was the president of her local Women's Liberal Association in Somerset before contact with the WSPU brought her 'a new perspective of the needs, position and possibilities of womanhood'.[67] Some organisers had previously worked for other suffrage societies. Margaret Cameron had been secretary to the London Suffrage Society while Mary Phillips had been an organiser for the Glasgow West of Scotland Association for Women's Suffrage Society. Both women found militancy more congenial than constitutional work, Mary Phillips admitting that she had thought her previous employment 'very dull'.[68] Nellie Martel, who was one of the WSPU's most popular itinerant speakers between 1906 and 1909, had worked for suffrage in Australia and was often introduced on WSPU platforms as 'a woman voter'.[69] Organising offered these women a continuity of experience, plus the chance to extend their talents in somewhat more challenging directions. Other women had experience of work that offered them scope to improve women's conditions. Lettice Floyd, who helped

Annie Williams in Halifax and Huddersfield, had been a nurse, as had both the Liverpool organiser Alice Davies, and Greta Allen who organised in Brighton in 1911. Charlotte Marsh had trained as a sanitary inspector, although she never practised, going into an organiser's job the minute her exams were finished.[70]

Experience was valuable but was not essential for an organiser. Most of them were young women at the start of their working lives. Among the 100 women for whom age data are available, a clear majority were in their twenties when they first began organising for the WSPU. Vera Wentworth and Nellie Hall were the youngest of these, recruited at the age of 19. The youthful profile was understandable given the demanding nature of the activities expected of organisers, though youth was not a prerequisite. Around 20 organisers were over 40 when they started suffragette work. Florence Haig organised during the General Election of 1910 at the age of 54, while Eleanor Penn Gaskill, who briefly organised in Middlesex, was 49 at the time. Older workers were no less active.

Emmeline Pankhurst, perhaps the WSPU's most indefatigable worker, had no settled home from 1907 when she began a life of itinerant campaigning interspersed with numerous prison sentences. Born in 1858, Emmeline was by then in her early fifties. She was also burdened by family responsibilities, as a widow with four children, although, admittedly, by this time her ties were more emotional than economic, as Sylvia was supported by her art-school scholarship, while Adela and Christabel were both on the pay roll of the WSPU. Emmeline was unusual but not unique in this among her fellow WSPU workers. Around 20 organisers were already married, and 3 – Theresa Billington, Annot Robinson and Elsa Gye – married during the WSPU's campaign.

Marriage and suffrage organising were particularly hard to combine if an organiser had children. Florence Bartlett, who went to prison under her maiden name of Slattery to avoid jeopardising her husband's work as a civil servant, remembered that she 'did not want to be' an organiser because she 'had young children [and] wanted to be free to work as [she] liked', although she did agree to take up the post when it was presented to her as a *fait accompli*.[71] Flora Drummond's second child, Keir, was born in 1909. By this point, Mrs Drummond was heavily involved in all aspects of the WSPU's work and had served a prison sentence during her pregnancy in 1908, although this was cut short when the authorities realised her condition. Keir's birth did not force her to cut down on activities, although a letter that she wrote to fellow-organiser Minnie Baldock suggested that the boy's grandmother was largely looking after him.[72]

Helen Archdale, who had three young children, relied heavily on fellow-organiser Adela Pankhurst, and also briefly employed Jennie Kenney, another of Annie's siblings, as a nanny. The demands that the movement placed on organisers' time were intense, and few other women managed to combine this with looking after a young family. It could be done only with exceptional levels of support, as Christabel Pankhurst admitted when she told Jennie Baines, the only other organiser with dependent children, to send 'best wishes, please, to Mr Baines who is making his sacrifice for the movement in sparing you'.[73] Even this was sometimes not enough. Despite her supportive husband, Louise Eates stopped suffrage campaigning after her daughter's birth, unable to face the dual pressures on her time.[74]

The means through which enthusiastic suffragettes transformed into organisers were as diverse as their individual backgrounds and circumstances. Early organisers were recruited directly by the WSPU leaders, drawn from groups of their immediate friends or associates, or from among the ranks of the Union's earliest members. As the numbers of organisers expanded, the process of recruitment broadened. Part of the organisers' work was to keep an eye open for any promising suffragettes who might make good organisers themselves. Mary Gawthorpe brought on some of her Manchester members in this way, while Annie Kenney had a keen eye for talented workers in the west of England where she 'trained speaker after speaker' and enlisted Mary Blathwayt, Elsie Howey and Clara Codd to the ranks of full-time workers.[75] Picking out likely new workers continued to be the main means of recruiting right up to the end of the WSPU's campaign. Mary Allen, the daughter of a railway manager, had been an active militant from about 1910, but had been forbidden from going to prison again on medical advice. She recalled how Mrs Pankhurst 'was quick to recognise' her 'unsuspected gift for organisation' and took her on to the WSPU staff in 1912.[76]

Other organisers such as Lettice Floyd, who worked with Annie Williams, and Adeline Redfern Wilde, who was based mainly in Birmingham but attempted to set up a branch in Stoke on Trent, were recruited by their district organisers and then worked alongside them in an assistant or honorary capacity. Very rarely an approach might come from the potential organiser herself. Jennie Baines had worked for out-of-pocket expenses for a time, but finally got tired of this and asked Emmeline Pethick Lawrence directly to put her onto the staff. This was a slightly more unusual route, and Pethick Lawrence agreed to the request only after securing 'the agreement of the Committee', suggesting that there may have been more consultation among the leadership about the recruitment of individuals than they themselves may have perceived.[77]

Emmeline Pethick Lawrence's appeal for more organisers in 1909 was aimed at a particular kind of volunteer, but it was not exclusive. As the WSPU's treasurer, she kept a vigilant eye on all expenditure, but was anxious not to deter any potential organisers unable to give their services for nothing. She explained,

> It may be that some girl will read this and say 'oh, I wish I were fortunate enough to be in an independent position. But I must work for my living ... Well, if you feel like that, write or better still come and see me ... every would-be organiser has to undergo a training and testing of three months and during that time a sum to cover board and lodging expenses is paid to her. At the end of that time she will discover whether or not the work suits her. If she is fitted for the work she will become one of the staff organisers. We must have women of the right spirit and the right temperament. The method and routine of the organisation we can teach them.[78]

The ways in which organisers learned this 'method and routine' remain elusive. Although many suffragettes recalled having worked as organisers in later life, very few of them described a training process in any detail, but concentrated on the actual work which they did. One organiser, Rachel Barrett, did mention a group of 'probationary organisers' to another worker, Annie Williams, but gave no detail of their training other than to suggest that the new workers would be in London for about a month.[79] The best evidence of the process is Emmeline Pethick Lawrence's appeal, which suggested that the training could take place either 'at headquarters in London' or, alternatively, carried out elsewhere under one of the 'chief officers'. The only organisers to allude to a period of training seem to have taken the second alternative and been trained "on the job" by more experienced workers. Olive Bartels first met Grace Roe while at art college. Grace herself had joined the WSPU and been asked to go on to the organising staff in 1909. Speaking in 1976, Olive recalled simply wanting to become an organiser, and then, when her mother approved her choice of career, going to work in Chelmsford where she learned how to work up a district first hand, with Grace as her 'sort of boss'.[80] Clara Codd was apprenticed to Annie Kenney in Bristol after impetuously handing in her name at the end of a public meeting, asking if she could be of any use. She was then working as a governess, so Annie Kenney offered her the option of a short trial period. Clara duly received 'a letter ... asking me to come over to Bristol for my summer holidays. [Annie Kenney] could not afford to pay me, that was the Union's business, but she could put me up, if I did not mind sharing a large double bed'.[81]

Annie Kenney's working practice required her trainees to possess a good deal of initiative. Clara Codd recalled that although she was 'an excellent' organiser, her new boss was not particularly directive: 'When she chose a helper and gave him [sic] work to do she trusted him [sic] absolutely and never interfered.'[82] Clara proved a capable worker, and was kept on when Annie managed to persuade a wealthy local member to give her 10 shillings a week for 'passing needs'.[83] Yet despite imbuing her assistant with feelings of trust and responsibility, Annie Kenney was rarely far away. Mary Blathwayt, who was to be her next trainee, frequently mentioned Clara Codd in her diary for 1908, but her descriptions show Clara working alongside Annie Kenney and Aeta Lamb, who was then in the west of England, and not on her own. This sort of training was sufficient for most organisers; certainly these examples succeeded. Although Clara Codd stayed in the WSPU only for a year, she moved on to do similar work, organising for the theosophical movement. Mary Blathwayt remained in post until her health broke down in 1911. Olive Bartels stayed at work until well into the First World War, and was eventually put in charge of the entire Union when Christabel Pankhurst was in Paris and Annie Kenney in prison.

Evidence for a different form of training can be traced in the deployment patterns of certain organisers. There were some new recruits who first appear listed as organiser for one of the smaller London districts, which did not usually have such a person in situ. Helen Jollie, who worked in Aberdeen and then Liverpool between 1912 and August 1914, was first listed as an organiser in February 1912 when she was linked to the Kingston upon Thames branch. Grace Roe started out in Brixton before being sent to her own district. All London branches were within easy reach of the WSPU headquarters and did not really require organisers in the way that other provincial centres did, so it appears that they were sometimes used by the WSPU to give new organisers a taste of the work with the support of Headquarters on hand before sending them to more distant postings.

The training offered to WSPU organisers had to help them overcome a surprising diffidence which affected many new workers, irrespective of their previous experience or social status. Mary Clarke, Emmeline Pankhurst's sister, led branches on the south-east coast before her early and unexpected death from a brain haemorrhage in December 1910. Her obituary noted that although she 'quickly became a remarkably successful organiser, winning the love and confidence of members wherever she went', she was far from confident in her own abilities. Rather, 'when the post of Organiser was offered to her, she could not believe that she would be able to fill the onerous duties of leadership' which it brought.[84] The

WSPU's leaders were emphatic that an effective organiser should be able to 'get voluntary workers to do all kinds of work and not to do everything [her]self', though the reality could be quite different.[85]

Public speaking was one duty which was more than likely to fall to the organiser, and was the one which caused the most anxiety. Alice Milne wrote in her diary that she 'detest[ed] speaking and would be far better in an office', when in April 1907 she was 'instructed to go "organising" for two months in Lancashire' with the more experienced Annie Kenney.[86] Elsa Gye, who organised in Nottingham, Derby, and Camberwell and Peckham from 1908, was at first so terrified at the prospect of having to speak that she asked Mrs Pankhurst to speak for her when she appeared on a national WSPU platform at a meeting to celebrate her release from prison in April 1909.[87] The WSPU devised a programme to overcome such apprehension. Rosa Leo, an elocution teacher with suffragette sympathies, was persuaded to deliver a series of classes for members starting in March 1910. Held at the home of the Brackenbury sisters, the classes were free aside from a nominal charge of 3 pence to cover literature costs. There, members learned a variety of skills, including handling hecklers.[88] Annie Kenney recalled that suffragettes 'were taught never to lose our tempers, always to get the best of a joke and to join in the laughter ... even if the joke was against us', a policy which she felt made speakers 'quick witted and good at repartee'. Speaking held no terrors for Annie, who, according to Margaret Haig, trained other speakers by advising them to tell people 'firstly what you want, secondly why you want it, and thirdly how you meant to get it'.[89]

Once trained, organisers were set to work – in London, around the country or in a mixture of fixed and itinerant work. Wherever the job was based, the work was punishing. Annie Kenney, the WSPU's longest serving organiser, believed that 'nuns in a convent were not watched over and supervised more strictly than were the organisers ... of the Militant movement during the first few years ... work and sleep to prepare us for more work was the unwritten order of the day'.[90] Theresa Billington concurred and felt that the pace of work increased between 1905 and 1906:

> In the Manchester preparatory period, our suffrage activities had been added on to the regular duties by which we lived, and this had given us a strenuous time, but the London work eclipsed it utterly, calling us to ceaseless effort ... there were week ends and evenings to fill with clerical work and planning ... and always there were meetings, meetings, meetings ... when we could no longer keep going we tumbled into our Chelsea beds and slept – oh how we slept![91]

The demands that the WSPU placed on organisers were ultimately too much for some, and there were substitutions and casualties throughout the life of the campaign, as well as new recruitments right up to its end.

Those who remained in post as organisers were sustained by friendship and a deep sense of loyalty to the WSPU and to its leaders, who were adept at creating surrogate families for women who had given up home, friends and career for the cause.[92] A frisson of excitement also helped retain their enthusiasm. Many organisers were young women who had led quite sheltered and restricted lives before joining the WSPU, with their friendships and social activities controlled by dominant ideals of feminine behaviour. This applied to women of all classes. Annie Kenney, who as a Lancashire mill girl ought to have embraced horizons bounded by family, work and eventual marriage, recalled that

> the changed life into which most ... [organisers] entered was a revolution in itself. No home life, no-one to say what we should do ... we were free and alone ... scores of young women scarcely out of their teens, sent together in a revolutionary movement ... fearless and self-confident.[93]

Such feelings did much to inspire organisers and keep them focused as they embarked on their new careers as political workers, in London and beyond. They were more than necessary, as many organisers would find that their work in the WSPU demanded every resource they possessed.

Notes

1 See Teresa Billington Grieg, 'The birth of the Women's Freedom League', in Carol McPhee and Ann Fitzgerald (eds), *The Non-Violent Militant: Selected Writings of Teresa Billington Grieg* (London: Women's Source Library, 1987), p. 104; C. Pankhurst, *Unshackled*, pp. 44–5.
2 Mitchell, *The Hard Way Up*, p. 164; Gawthorpe, *Uphill to Holloway*, p. 228; E. Sylvia Pankhurst, *The Suffragette* (London: Gay & Hancock, 1911), p. 56; *Women's Franchise*, 27 June 1907.
3 The figure is somewhat approximate as the geographical boundaries of districts could shift over time. Lancashire, for instance, was configured in three ways: in November 1907 Jennie Baines and Mary Leigh were deployed to organise a campaign among local factory workers; in June 1908 Mary Gawthorpe was appointed as regional organiser (to be succeeded in 1911 by Miss V. Hughes); and in August 1909 Dora Marsden was put in charge of the district of north-west Lancashire.
4 The women who form this sample are identified in the biographical appendix.
5 See Frederick W. Pethick-Lawrence's pamphlet *Annie Kenney: A Character Sketch* (London: Labour Record & Review, n.d.[1907]); E. S. Pankhurst, *The Suffragette*, pp. 19–23; C. Pankhurst, *Unshackled*, pp. 44–5; Emmeline Pankhurst, *My Own Story* (London: Eveleigh Nash, 1914), p. 44.

6 E. Pankhurst, *My Own Story*, pp. 44–5.

7 Kenney, *Memories*, pp. 58–61.

8 Jessie Kenney, 'The flame and the flood', Book 2, unpublished typescript, Kenney Papers, KP/JK/4/2, University of East Anglia; *Votes For Women* (hereafter *VFW*) 8 May 1908.

9 Jennie Baines, profile, *VFW*, 7 May 1908.

10 *Labour Record & Review*, November 1906; see also Lucy Minnie Baldock Papers, SFC.

11 Alice Hawkins, profile, *VFW* 18 June 1908.

12 Statement by Alice Hawkins, *Suffragette*, 24 January 1912.

13 *Labour Record & Review*, July 1906.

14 Teresa Billington Grieg, 'Running away from home' and 'Study and work in Manchester', in McPhee and Fitzgerald (eds), *The Non-Violent Militant*, pp. 56–7, 65–70.

15 E. S. Pankhurst, *The Suffragette*, pp. 65–6.

16 For details see Mitchell, *The Hard Way Up*, pp. 126–32

17 E. S. Pankhurst, *The Suffragette*, p. 49.

18 Notes on Alice Milne's diary, 24 September 1906, Box 397 A/6, Teresa Billington Grieg Papers, Women's Library (hereafter TBG Papers).

19 Gawthorpe, *Uphill to Holloway*, p. 218.

20 'Annie Rhonda Craig', in A.J.R. (ed.), *The Suffrage Annual and Women's Who's Who* (London: Stanley Paul, 1913).

21 Gawthorpe, *Uphill to Holloway*, p. 88.

22 Edith New, profile, *VFW*, 7 May 1908.

23 Annot Erskine Robinson, Obituary, *Women's Leader*, 6 November 1925.

24 Adela Pankhurst, profile, *VFW*, 7 May 1908.

25 Rona applied for a Gilchrist Scholarship to study home science and economics. She appears to have returned to college, although later Mary Gawthorpe unsuccessfully attempted to get her a job at the *Freewoman*: see Mary Gawthorpe to Dora Marsden, 16 October 1911, and Dora Marsden to Mary Gawthorpe, 8 March 1912, in Dora Marsden Papers, Princeton University (hereafter DM Papers); Rona Robinson's curriculum vitae, Mary Gawthorpe Papers, Tamiment Library.

26 *Labour Record & Review*, March 1906.

27 *VFW*, 15 October 1909.

28 Scrap notes on Louise Eates, SFC.

29 Watts Papers, Nottingham Record Office; Margaret Cameron, profile, *VFW*, 22 July 1909.

30 'Elsie Howey', in A.J.R. (ed.), *The Suffrage Annual*.

31 'Rosamund Massy', in *ibid.*; unidentified press cutting, 24 July 1914, Janie Allan Papers, National Library of Scotland, Acc. 44498/2.

32 Antonia Raeburn, *The Militant Suffragettes* (London: Michael Joseph, 1973), p. 198.

33 Crawford, *The Women's Suffrage Movement*, p. 76.

34 'Clara Elizabeth Giveen' and 'Arabella Charlotte Scott', in A.J.R. (ed.), *The Suffrage Annual*.

35 'Olive Bartels', *Calling All Women*, 1967; for Mabel Tuke, see Crawford, *The Women's Suffrage Movement*, pp. 689–90.

36 For family backgrounds of Janie Allan and Lilias Mitchell, see Leah Leneman, *A Guid Cause: The Women's Suffrage Movement in Scotland*, 2nd edn (Edinburgh: Mercat Press, 1995), pp. 253, 266. For Maude Joachim, see Roger Fulford, *Votes For Women!*

(London: Faber and Faber, 1957), p. 278; for Laura Ainsworth and Nellie Crocker, see profiles, *VFW*, 22 July 1910, and 7 May 1908. Katherine Douglas Smith and Mary Phillips discuss this in their entries in A.J.R. (ed.), *The Suffrage Annual*. For Phyllis Ayrton's father, see Cynthia Maguire to Jessie Kenney, 15 July 1964, Mitchell Collection, Museum of London; for Dorothy Evans, Olive Walton and Evelyn Sharp, see their entries in Crawford, *The Women's Suffrage Annual*, and also Codd, *So Rich a Life*, and Phoebe Hesketh, *My Aunt Edith* (Preston: Lancashire County Books, 1992 [1966]). Other details are taken from the 1901 Census.

37 Christabel Pankhurst to Henry Harben, 7 August 1913, BL Add. Mss 58226/34–9, Harben Papers, British Library.

38 *VFW*, 25 February 1910.

39 See, for example, Pugh, *The March of the Women*, p. 212, which describes middle-class militancy as shocking but lacking 'the effect that extensive *working-class* involvement would have had'.

40 Brian Harrison, interview with Olive Bartels, 27 March 1976, Women's Library.

41 Helen Archdale, unpublished memoir, reproduced in D. McPherson, *The Suffragette's Daughter*, p. 33.

42 See Caroline Morrell, *Black Friday: Violence Against Women in the Suffragette Movement* (London: Women's Research and Resources Centre Publications, 1981).

43 There is some evidence that this may have been raised towards the end of the campaign: Annie Kenney reportedly received £4 4s at the time of the 1913 conspiracy trial, while Mary Phillips had her salary increased to £2 15s in 1912.

44 Mitchell, *The Hard Way Up*, p. 167.

45 *Ibid.*

46 Gawthorpe, *Uphill to Holloway*, p. 218.

47 *Ibid*, pp. 228–9.

48 Profiles of Vera Wentworth and Gladys Roberts, *VFW*, 18 June 1908 and 2 July 1909; Jessie Stephenson, 'No other way', unpublished typescript autobiography, SFC; Marguerite Anne Sidley, autobiographical statement, SFC. For Burkitt see Crawford. *The Women's Suffrage Movement*, p. 87.

49 F.S. to Betty Balfour, 2 October 1909, and Margot Asquith to Frances Balfour, n.d. (October 1909), GD433/2 338, Balfour Papers, National Archive of Scotland.

50 H. Brackenbury to Lady Lytton, 26 February 1909, Camellia Collection.

51 S. Walker, 'Helen Pethick Lawrence: a memoir', unpublished typescript, Women's Library, p. 19.

52 Stephenson, 'No other way', p. 224.

53 Emmeline Pethick Lawrence, 'Wanted, more officers', *VFW*, 11 February 1909.

54 See Rona Robinson's curriculum vitae, Mary Gawthorpe Papers; further information about her university career was kindly supplied by the archivist of the John Rylands Library.

55 See, for example, *VFW*, 19 February 1910, where she discusses St Augustine, Queen Bertha and Queen Elizabeth 1.

56 *American Heritage*, February 1974, copy in Mitchell Collection, Museum of London.

57 Mary Phillips, 'Rachel Barrett, obituary', *Women's Bulletin*, 18 September 1953.

58 *VFW*, 22 July 1910; Walker, 'Helen Pethick Lawrence'.

59 Anon., 'Biographical notes on Aeta Lamb', SFC.

60 *VFW*, 11 February 1909.

61 Archdale, in Macpherson, *The Suffragette's Daughter*, p. 32.

62 Haig, *This Was My World*, p. 120.

63 Nellie Hall, interview, *Canadian Weekly*, 16 October 1965, copy in Nellie Hall Hunpherson Papers, Birmingham City Art Gallery.

64 Archdale, in Macpherson, *The Suffragette's Daughter*, p. 31.

65 *Ibid.*, p. 42.

66 Scrap notes on Louise Eates, SFC.

67 *VFW*, 7 May 1908.

68 *Calling All Women*, February 1970.

69 Nellie Martel, autobiographical statement, *VFW*, 7 May 1908.

70 Alice Davies, profile, *VFW*, 25 November 1910; for Lettice Floyd and Greta Allen, see their entries in A.J.R. (ed), *The Suffrage Annual*; for Charlotte Marsh, see Marion Lawson, *Memories of Charlotte Marsh* (London: Suffragette Fellowship, 1961).

71 Scrap notes on Florence Bartlett, SFC.

72 Flora Drummond to Minnie Baldock, 20 December 1909, SFC.

73 Christabel Pankhurst to Jennie Baines, 19 September 1909, Baines Papers, Fryer Library, University of Queensland.

74 Scrap notes on Louise Eates, SFC.

75 Kenney, *Memories*, p. 120.

76 Allen and Heyneman, *Woman at the Crossroads*, p. 64.

77 Emmeline Pethick Lawrence to Jennie Baines, 7 April 1908, Baines Papers.

78 *VFW*, 11 February 1909.

79 Rachel Barret to Annie Williams, 3 May 1912, SFC.

80 Olive Bartels to Brian Harrison, 27 March 1976, Harrison Tapes.

81 Codd, *So Rich a Life*, p. 46.

82 *Ibid.*, pp. 46–7.

83 *Ibid.*, p. 48.

84 *VFW*, 6 January 1911.

85 Kenney, 'The flame and the flood', fragments towards Book 2.

86 Notes on Alice Milne's diary, April 1907, Box 398/B7, TBG Papers.

87 *VFW*, 9 April 1909.

88 *VFW*, 25 February, 4 March, 16 September 1910. Miss Leo also offered Union members one-to-one tuition in private classes, at a fee of a guinea per lesson.

89 Haig, *This Was My World*, p. 122.

90 Kenney, *Memories*, p. 110.

91 Fragment, 'Early WSPU history', Box 398 B/8/2, TBG Papers, Women's Library.

92 See Brian Harrison, 'The act of militancy: violence and the suffragettes 1904–14', in Brian Harrison, *Peaceable Kingdom: Stability and Change in Modern Britain* (Oxford: Clarendon Press, 1982), pp. 26–81.

93 Kenney, *Memories*, p. 110.

2

'They wanted me here':
organisers and the itinerant life[1]

ONCE THEY WERE recruited and trained, the WSPU's first organisers were set to work wherever they could best be used. Although they worked near to the Union's headquarters in Manchester (and later, London) they were by no means desk-bound. Suffragettes made full use of a lively tradition of mobile propagandising. This had served radicals in Britain since the peasant uprisings of the fourteenth century, but, by the end of the nineteenth century, other political factions had noticed its potential to an expanded electorate. Liberals and Tories attempted propaganda tours but it was the socialist parties who really made the tactic their own. Using the new railways, socialist speakers travelled the length and breadth of Britain, holding innumerable meetings to develop and strengthen a system of local branches. Outdoor meetings remained a key part of this work, but socialists made increasing use of a network of halls and indoor venues, often built and owned by local branches to enhance the social and cultural dimensions of their political work. The ILP and the broader socialist culture which surrounded it made particular use of women speakers. Caroline Martyn, Enid Stacy, Katherine Bruce Glasier, Margaret and Rachel Macmillan and Isabella Ford were among the best-known of these, and their popular meetings drew large crowds.[2]

From 1895, the *Clarion* van afforded women further opportunities to act as socialist propagandists. The van, initiated by Julia Dawson, the *Clarion*'s women's page editor, carried speakers on tours throughout Britain aimed particularly at taking the socialist message into rural communities. Although men and women lived and worked together in the van (a feature that gave rise to some interesting discussions about socialists' morality), Julia Dawson had from the outset believed that it was 'meant to be the Clarion women's van', and it inspired several imitators among political campaigners in the years before the First World War.[3] Women began electioneering. Jeannie Churchill and Georgina Curzon

of the Conservative Primrose League took to their bicycles to secure electoral success for their husbands.[4] The Women's Liberal Federation pursued similar initiatives. By the General Election of 1906, these changes,
along with suffragette interventions, prompted the *Daily Telegraph* to
remark that the 'ladies' were taking 'a more prominent and systemised
part' than had ever been the case.[5]

The WSPU picked up on this trend for party-political feminism and
combined it with a northern tradition of socialism centred on taking
a message out to the people wherever they were. Early suffragettes had
learned to propagandise in the ILP and imported socialist techniques into
their new work. Street-corner and factory-gate meetings were a particular
favourite, while the interchangeable membership of the early WSPU and
the ILP opened the socialist halls and Clarion clubs of Lancashire and
Yorkshire to the first suffragette speakers. Such meetings were extremely
cost-effective, reaching a comparatively wide audience for the minimum
outlay. The outdoor meeting could also catch the interest of those who
might not feel motivated to attend an indoor event, but who may nevertheless be convinced after hearing a speaker when passing by. Although
unpredictable, such chance encounters could have great benefits for the
WSPU. Edith New, the former pupil teacher who was appointed to the
WSPU's staff in January 1908, had been moved to join after attending one
of its earliest meetings in Trafalgar Square, while many suffragette prisoners cited the importance of open-air propaganda on influencing their
decision to take militant action.[6]

The arrests of Christabel Pankhurst and Annie Kenney at the Free
Trade Hall in October 1905 made the WSPU known beyond Manchester, and thereafter its work began to expand. Its first political campaign
was launched to coincide with the General Election of January 1906. The
campaign, begun almost immediately after the Free Trade Hall arrests,
marked a shift in WSPU policy. For over forty years, great attempts had
been made by suffrage campaigners to persuade public and political
opinion both of the necessity of votes for women and of the moral just-
ness of the suffragette cause, and, although the WSPU had favoured more
public manifestations over private petitions, it had not yet departed from
the underlying premiss that persuasion was all that was required for the
vote to be won. Now, while persuasion remained a crucial dimension of
WSPU work, especially where recruitment was concerned, Liberal politicians, ministers in particular, were increasingly conceived as a group
which had to be defeated rather than convinced. By adopting militancy,
the WSPU had put itself on a war footing, with the Liberal Government
designated 'the enemy'.[7]

2 Theresa Garnett, Nellie Crocker, Gladys Roberts and Edith New
during an election campaign, c.1910

This was bold talk, but drawing up battle lines posed serious tactical problems for a WSPU which remained small and poorly resourced. Its half-dozen proven speakers had been sent out alone to orate, but the more risky tactic of deliberate disruption required at least two, doubling the travel costs. Theresa Billington asserted that it was only a donation passed on by Keir Hardie, thought to have come from the radical millionaire Joseph Fells, that enabled a handful of suffragettes to spend 'their days in trains and their evenings in questioning and interrupting the Liberal party nominees'.[8] Even with financial help, a full-scale campaign was impossible. Christabel decided to concentrate efforts on Winston Churchill, 'the most important of the Liberal candidates ... standing for constituencies within easy reach' of Manchester, and on others who ventured north, such as Asquith in Sheffield, Campbell Bannerman in Liverpool and Lloyd George in Altrincham.[9] This sustained harassment kept the WSPU in the public eye during the election, but its geographical limits meant that suffragettes were forced to wait for the politicians to come to them. After the election, which had seen the WSPU become a familiar fixture at political meetings and in newspaper headlines, a furious Christabel was forced to watch 'the Liberal leaders, with their Parliamentary rank and file, with[draw] to Westminster', putting themselves far beyond the reach of the WSPU, 'except during their occasional sallies to the constituencies'.[10] She realised, astutely, that action would be required if the WSPU was to capitalise on its new-found prominence and not fall back into provincial obscurity when Parliament resumed. Consequently, despite her mother's real concerns as to how any expansion of WSPU work might be financed, it was decided to send Annie Kenney to London, both to 'rouse' the city and to ensure that the WSPU remained firmly in the consciousness of the new Government.[11] Annie duly set off from Manchester in January 1906 with £2, almost all the money that remained of the WSPU's election fund, charged with establishing a branch in the capital.

The move transformed the WSPU from a northern-based group of volunteers to a political party with a paid staff and large headquarters in the capital. This new perspective did not eclipse the WSPU's regional work, although the purpose and form of campaigns in the provinces and elsewhere became increasingly complex. As its workforce grew, the WSPU was able to make numbers of workers available for short-term deployment throughout Britain in a series of itinerant campaigns. Most of these workers were now based in London, although a small number still lived in the provinces where they could be called on when required. The itinerant campaigns fell into four main groups: by-election campaigns; short-term building campaigns for a particular protest or event; building campaigns to start off a new branch; and holiday campaigns. A team of itinerant organisers worked on all of these between 1906 and 1914, travelling the length and breadth of Britain, often with little or no notice, as the Union demanded.

The WSPU's new focus on government and Parliament, combined with its determination to attack the new Liberal administration at any opportunity, made by-elections a key site for suffragette agitation. These saw the WSPU's first sustained use of mobile propagandists. While there was a degree of unpredictability about the timing and number of by-elections, the strategy of concentrating propaganda around them was not as haphazard as modern observers may suppose. Edwardian by-elections were frequent. Contemporary parliamentary rules dictated that any MP who became a minister must immediately resign his seat and seek fresh electoral endorsement of his new position, thus ensuring that a good number of contests would take place in the life of any Parliament.[12] Cabinet reshuffles could thus precipitate a number of simultaneous by-elections, which offered suffragettes the prospect of implementing sequential campaigns against their Liberal opponents across a number of constituencies. The fact that many of these elections were prompted by ministerial appointments or promotions guaranteed that many by-elections involved the key ministers or the rising stars of a party, and consequently offered the WSPU the enticing prospect of some high-profile Liberal scalps.

At first, Christabel Pankhurst tried to use by-elections to increase the number of pro-suffrage MPs in Parliament by obtaining a pledge from candidates in favour of women's suffrage. She hoped that such a pledge might be easy to extract in the hot-house political atmosphere of a by-election campaign, and first suggested the tactic in April 1906, when a vacancy arose at Eye in Suffolk. Writing from Manchester, where she was completing her law degree, to the new London committee, Christabel urged them to go to Suffolk: 'Intimate to the Liberal candidate that, unless he could obtain a pledge from his Government to give votes to women, [the WSPU] should oppose his return, and ... take a similar course in the case of every future Government nominee'.[13] The WSPU had few available organisers at this point, but realised that someone was needed to lead this campaign. After raising £5 from sympathisers in Manchester, Flora Drummond, who had been oscillating between her local typewriting and the WSPU's London work, was dispatched 'to fight the election single-handed'. Her vociferous campaign, which was sufficient to convey 'the impression that ... several [suffragettes] were working from different centres', was credited with persuading both the Conservative and the Liberal candidate to declare themselves in favour of women's suffrage.[14] Making suffrage a 'test question' was a risky tactic, as Liberal women had discovered in the 1890s, for once an MP was safely ensconced in Westminster, his enthusiasm for the topic could easily evaporate, while voteless women remained unable to call him to account in any way. Although she was pleased with Mrs Drummond's reception at Eye, Christabel now felt that a series of embarrassing defeats for Liberal candidates, whatever their personal views on suffrage, would prove 'the best way of forcing the Government to act' on the issue of votes for women.[15] In August 1906 she unveiled the WSPU's new policy of opposition to the Government's candidate at the Cockermouth by-election. All subsequent official intervention by the WSPU at by-elections was carried on under the slogan 'Keep the Liberal Out'.

The WSPU campaigned in all ensuing by-elections where a government candidate was standing until the outbreak of the First World War. While the overall effectiveness of this campaign is difficult to judge, it is clear that suffragette intervention could achieve its aim of preventing a Liberal victory. The most notable casualty was Winston Churchill, who was promoted to President of the Board of Trade in the spring of 1908. Henry Campbell Bannerman's resignation and Asquith's move to the premiership set off 'something almost like a miniature General Election', with nine by-elections held in rapid proximity.[16] Much of the national press agreed that Churchill's defeat at Manchester was attributable at least in part to the WSPU, with the pro-Liberal *Manchester Guardian* stating that the Liberals had 'enormously under-rated the influence of the hostile feminine organisations' working against him.[17] Churchill then decamped to the next available vacant seat – at Dundee – preceded by a group of WSPU organisers led by Mrs Pankhurst who had correctly anticipated his choice of constituency. Ministers were clearly irritated by this new tactic. Although the WSPU failed to keep him out of Parliament for a second time, Churchill was sufficiently concerned by their efforts to be moved to question Asquith in the House as to whether the Corrupt Practices Act might be amended to combat 'organisations which worked against the Government' at elections, a course of action which the WSPU, not unrealistically, felt to be 'aimed principally at' itself.[18]

Elsewhere, the WSPU's influence was less easy to discern. Liberal candidates were successfully returned, despite sustained intervention, in the other by-elections that accompanied Churchill's defeat – at Dewsbury, Kincardineshire, Wolverhampton and Montrose.[19] The WSPU's strategy was also hit by consecutive Liberal successes in the two General Elections of 1910 as the Government's affirmation by the electorate on both occasions made the WSPU's aim of bringing it down via a series of by-election defeats appear much less realistic. A further shot across the bows of the WSPU's by-election activities came with the decision by the NUWSS in 1912 to establish an electoral fighting fund which would offer the Labour Party the direct support of constitutional suffragists in elections. Prior to this, other suffragists would frequently vacillate among the competing parties in different constituencies, while the WSPU's anti-Liberal strategy at least had the strength of remaining consistent. By-elections thus became less vital to its work from this point, although the WSPU continued to retain a presence at most contests up to the outbreak of the First World War, including concurrent campaigns in Poplar, Bethnal Green and Leith in February 1914.[20]

Whether or not they actually affected the outcome on polling day, by-elections offered the WSPU the opportunity of many column inches of press coverage. With no parliamentary platform, this was a useful way of spreading the suffragette message, and during the peak years of these campaigns the WSPU relied heavily on a pool of paid organisers to exploit the occasions. In the year after the campaigns at Eye and Cockermouth, the WSPU expanded its staff to include 'upwards of thirty regular by-election campaigners who could always be relied upon' for immediate deployment.[21] Around half of them were paid organisers, while the remainder were regular volunteers, with no other commitments, who could guarantee constant availability.[22] As a result of this pattern of deployment many organisers did little else besides by-election work at this stage, particularly during the hectic round of contests in the spring and summer of 1908. This had many advantages. It allowed for the rapid dispatch of a team of available and experienced campaigners. Notice of elections could be quite short. Alice Milne, the young secretary of Manchester WSPU, learned one evening that she was to go to mid-Glamorgan with Mrs Pankhurst the following day, and missed the Cardiff train in her confusion, arriving on the next one to find Mrs Pankhurst anxiously waiting on the platform.[23] As the Government's concern over the impact of the WSPU's campaign on its candidates (or perhaps its irritation at the suffragettes' presence) increased, writs were moved with the bare minimum of notice in an attempt to wrong-foot opponents. Sadly for the Government, this seldom had any effect on the WSPU, as suffragettes were frequently breaking ground in constituencies from the moment an election looked likely, without waiting for the announcement. They became skilled at picking the right constituency. The Manchester campaign against Churchill opened before official notice was given when Christabel Pankhurst was convinced by a speculative article in the *Morning Post*. She warned Jennie Baines, the organiser on hand to start the campaign, that the announcement would 'come very quickly, so we must do plenty of work beforehand'.[24] Mrs Baines was instructed to 'spend as much time as you can in the constituency, holding open air meetings and rousing up the people', which she duly did.[25]

The deployment of experienced organisers made a huge difference to the work that the WSPU was able to achieve in a short by-election campaign. Organisers arrived in a new area with full knowledge of what needed to be done and how best to do it. Headquarters would be taken if possible, and a phenomenal number of public meetings, reaching up to twenty a day, would be arranged, often aimed at specific groups of voters such as workers in a particular trade or factory.[26] Organisers were expected to bring on local workers to help, but appreciated that they would be less experienced and would need encouragement and direction. In most cases, this was welcomed. Leila K McNeil, a student at Glasgow University, was involved with the student suffrage society when a by-election was called in 1909. She recalled how, just as the candidates and their party workers descended on the constituency, 'Mrs Pankhurst and her cohorts arrived in full force … [and] the local WSPU office sent an urgent call' to the student suffrage society. Soon, Leila was busy writing 'a daily schedule of all the help we could offer and every morning reported to Mrs Pankhurst at her headquarters to complete the details of our work according to her programme'.[27] As Leila and the other militants were out-numbered by constitutionalists in the student society, they could not pos-sibly have managed to run an effective campaign on their own, but were only too glad to be organised from outside.

If an organiser was already in place in a district, itinerant workers could still be useful. Deploying workers to by-elections from a national centre ensured that branches which happened to be in the vicinity did not have to shoulder the financial burden alone. The WSPU's treasurer, Emmeline Pethick Lawrence, kept election accounts separate, explaining to Jennie Baines that she 'like[d] to appoint a deputy Treasurer and pass all the expenditure through her hands, then I get all the accounts of the By-election together and am able to make a clear statement for the Audi-tor'.[28] This was a sensible precaution: WSPU annual reports reveal that between 1 March and 31 August 1907, the board and lodging costs alone at the 7 by-elections which had been covered were over £182.[29] The money provided from headquarters to most branches over the same period would have been much less – £48 for the organiser's salary, plus occasional donations from the national petty cash.[30] Any other money would have to be raised by a branch, so a separate fund for by-elections relieved what could have become a severe pressure. It did, however, throw much of the worry back onto the shoulders of the itinerant organisers, which could cause problems for them, as will be seen.

As well as keeping the pressure on the Liberal Party and provid-ing welcome publicity openings, by-election campaigns extended the WSPU's reach, expanding branches into new areas and establishing new centres. This had always been part of the aim. Hannah Mitchell remem-bered that although the Liberal candidate had been returned in Hudders-field in late 1906, the campaign itself had been 'a wonderful experience, like putting a match to a flame', with over seventy meetings held in a few weeks, many aimed specifically at women.[31] At the close of the cam-paign Emmeline Pankhurst and Nellie Martel presided over a meeting at which a new branch was inaugurated, and left the town convinced that this would prove 'a valuable asset to the WSPU' in future work.[32] Mary Gawthorpe similarly refused to be downhearted about the result at Hud-dersfield, which she felt overlooked the equally important dimension of persuading women of the rightness of their claim: 'This is what we are aiming at', she told Frederick Pethick Lawrence, 'the arousing of the women … in this I see the greatest hope of all'.[33] Mary was equally buoy-ant in November 1907 about her work in Hull, where she was in no doubt as to the 'wonderful educational value' of what the WSPU was doing in the city. Although Guy Wilson was returned for the Liberals, Mary felt that because of suffragette intervention Hull would 'soon have a WSPU of its own'.[34] A branch was duly established the following year as a 'permanent result' of the by-election campaign.[35] Six months later, although the national Union had paid Hull little attention in between, Nellie Martel was impressed by the turn-out at her meeting there, which she felt 'spoke volumes for the spread of the movement' in the city.[36] Mrs Martel, one of the WSPU's most active by-election campaigners, was certain that suffragettes were 'educating with [their] agitation' on such occasions.[37] By-elections drew in volunteers from beyond the immediate constituency, many of whom lived in small villages where a separate WSPU branch was impracticable. In these instances, the closest organiser would be sent the woman's details, ensuring that no potential recruit was lost. In north-west Manchester, Christabel Pankhurst found herself working alongside an old school friend, Miss Hewitt, then living in Hale. Christabel sent her friend's details to Jennie Baines and Mary Gawthorpe, and Miss Hewitt was soon involved in WSPU work herself, including a spell as an itinerant worker in Newhaven and as an organiser in Preston.[38]

The second kind of itinerant work which fell to organisers was the 'building' campaign which would send them off for short bursts of intensive work. Sometimes such campaigns were to open up new regions. Annie Kenney, Teresa Billington and Christabel Pankhurst went to Scotland in the autumn of 1906 to set up new branches in an area largely untouched by the WSPU. Cold-calling politics was not easy. Teresa was pleased with the suffragettes' progress in east Fife, but felt that other places needed more attention. Aberdeen, in particular, failed to 'capitulate on the first attack', although their visit left 'a few staunch women' to 'hold the fort and keep the question to the fore in such ways as they can'.[39] Again these unexpected new recruits proved invaluable. Helen Fraser admitted that she had no real interest in suffrage, but was so convinced by Teresa Billington at the meeting she attended that she agreed to act as chairman for the next meeting and was soon on the WSPU payroll herself.[40] Yet, as a percentage of the women who were addressed by organisers during building campaigns, converts remained in the minority.

Alice Milne, who was sent to Sheffield at the same time as the Scottish campaign was in full swing, had a more difficult task. Her diary recorded a 'long weary day', with many obstacles. The local 'working girls [were] not interested in votes', while some socialist women were 'angry about Cockermouth' and the WSPU's decision not to support the Labour candidate at a recent by-election there.[41] Despite this, Alice did gather 'enough supporters to form a branch'. She also promised them a visit from Mary Gawthorpe for a week of solid work. The presence of a better-known speaker – and Mary was one of the rising young stars of the WSPU at this stage – could make all the difference, and, although Mary remembered 'ten days of stiff work organising noon meetings at factory gates, cottage meetings, evening open-air meetings' in the city, no memories of problems remained.[42] Yet building campaigns could daunt even the most cheerful of organisers, and Mary also recalled that her next assignment, Birmingham, proved 'a hard nut to crack'. Here there were 'no solid ranks of sympathetically inclined comrades; but the vastness of [the city] to penetrate, to impress and persuade'.[43]

Building campaigns were easier for workers if there was a specific objective in view beyond that of starting up a new branch. National events, such as 'monster' demonstrations or the militant 'Women's Parliaments' in London could spearhead local campaigns over quite large regions. Mary Gawthorpe headed a campaign in her home district of Yorkshire in the winter of 1906–7 in which she managed to form 'ten branches of the Union within a few weeks', most of which sent delegates down to the next Women's Parliament, in February 1907. This promising start was followed up by Annie Kenney and Adela Pankhurst, who returned to the region for 'a wild, wet and stormy campaign', building for the next meeting in March.[44] Recruitment was more difficult when arrests might be involved (as the discussion of militancy in chapter 5 explores), and Annie recalled that she faced 'the tempers of some of the men whose wives we had coaxed … into giving in their names', who were less than happy about the prospect of losing them to prison.[45] Yet there were also advantages. Margaret Haig was struck by the camaraderie among provincial women who travelled together for events in London: 'after the great Albert Hall meetings [we] arrived at three in the morning … the local branch … used to arrange a party and make terms with the railway authorities … and so we all came home together'.[46] The days' events, the speeches and the spectacles would be shared and revisited, ensuring that the excitement remained long after the actual meeting had finished. Building a branch was much easier when there was a focus of this kind to establish a sense of identity among local members.

The third task that took itinerant workers into new areas for short periods was the holiday campaign. Taking a holiday had become a regular feature of British life across social classes by the Edwardian era, and the holiday campaigns run by the WSPU capitalised on the opportunities that popular resorts offered for new audiences. The idea of a co-ordinated holiday campaign in the summer was first raised in *Votes for*

Women in August 1908, when Emmeline Pethick Lawrence reported that several members had informed her 'of their intention to have a "Votes for Women" propaganda in the seaside places or the country towns and villages where they are going to spend their holidays'.[47] Several women took up the idea, and spent some of their holiday on suffrage work, either individually or by joining in with campaigns that were already running. Miss E. M. Middleton from Sheffield was just one who spent 'a fortnight of [her] holidays at Bristol helping Miss Annie Kenney'. She noted that 'the work [was] instructive and as most of the day is spent in the open air, it is healthy too'.[48] Annie had not originally thought of running a holiday campaign, but the number of suffragettes wanting to spend some time in the West Country and propagandise at the same time changed her mind. Other organisers also recognised the potential that holiday resorts offered for this work. Mary Gawthorpe had so many accounts from her Manchester members, 'recently returned from the seaside and other pleasure resorts', of 'the universal interest displayed in the cause' that she rushed off alone, to Harrogate, 'to conduct a week's campaign', though she knew no one in the town, and raised over £5 in a week by addressing meetings in cafés and hotels as well as in the pump room.[49]

The success of these sporadic ventures led to more sustained efforts in this direction in future years. In June 1909, Mary Gawthorpe reported that members from Manchester had made the most of Whitsun week and 'carr[ied] the Votes for Women flag into all the seaside and pleasure resorts to which the Manchester citizens have flocked', particularly Southport. Some district organisers were then sent to certain of the more hopeful districts, with some attempt made to place them where residents of the areas covered by their branches might holiday. Gladice Keevil, the Midlands organiser, went to work in west Wales in the summer of 1909, while Annie Kenney helped co-ordinate campaigns in Devonshire resorts, and Mary Gawthorpe took north Wales and the Lancashire coast. For paid organisers, the holiday campaign was considered part of their deployment, although they were always encouraged to take their own holidays afterwards, when they should have a complete rest from WSPU work.[50] Other workers were also encouraged to participate alongside organisers, especially 'those who are unable through pressure of work or social considerations to do much in the towns where they ordinarily live', although as volunteers they were expected to spend their holidays in such work.[51] Edith Mansell-Moulin, who later spoke at Hyde Park demonstrations and founded the Forward Cymric Suffrage Union, started her public work during a holiday in Keswick in 1909, convinced that she 'must be doing something as I cannot be in prison with the noble heroines'.[52] Such sentiments ensured that organisers could rely on a constant supply of co-workers who would forgo their own holidays for the WSPU, encouraged by comments like this from *Votes for Women*:

> [H]oliday work has many advantages. The members will in many cases feel that they are opening up new ground and drawing into the movement people who might otherwise remain indifferent; and as in most seaside places meetings are permitted on the sands, there is no expense entailed … workers should … have a good stock of membership cards … and there should be helpers who will take the names and addresses of all in the crowd who seem interested so that the work may be followed up from head office.[53]

Itinerant campaigns undoubtedly inspired converts, but placed particular strains on organisers. As with other suffrage work, much of this was financial. Campaigns were supposed to be carried out on strict, fixed budgets, and organisers felt the brunt of this. One area that was constantly contentious was the question of where an organiser was supposed to stay when she was sent into an unfamiliar area at short notice. In most instances, organisers were expected to 'find board and lodgings' out of their overall budget, although Emmeline Pethick Lawrence did sanction a separate allowance for this during by-elections 'to enable organisers to present a good appearance' at such times.[54] Self-presentation mattered to the WSPU. Cicely Hamilton, who spoke at many public meetings for the Union, remembered 'the importance … attached to [organiser's] appearance' at such events, and how they were expected to look feminine above all.[55] This could be especially difficult during itinerant campaigns when weather and travel could take its toll on a restricted wardrobe. When the newly-appointed Helen Archdale began her first itinerant campaign in Aran she and her three companions landed

> from a steamer and had about seven miles to drive in a horsed wagonette … it was pouring with rain and at every hill we got off to ease the horse. As we trudged along, we heartily sang the old song … 'she's off with the raggle-taggle gypsies oh' which … seemed particularly appropriate.[56]

Although Helen and her colleagues saw the humour in their situation, they were less likely to convince the indifferent crowd if they did not look like serious political workers. As itinerant campaigning mounted, the distinction between election and non-election work became less firm and more costs became claimable. Jennie Baines managed to get the committee to agree to spending £1 10 shillings on a coat for Mary Leigh during a campaign in November 1912.[57] Such generosity could not always be relied on. When Dora Marsden bought a coat for her friend Florence Clarkson to wear in the General Election campaign of 1910, Beatrice Sanders refused to refund the cost on behalf of the WSPU's financial department, particularly as she had not sought prior permission.[58] Emmeline Pethick Lawrence kept a tight hold on the purse strings and regularly berated organisers whom she suspected were developing 'a tendency ... to be more than necessarily extravagant with board and lodging', now that she had relaxed the rules over accommodation.[59] Her concerns were not unfounded. Annual reports show that between March and August 1907 the WSPU's total national expenditure was £2, 700. Of this, special board and lodging for organisers came to £41 13s 11d and the cost of board and lodging at 7 by-election campaigns added another £182 7s 2d. Total organisers' salaries for the same period came to £680 13s 8d, so the new expenses were increasing costs by around one-third. Organisers were now pressured to recoup the money in other ways. Jennie Baines, who was following cabinet ministers around the country in the autumn of 1907, was given £4 from petty cash, but was entreated: 'For heaven's sake ... raise a little money somehow or other in your campaign ... we are spending an awful lot ... and your poor Treasurer has sleepless nights'.[60]

Organisers found that their employers tried to curb their accommodation costs in more direct ways. In certain districts, sympathisers offered bed and board which organisers were expected to use. Annie Kenney felt that the 'question of hospitality was a serious one with organisers' as 'it saved hotel bills'.[61] Certainly, many WSPU sympathisers saw this as part of their work for the cause, and one, Mrs Macdonald from Aberdeen, put an entire house at the disposal of the WSPU for two years.[62] In Margate, Laura Lennox offered 'hospitality to a speaker for a night or two' immediately after joining the WSPU herself.[63] Miss Turner of Brighton believed that 'entertaining the speakers' was her main suffrage work, and was proud of being able to claim that 'more of our leaders ... have stayed with me than in any other home'.[64] Accommodation with friends could prove extremely pleasant, but other arrangements were less congenial. Headquarters sent out lists of rather spartan hotels to organisers who were encouraged to use them. Jennie Baines stayed at the Salvation Army Hotel in Liverpool during a campaign in December 1907, as did Mary Phillips the following year.[65] As soon as her campaign was over, Mrs Baines received a letter from Christabel Pankhurst sending her to Sunderland and suggesting that she stay in the Temperance Hotel. She would not be its first suffragette visitor, but was told that when booking she ought to 'mention that Mrs Drummond who stayed ... on Tuesday has sent you'.[66] Annie Kenney and Mary Blathwayt also stayed at a Temperance Hotel in Shropshire in May 1908.[67] Organisers who could not face such sur-roundings sometimes made excuses for seeking out a bit more comfort. Kitty and Jessie Kenney moved from cheap lodgings into a more extrava-gant hotel during a campaign in August 1909, claiming that they had little choice as 'the room in the cottage ... was not clean'.[68]

Restricted expenses were used to dissuade organisers from bringing too many helpers into a district. This was desirable in order to 'bring on' local workers by forcing them to undertake work themselves. Organis-ers were often less convinced, however, especially when faced with the disappointment and irritation of local workers who wanted to present their neighbours with the big names of the movement at indoor meetings rather than braving street-corner crowds themselves. Jennie Baines had visits from Emmeline Pankhurst and Emmeline Pethick Lawrence as well as Christabel Pankhurst during a campaign in Birmingham in May 1909, but was still unhappy with the number of meetings that the leaders were able to address for her. Christabel became firm: 'I shall *not* be able to be at the meeting', she wrote; 'you must try to manage without anyone coming over. I cannot possibly attend', although she did agree to send a letter of greeting which could be read out by a less confident speaker.[69] As popular speakers received repeated requests from all over the country, they had to become guarded with their time. Emmeline Pethick Lawrence refused another invitation from Jennie Baines in November 1909, but suggested that she tried some of the newer organisers, explaining that it was now a good idea to 'fall back upon other people ... we have got to bring out other public speakers ... the other names will get well known if we give them a chance'.[70] Emmeline also felt that it was important to reduce the number of speakers appearing at each meeting, and suggested that having three organisers together on a platform amounted to 'a great waste of our resources'. That was true, but a lack of tried and trusted speakers caused problems for itinerant workers who had little time to get to know a dis-trict or its workers before having to ask them to do something.

There were dangers, too, in sending out new workers. Margaret Haig acquired public-speaking experience on an itinerant tour of Devonshire with her schoolfriend Prid, but admitted that their meetings often began with quarrels over who should speak first. Inevitably, 'if one spoke second, the other might have taken away all the points one meant to make, and we were neither of us ... able to deviate by the fraction of an inch from the lines of a speech projected'.[71] Cicely Hamilton was also sent out as an untried speaker, but proved a lucky gamble. Although her confident tone (she was a trained actress) had impressed an organiser who had heard her ask a question at a WSPU meeting, Cicely felt that the real reason was the organiser's desperation – she had been let down for a meeting the next day – rather than Cicely's own talent. 'The movement was an epoch of many meetings [and] organisers were often hard put to it.'[72] In other instances itinerant organisers who lacked the skills, the time – or the courage – to instantly appraise local volunteers often ended up doing most of the speaking themselves. This ensured that all meetings would be fronted by a competent orator, but increased the strain of an already demanding job.

Some of the pressure of itinerant work was eased when a campaign was fixed for a district that already had a functioning WSPU branch. Organisers could then reasonably expect to have some of their arrangements made for them. Accommodation would usually be fixed, especially if there was already a district organiser in place. Mary Blathwayt, in Bath, was charged with accommodating two helpers from Liverpool who arrived to work up a series of meetings in the West Country in October 1908, but ended up putting up one, a Miss Stephenson, herself.[73] Booking hotel rooms became a regular part of the work of district organisers, and even featured in the 'sample diary' which was given to them as part of their training. This fictional record of a typical week's work noted that on the Friday afternoon the district organiser: 'Met Mrs Pankhurst, took her to her Hotel and had a talk with her about the evening's programme.'[74] The choice of Emmeline Pankhurst as the example is quite telling, as she probably spent more time on the road than any other WSPU worker, and was sometimes anxious about the firmness of long-distance arrangements. Much of her correspondence, written from hotels or trains, revealed the anxiety that beset even the most experienced itinerant workers as they tried to co-ordinate their plans over a long distance. In a typical note written to Caroline Phillips in December 1907, Emmeline announced: 'I expect to be in Aberdeen on Thursday the 12th. I leave Kings X at 10 am arriving Aberdeen 10.50 pm … I don't know whether you can make arrangements for me to stay with friends. If not perhaps you will take a room for me at the hotel.'[75] Organisers often arrived in an unfamiliar town late at night or at short notice, and had no alternative but to hope that somebody would be at the station waiting for them.

The disorienting effect of frequent travel was compounded by intense feelings of loneliness, which many organisers found the worst feature of their work. It was difficult for an organiser to confide feelings to the local members she was supposed to direct and inspire. Only another organiser could really understand the strains. Mary Phillips had been working for the WSPU for about five months, and had just been released from her first imprisonment when in April 1908 she was sent without warning to Dundee to help out with a by-election campaign. Ex-prisoners were quite a crowd-puller for the WSPU, so were particularly at risk of having unexpected moves pushed on them. In an otherwise lively letter, written at midnight while drying off in front of a fire after a wet outdoor meeting, Mary confessed to her fellow-organiser and ex-prisoner Annot Robinson that she was not enjoying the solitary aspect of her work:

> I'm all alone tonight and want to gossip to somebody … At first I stayed with Mary Gawthorpe at the house of a local member, but it was too far from my … committee room, so I shifted into lodgings yesterday. It's so beastly lonely, I think of prison every time I sit down to my solitary meals! I'm going on strike, or to the Freedom League or something desperate, if they don't fish up somebody to share my room soon! Miss Joachim and Elsa Gye are both in the constituency, but I haven't seen them yet …[76]

No worker was immune to these sentiments, no matter how dedicated she may have been. Even Mrs Pankhurst, whose presence was eagerly competed for by district organisers who booked her months in advance, 'often felt herself a lonely outsider … a bird of passage in some hotel', according to her daughter Sylvia.[77] The sense of a common purpose, often forged under the intense pressures of itinerant campaigns, hostile crowds and perhaps time shared in prison, was the only thing that could really combat such feelings, and itinerant workers tended to stay together whenever possible, taking pleasure in each others' company. Such camaraderie offered the best antidote to the discomfort and loneliness that plagued itinerant workers. Mary Gawthorpe, who undertook many such journeys herself, recalled in her autobiography that in the first campaigns organisers 'usually stayed with Labour comrades keen on suffrage', and that although their surroundings were 'never by any means wealthy … the offering of a congenial environment was true wealth'.[78] Jessie Stephenson, who became the Manchester organiser, began her work for the WSPU in a short by-election campaign in Jarrow, giving up her annual holiday in order to be able to do so, and remembered the 'jovial … fun and repartee' of breakfast at the County Hotel, where she would join Mrs Pankhurst, Mary Gawthorpe and Dr Helena Jones to plan the day's work.[79]

When friendly faces and congenial surroundings were available, the job of organising was much easier. In the spring of 1908 Mary Blathwayt and Annie Kenney campaigned around the seaside towns of the west of England. This was Mary's first taste of suffrage work, as she had only just been appointed an assistant organiser, but the pleasure of her suffragette friendships helped her to overcome misgivings about the difficulty of the task in hand or her surroundings. In her diary account based on letters from Mary, her mother Emily Blathwayt recorded that her daughter was 'intensely happy' travelling with Annie and other volunteers, particularly because in Torquay they were 'staying in a big house with lovely garden'. The women next visited Paignton where 'Miss Hughes and a friend ... put them up'.[80] Yet nothing was certain on propaganda tours, where circumstances – and feelings – could change daily. By June, things were not quite so pleasant, and Mary found that the boarding house where they stayed in Weston Super Mare was distinctly down-at-heel, curtly remarking in her own diary that it was 'kept by two ladies who have lost a lot of money and so must do something'. Conditions in Pembrokeshire were uncomfortably cramped, with Mary, Annie Kenney and Katharine Douglas Smith in one small room.[81]

Intense and demanding work was not eased by circumstances of this sort, and organisers tried to fit distractions into their working day to alleviate the stress. Sometimes these were quite simple. When Margaret Haig set off with her schoolfriend Prid 'to spend a summer holiday learning to speak', their choice of region was not purely political. The two headed for Devonshire, 'partly because it was as yet practically untouched by the militant movement, partly ... because we liked Devonshire cream and we thought we might as well combine a little pleasure with business'.[82] Even when the choice of district was predetermined, other diversions could help. Mary Blathwayt and Vera Wentworth had a particularly difficult time working in Plymouth in July 1909. The local branch had opted to affiliate to the National WSPU following the re-organisation of September 1907, but was now revisiting the decision, and Mary and Vera spent most of their time appeasing local branch members who wished to form an independent branch again. The two young organisers found some relief from the carping in swimming sessions in the sea before breakfast.[83] Supporters who offered to host visiting speakers could also do their part to ease the pressures. Annie Kenney recalled how workers who visited the West Country benefited from 'the number of large country houses that were open to us at all times'.[84] Of these, the Blathwayt's own house near Bath was the most popular. There, suffragettes enjoyed musical evenings, walks in the suffragette arbour that Colonel Blathwayt was creating in the grounds of his house, or games on the 'fire escape' which Mary herself rigged up from her bedroom window.[85]

Pleasant though such diversions undoubtedly were, they could not overcome the constant and unsettling sense of uncertainty that beset organisers specialising in itinerant work. As by-elections loomed or cabinet ministers spoke around the country, WSPU organisers followed, often with little or no notice. Their own wishes didn't come into it: 'I was to come back to London this week', Mary Phillips wrote to Annot Robinson in April 1908, 'but "Suffragette proposes, Government disposes" and of course when this vacancy occurred they wanted me here.'[86] Even popular speakers could not escape. Alice Milne noted how upset Mary Gawthorpe was in October 1906 when she arrived for a planned campaign in Manchester, to be greeted by a telegram sending her back to Birmingham.[87] Other workers faced additional anxiety. Jennie Baines was one of the few organisers to have young children. As her family was in no position to afford child care, Mrs Baines usually worked around the north west, but this did not always work out. Although she was careful to acknowledge the sacrifices of the entire Baines family, Christabel Pankhurst had no hesitation in deploying Mrs Baines throughout the country when necessary, often hounding her with instructions for the next campaign before the current one had finished. In July 1907, she was sent to Huddersfield on her return from Jarrow, then in November that year she was told 'to go straight to … Rochdale … As soon as you leave Bristol', and was again sent 'to Norwich after the Leeds election' in the spring of 1908. There was little hope of rest in Norwich either – Mrs Baines was also asked to 'take your bicycle' to work up the surrounding district and 'spend a day or two in Yarmouth' to that end[88] The more popular speakers, whose presence was repeatedly requested from branches throughout the country, felt the relentlessness of such work most keenly. Constance Lytton, who was undoubtedly one of the WSPU's most prestigious recruits, found herself frustrated by her inability to dictate her own timetable, apologising to Annie Kenney that although she had 'planned to speak' for her as promised, 'Headquarters … have again decided differently and I have been booked for Birmingham, Liverpool and other districts'.[89] Against the demands of the movement, the individual organiser had little voice.

Hard though this work was, the WSPU's leaders did not ask employees to do things that they were not demanding of themselves. Emmeline Pankhurst wrote lightly of her punishing schedule to Alice Morgan Wright:

> Since I saw you last I have been in many places. Last week I was in Wrexham[,] Chester[,] Liverpool[,] Cardiff. This week Leicester[,] Market Harboro'[,] Newcastle on Tyne[,] Sunderland[,] North Shields.
> Tomorrow I go to Wolverhampton & hence to Lincoln. Then back to London … So you see I am kept well at it.[90]

Others made even greater sacrifices, which they recognised only with hindsight. 'My life was my work; and nothing but work was my life', Annie Kenney wrote in her autobiography some twenty years later.[91] In such an atmosphere, many things were put aside. Nellie Hall turned down a marriage proposal in 1914, without consideration, 'because I couldn't marry until we won our fight'.[92] Mary Gawthorpe, who's own engagement was broken off during the campaign, later confessed that when another admirer brought her a bunch of flowers at the end of a meeting she was so focused on her work that she entirely mistook his meaning. 'Some of us', she explained, 'were very much pulled off from our womanly base in those days.'[93] Grace Roe suggested that, towards the end of her life, even Christabel Pankhurst acknowledged that she had missed out on a social life in her youth.[94] Yet at the height of the campaign, few such admissions were forthcoming. Rather, the itinerant work continued at a pace which placed unfeasible demands on organisers.

The rapid pace of short campaigns which saw organisers and volunteers catapulted into unfamiliar districts invited confusion, adding to the overall strain of the job. In September 1908, Christabel Pankhurst told Jeannie Baines to postpone a meeting she had been working to arrange in Lancaster and head straight for Newcastle instead where a by-election campaign was proving a 'tough fight'. Such was the air of confusion that two copies of the letter were dispatched, one to Mrs Baines's home in Stockport and another to Rawtenstall, where she was about to start yet another campaign, and in both of them Christabel reminded her that organisers needed to let London know their whereabouts the minute they arrived in a new destination 'so that we can get in touch with you at a minute's notice'.[95] Although Headquarters had telephones, these were not always secure, nor commonplace in the provinces. Most details were arranged by post, often using forwarding addresses or hotels, and things could easily go astray. Mary Blathwayt was dismayed to find that she had lost 'a roll of posters [that did] not come on with the luggage' during one campaign.[96] Such losses were not only irritating, they diminished what could be achieved, as the time-scale of itinerant propagandising did not allow for extra orders to be placed with the literature department in London. Nor was it just propaganda that could be misplaced. Other losses could be even more problematical, as the rapid movement of women around the country led to confusion as to who was meant to be where at any given time. Millicent Browne, working in north Wales in the summer of 1909, wrote frantically to Mary Gawthorpe, who was overseeing this particular campaign, that she had failed to join up with her co-workers as first planned:

> Miss Barry hasn't sent me any work. I left her a note because I didn't see her when I decided to go. But I have heard no word of her ... [she] went off with friends and I fear changed her lodgings ...[97]

Although her tone when discussing forthcoming meetings became more buoyant, Miss Browne was clearly disoriented. The letter, which was written hastily on the back of a handbill advertising a meeting at which both she and Mary Gawthorpe were the speakers, declared that work was 'going on pretty well in Llandudno', with the place name struck through and replaced with Rhyl. 'It became a question of where next', observed Helen Archdale, who was able to set out on itinerant campaigns only because of the help of a series of sympathetic suffragette nannies, including Jennie Kenney.[98] The pace was frenetic, and some organisers would not be able to keep up.

When an organiser reached her new destination there was no time for recuperation. In one Sabbatarian part of Scotland, Annie Kenney found herself unable to arrange meetings on Sunday. This gave her a welcome opportunity for 'a day of rest', which she spent 'in writing a report to Christabel, addressing envelopes ... and retiring early to be ready for another strenuous week' – not the most relaxing weekend.[99] In less observant regions, an organiser did not have even this limited opportunity but had to plunge straight into work. The number of meetings the WSPU expected was phenomenal. Theresa Billington, who left a file of notes based on the diary that Alice Milne kept during the hectic month of September 1906, remarked that this document revealed 'the expectation of service with which [organisers] had to comply'.[100] Alice was involved in setting up meetings in Bolton, Sale, Sheffield, Eccles, Bury, Manchester, Liverpool, Ashley Bridge and Seedly before being dispatched to Glamorgan on September 25. Even when an organiser was in a district for a couple of weeks, the workload did not lessen. During the Huddersfield by-election 'all the available halls' were booked by organisers who held meetings every day, afternoon and evening.[101] Marguerite Sidley was dispatched to south Leeds in January 1908, and 'lost no time in getting to work', arranging twenty-two meetings in her first week.[102] The following month, Gladice Keevil surpassed this with twenty-seven meetings in a single week in Worcester, including separate meetings for women, and dinner-hour meetings outside factories with a predominantly female workforce.[103] The pace of work, exacerbated by uncomfortable or cramped sleeping conditions and irregular meals, could exact a heavy toll, and the health of many itinerant campaigners was compromised. Aeta Lamb worked at several by-elections in 1907 and 1908, but found that this 'reduce[d] her to an appalling state of weariness'. The sympathetic colleague who worked alongside her at several of these remarked without irony that, unlike more stalwart campaigners, after the Dundee election of 1908 'where we had been holding meetings – not only all day but all night as well – Aeta had to be sent to bed where she lay delirious with fatigue for twenty-four hours'.[104] Annie Kenney frequently ended her speaking tours at the home of the Blathwayts where she would retire to bed, ill from overwork.[105] The series of health problems which finally forced Mary Gawthorpe to retire from her organiser's post were considered by many of her friends to have been exacerbated by her punishing work schedule.[106]

The WSPU leaders, many of whom undertook punishing touring schedules themselves, were aware of the demands of itinerant work. They also recognised that much of the value of organisers lay in their experience and the continuity they were able to bring to itinerant work, which would be seriously compromised by repeated bouts of ill-health. Nevertheless, official responses to sickness among organisers varied. Emmeline Pethick Lawrence, who had almost suffered a breakdown herself during her first imprisonment, was constantly at pains to remind itinerant workers to pace themselves and not overstrain themselves: 'Health is infinitely precious to us ... and must not be risked for anything but the most strong and pressing duty', she explained to Mary Phillips in 1909.[107]

Christabel Pankhurst's response was less predictable. Blessed with robust health herself, she could be perplexed or irritated by illness in others, even in those close to her. The attack of polio that killed her brother Harry in 1910 bewildered Christabel, and prompted her to confess to Jennie Baines: 'Illness is such a new thing in our family.'[108] She could be conciliatory towards organisers who were literally tired out. When Marguerite Sidley, a worker at Clements Inn, was taken ill in the autumn of 1907, her doctor suggested that outdoor work might be beneficial, so she was sent off to the Hull by-election then to Liverpool for a short building campaign. Unfortunately, she also had a horror of speaking in public and found Liverpool women 'very slow to move', putting her in a hopeless position.[109] Christabel asked the more experienced Jennie Baines to come and help her, but warned her to excuse Miss Sidley from meetings as she was in '*very* poor health'.[110] Yet on other occasions, Christabel was less benevolent. The dependable and effective Mrs Baines was not fit herself, suffering from repeated attacks of chorea. Christabel could scarcely mask her irritation on learning of a relapse in February 1909, and demanded to be told 'on what date you will be free to resume full work', although she then softened this with the excuse that the information was necessary 'because of all these by elections'.[111] She welcomed news of Mrs Baines's recovery the following month, but again pressed her: 'how long does the doctor think it will be before you are ready for active service once more?'[112] Rachel Barret, who suffered a breakdown that forced her to give up WSPU work for a year in 1908, found that the chief organiser's sympathy for her staff was bound up with anxiety about the effect their illness might have on the movement. 'I am more sorry than I can say', Christabel wrote, conceding that 'to be overtaken by ill health … must be a great unhappiness', but concluded by expressing 'how much we shall look forward to having you at work with us again'.[113] As organisers comprised the WSPU's most vital asset it was commonly their return to their posts rather than to full health that most concerned their employers .

If the stress of itinerant campaigning did not damage an organiser's health, she still faced other dangers. Although the particular pressures of militancy will be explored in chapter 5, some points need to be made here in relation to the treatment that organisers often received during their peripatetic campaigns. The WSPU consistently emphasised that its violence was always a reactive rather than a pro-active phenomenon. Nowhere was this argument more sustainable than in the face of much of the treatment meted out to itinerant campaigners. By stepping outside of what was expected of women in political work, it appeared that many of the suffragettes' opponents felt that they had made themselves fair game and could be assaulted with impunity. Even government officials took this line. One regular WSPU activity was the prison-gate meeting, at which supporters would gather nightly to address meetings outside prisons housing suffragette prisoners. When George Touche, MP for North Islington, complained to the Home Office in 1913 that police were doing nothing to protect women gathering outside Holloway Prison from local youths who broke up their lawful gatherings, the official response made it clear who the Government felt to be at fault. It questioned 'Mr Touche's assumption that persons meeting outside a prison in order to demonstrate their sympathy with convicted prisoners inside are entitled to as much protection from the law as a lawful public assembly'.[114] In the eyes of the Liberal Government, the WSPU was putting itself beyond the law in certain instances, and thus forfeiting its protection in all others. 'Persons parading their sympathy [with suffragettes] provoke reprisals'.[115]

Itinerant speakers were particularly at risk during election campaigns, when political feelings were already running high. Suffragettes interviewed by Antonia Raeburn in the 1970s described an acknowledged 'tradition' by which 'the Liberals would break up the meetings of any opposing party' in many constituencies.[116] Even the WSPU's own propaganda acknowledged the levels of violence against its workers, although public accounts tended to end with a suffragette victory in the eyes of a hostile crowd. Nellie Martel, who worked entirely as an itinerant organiser until 1908, offered to *Votes for Women* a typical report of such an encounter during the a Herefordshire by-election in February 1908:

[Whitchurch] has no street lamps, and I took my stand on a lorry with a candle lantern. Just as I commenced to speak I was struck with a stone, and someone beat on a tin tea tray. I stopped speaking, and told them that if they did not want to hear I did not want to speak, I was rather tired ... although asked by one or two to proceed with my speech, I was determined not to speak unless the noisy individuals asked me to go on.[117]

Eventually, she reported, she was given a forty-five- minute hearing, followed by an apology conveyed by the local police constable who informed her that 'had [the men] known I was only asking for votes like men, they would not have interfered, but if I would come again they would bring everyone to hear me'.[118] Although she did not say so, this response was a marked improvement on events in mid-Devon the previous month. There, the Liberal candidate had been defeated, and the WSPU's part in this publicly acknowledged by the *Manchester Guardian*, which suggested that 'their activity, the interest shown in their meetings, the success of their persuasive methods in enlisting popular sympathy' left observers in 'no doubt that the Suffragists [*sic*] did influence votes'.[119] Local liberals, many of whom were 'notorious ... roughs', did not take defeat lightly.[120] Mrs Pankhurst and Mrs Martel, the only two WSPU organisers remaining in Newton Abbot when the vote was declared, were sceptical of the warnings they received from local women, and were walking back to their lodgings when they were mobbed by young Liberals, who advanced on them with cries of 'Those women did it.'[121] Although a grocer's wife attempted to hide them in her husband's shop, they were eventually cornered and badly beaten; leaving Mrs Pankhurst with an injured ankle that troubled her 'for many years'.[122] Mary Gawthorpe was knocked unconscious by a pot-egg thrown at her during the Rutland by-election in the summer of 1907, in the course of a concerted campaign against the WSPU which Sylvia Pankhurst believed was initiated by 'a well-do-do- Liberal [who] was paying a band of youths to disturb our ... meeting'.[123] The WSPU played down such events, but the local press was always keen to sensationalise accounts that ridiculed the notion of women politicians.

Violence against suffragettes could be worse in districts where the women −or their assailants − were unknown. Ada Flatman, who organised with few problems from crowds in Liverpool between 1909 and 1911, met with persistent trouble from 'organised bands of young men' in the Isle of Man during a holiday campaign in 1909, many of whom she recognised as holidaymakers from Liverpool.[124] Attacks during building or holiday campaigns were particularly difficult to deal with, as they were perceived as so senseless. The more optimistic suffragettes might claim that the violence meted out to them during by-elections at least indicated that their political presence was being acknowledged, albeit in an unwelcome manner. Other attacks were indicative more of male opposition to the WSPU's very public appearances than of a coherent party-political response. Mary Allen, who was an organiser from 1912, sketched a vivid portrait of some of the things she encountered. She recalled: 'The boxes on which we mounted on street corners were likely to be kicked form under us; stones and rubbish flung, and upon our departure, in the inescapable tussle, our clothes might literally be torn from our backs.'[125] The treasurer's insistence on the cheaper venues increased the risk to speakers who were accessible and vulnerable to hostile crowds. Annie Kenney and an anonymous local speaker were towed away by a crowd one evening, unable to get down from the lorry which they had hired as a platform. Fortunately, the crowd were in good humour, and deposited the women outside the local lunatic asylum as a rather forced joke, but other speakers were less lucky.[126]

Itinerant campaigns offered organisers some of the worst experiences of their suffragette careers. The compensation came in the intense camaraderie, often forged through shared misery, that developed between women as they moved around the country in pursuit of new recruits or Liberal ministers. There was also a glamour to the work. Relatively unknown women were dispatched to provincial towns where, as representatives of a growing national movement, they could find themselves at the centre of attention, not all of it hostile. Yet most organisers ultimately found the pace of constant itinerant campaigning too much, and were keen to find alternative ways of using their talents. As the WSPU reassessed its approach to regional work from 1907, a new role was defined. Many organisers were now sent into provincial centres for much longer periods, from where they would be seconded to itinerant work on a less regular basis. The district organiser was now the key figure in the WSPU's national campaign.

Notes

1 Mary Phillips to Annot Robinson, 8 April 1908, Annot Robinson Papers, 718/17, Manchester Central Library.
2 For more detail on their activities, see for example June Hannam and Karen Hunt, *Socialist Women: Britain, 1880s to 1920s* (London: Routledge, 2002), pp. 32–6.
3 *Clarion*, 16 May 1905.
4 See Beatrice Campbell, *The Iron Ladies: Why Do Women Vote Tory?* (London: Virago, 1987), pp. 11–13.

5 *Daily Telegraph*, 6 January 1906, cited in *Labour Record & Review*, January 1906.
6 Edith New, profile, *VFW*, 7 May 1908; see also prisoners' testimonies, e.g. Alice Burton's in *VFW*, 2 April 1909.
7 C. Pankhurst, *Unshackled*, p. 61.
8 Teresa Billington Grieg, 'Early WSPU history', TBG Papers, Box 398, B/8/2.
9 E. S. Pankhurst, *The Suffragette*, p. 43.
10 C. Pankhurst, *Unshackled*, p. 61.
11 See Kenney, *Memories*, pp. 58–61; also E. S. Pankhurst, *The Suffragette*, p. 54; C. Pankhurst, *Unshackled*, p. 61.
12 For a full, yet succinct, outline of the relevant laws, see Constance Rover, *Women's Suffrage and Party Politics in Britain* (London: Routledge & Kegan Paul, 1967), p. 78.
13 E. S. Pankhurst, *The Suffragette*, p. 66.
14 *Ibid.*, pp. 66–7.
15 Raeburn, *The Militant Suffragettes*, p. 22.
16 E. S. Pankhurst, *The Suffragette*, p. 224; see also *VFW*, March–May 1908.
17 *Daily Mirror*, 24 April 1908, cited in *VFW*, 30 April 1908; the other organisation was of barmaids.
18 *VFW*, 14 May 1908.
19 For discussion of the impact of the WSPU's by-electioneering on Liberal votes, see Pugh, *The March of the Women*, pp. 231–40.
20 *Suffragette*, 13 February 1914.
21 E. S. Pankhurst, *The Suffragette*, pp. 165–6.
22 *VFW*, March 1908.
23 Notes on Alice Milne's diary, 24, 25, 27 September 1906, TBG Papers, Box 397, A/6 and 398 B/7.
24 Christabel Pankhurst to Jeannie Baines, 1 April 1908, Baines Papers.
25 *Ibid.*
26 E. S. Pankhurst, The Suffragette, p. 166.
27 Leila K. McNeill, mss statement, ACC4703, National Library of Scotland.
28 Emmeline Pethick Lawrence to Jennie Baines, 7 April 1908, Baines Papers.
29 WSPU Second Year Intermediate Report (August) 1907.
30 Kenney, *Memories*, p. 124.
31 Mitchell, *The Hard Way Up*, p. 163.
32 *Women and Progress*, 7 December 1906.
33 *Labour Record & Review*, December 1906.
34 *VFW*, December 1907.
35 *Ibid.*, February 1908.
36 *Ibid.*, 4 June 1908.
37 *Ibid.*, February 1908.
38 Christabel Pankhurst to Jennie Baines, 20 May 1908, Baines Papers; M. J. Hewitt to Mary Gawthorpe, undated postcard describing her work in Newhaven, Mary Gawthorpe Papers, Tamiment Library, New York.
39 *Labour Record & Review*, October 1906.
40 Leneman, *A Guid Cause*, p. 42.
41 Notes on Alice Milne's diary, 2 September 1906, Box 397 A/6, TBG Papers.

42 Gawthorpe, *Uphill to Holloway*, p. 230.

43 *Ibid.*, p. 235

44 Kenney, *Memories*, p. 114.

45 *Ibid.*

46 Haig, *This Was My World*, p. 134.

47 *VFW*, 6 August 1908.

48 *Ibid.*, 27 August 1908.

49 *Ibid.*, 27 August 1908, and 17 September 1908.

50 Emmeline Pethick Lawrence to Mary Phillips, 23 August 1909, Mary Phillips Papers, Camellia Collection; see also Christabel Pankhurst to Jennie Baines, 23 November 1909, Baines Papers.

51 *VFW*, 23 July 1909.

52 *Ibid.*

53 *Ibid.*

54 Emmeline Pethick Lawrence to Jennie Baines, 7 April 1908, Baines Papers.

55 Cicely Hamilton, *Life Errant* (London: Dent, 1935), p. 75.

56 Archdale, in Macpherson, *The Suffragette's Daughter*, p. 35.

57 TNA, DPP 1/19, Exhibit 62.

58 Beatrice Sanders to Dora Marsden, 9 February 1910, Dora Marsden Papers.

59 Emmeline Pethick Lawrence to Mary Phillips, 17 December 1908, Mary Phillips Papers.

60 Emmeline Pethick Lawrence to Jennie Baines, 14 November 1907, Baines Papers.

61 Kenney, *Memories*, p. 120.

62 *VFW*, November 1907.

63 *Ibid.*, 23 July 1909.

64 Scrap notes on Miss M. S. Turner, SFC.

65 Christabel Pankhurst to Jennie Baines, 28 November 1907, Baines Papers; Emmeline Pethick Lawrence to Mary Phillips, 17 December 1908, Mary Phillips Papers.

66 Christabel Pankhurst to Jennie Baines, 28 November 1907, Baines Papers.

67 Emily Blathwayt's diary, 8 May 1908. Blathwayt Diaries, Gloucester Record Office.

68 Mary Blathwayt's diary, 12 August 1909, Blathwayt Diaries.

69 Christabel Pankhurst to Jennie Baines, 13 May 1907, Baines Papers.

70 Emmeline Pethick Lawrence to Jennie Baines, 24 November 1909, Baines Papers.

71 Haig, *This Was My World*, p. 135.

72 Hamilton, *Life Errant*, p. 69.

73 Emily Blathwayt's diary, 18 October 1908, Blathwayt Diaries.

74 Organiser's sample diary, Mary Phillips Papers.

75 Emmeline Pankhurst to Caroline Philips, 10 December 1907, quoted in Purvis, *Emmeline Pankhurst*, p. 101.

76 Mary Phillips to Annot Robinson, 8 April 1908, Annot Robinson Papers.

77 E. Sylvia Pankhurst, *The Life of Emmeline Pankhurst: The Suffragette Struggle for Women's Citizenship* (London: T. Werner Laurie, 1935), p. 72.

78 Gawthorpe, *Uphill to Holloway*, p. 230.

79 Stephenson, 'No other way', p. 65.

80 Emily Blathwayt's diary, 29 May 1908, Blathwayt Diaries.

81 Mary Blathwayt's diary, 5 July 1908, Blathwayt Diaries.

82 Haig, *This Was My World*, p. 135.

83 Mary Blathwayt's diary, 12 and 15 July 1909, Blathwayt Diaries.

84 Kenney, *Memories*, p. 120

85 See, for example, Emily Blathwayt's diary, 5 March 1911, Blathwayt Diaries.

86 Mary Phillips to Annot Robinson, 8 April 1908, Annot Robinson Papers.

87 Notes on Alice Milne's diary, 16 October 1906, Box 397 A/6, TBG Papers.

88 Christabel Pankhurst to Jeannie Baines, 6 July 1907, 12 November 1907 and 11 February 1908, Baines Papers.

89 Constance Lytton to Annie Kenney, 22 September 1909, Kenney Papers.

90 Emmeline Pankhurst to Alice Morgan Wright, 11 February 1912, quoted in Purvis, *Emmeline Pankhurst*, p 177.

91 Kenney, *Memories*, p. 120.

92 *Toronto Globe & Mail*, 11 February 1965.

93 Mary Gawthorpe to John Galsworth, 30 April 1931, Mary Gawthorpe Papers.

94 Grace Roe to Nellie Hall, Christmas 1962, Nellie Hall Humpherson Papers.

95 Christabel Pankhurst to Jennie Baines, 8 September 1908, Baines Papers.

96 Mary Blathwayt's diary, 11 June 1908, Blathwayt Diaries.

97 Millicent Browne to Mary Gawthorpe, 30 July 1909, Mary Gawthorpe Papers.

98 Archdale in MacPherson, *The Suffragette's Daughter*, p. 35.

99 Kenney, *Memories*, p. 100.

100 Notes on Alice Milne's diary, Box 397 A/6, TBG Papers.

101 Mitchell, *The Hard Way Up*, p. 163.

102 *VFW*, February 1908.

103 *Ibid.*

104 Anon, 'Notes on Aeta Lamb', SFC.

105 For example, Emily Blathwayt's diary, 27 and 28 January 1909, and 7 July 1909, Blathwayt Diaries.

106 See, for example, Marguerite Sidley to *Standard*, 9 October 1912.

107 Emmeline Pethick Lawrence to Mary Phillips, 5 August 1909, Mary Phillips Papers.

108 Christabel Pankhurst to Jennie Baines, 13 October 1909, Baines Papers.

109 *Ibid.*, 21 November 1907, Baines Papers.

110 Marguerite Annie Sidley's biographical notes, SFC; Christabel Pankhurst to Jennie Baines, n.d. (?November 1907), Baines Papers.

111 Christabel Pankhurst to Jennie Baines, 6 February 1909.

112 *Ibid.*, 2 March 1909.

113 Christabel Pankhurst to Rachel Barrett, 20 May 1908, Camellia Collection.

114 TNA, Home Office (HO), 45/10695/231366/56.

115 *Ibid.*

116 Raeburn, *The Militant Suffragettes*, p. 45.

117 *VFW*, February 1908.

118 *Ibid.*

119 Quoted in C. Pankhurst, *Unshackled*, p. 86.

120 E. S. Pankhurst, *The Suffragette Movement*, p. 272.

121 Raeburn, *The Militant Suffragettes*, p. 45.

122 See *ibid.*, pp. 45–6; E. S. Pankhurst, *The Suffragette Movement*, pp. 272–3; C. Pankhurst, *Unshackled*, p. 86.
123 E. S. Pankhurst, *The Suffragette Movement*, p. 262.
124 *Liverpool Daily Post*, 3 August 1909; similar reports occur in *ibid.* on 18 and 21 August.
125 Allen and Heyneman, *Woman at the Crossroads*, p. 65.
126 Kenney, *Memories*, pp. 108–9.

3

'There was only one member . . . when I arrived':[1] working as a district organiser

THE FIRST DISTRICT ORGANISERS had much in common with itinerant workers. Indeed, many district organisers began their careers at by-elections or 'working up' particular districts. The key difference between itinerant and district work was that women who became district organisers were deployed for much longer – sometimes for a matter of years – and were expected to become a more permanent fixture on the local political landscape. District organisers were usually put in charge of a number of branches in a particular region. They ran their own campaigns, and enjoyed a reasonable degree of autonomy and job stability, although they were ultimately answerable to headquarters for their actions, and could still be required to move on from their posts at short notice if the needs of another area were perceived to be more acute.

Another distinction between the district organiser and the peripatetic itinerant worker lay in the way that the local membership saw her role. The majority of the WSPU's members rarely left their own area to participate in events in London, and they had little first-hand knowledge of their national leaders – iconic figures glimpsed from a distance on a platform, at the head of a demonstration or as images in the literature and propaganda that they sold. For most regional members the district organiser became the accessible official face of the Union and the means through which national policies were channelled down to the membership. The local members could also perceive their district organisers as more responsive. Although they did not often devise national policy, they had the authority to interpret or mould its implementation and were expected to display innovation in adapting directives to local conditions. Some of their initiatives could be taken up at headquarters and disseminated to other regions as examples of good working practice. In this way, the district organiser carried more responsibility for the success of the

WSPU's campaign than its national leaders. Without a team of success-ful district organisers throughout Britain, the WSPU would have found it impossible to achieve any coherence in its campaign, or any longevity once itinerant campaigners had returned to London.

The WSPU began its shift to the more long-term deployment of dis-trict organisers in 1907. The London base had been secured by this stage, and the WSPU also had its Manchester branch, plus active groups in other parts of the country, although their development had been due largely to chance and often depended on the will and determination of small groups of women to form a branch in their own town or city. The itinerant campaigns that Christabel Pankhurst announced in *Women's Franchise* in June 1907 were aimed at spreading the Union on a more methodical basis, and concentrated on six regions. There was another subtle difference, in that individual organisers were now put in charge of these regions for the duration of a campaign, thus identifying themselves with a region rather as well as with the WSPU overall. Nell Kenney was sent to the north east, Annie returned to Manchester and Adela Pankhurst was sent to south Wales. In Scotland, Teresa Billington Grieg announced the establishment of a federation, with Helen Fraser as its organiser. York-shire and the Midlands were also involved, and plans were laid to expand further into the West Country. This arrangement covered most of Britain, but stretched the WSPU's resources to their limit, and Christabel admit-ted that in London and the south she was 'obliged to rely chiefly on the London members since most of the organisers are at work in other parts of the country'.[2]

Effective contact with the branches became even more important in September 1907, following the split in the WSPU which precipitated the formation of the WFL. Prior to this, the relationship between branches and the centre had been rather loose, although branches could send del-egates and resolutions to the WSPU's national conference. Now that the WSPU had become avowedly autocratic, such formal affiliate structures were deemed to be unnecessary. Women now joined their local branch, although, as Emmeline Pankhurst explained to Miss Thompson, the lead-ers hoped that 'members of the local Unions ... [would] become members of the National WSPU as well'.[3] There was also a growing suspicion among the WSPU leaders that some of the newer provincial recruits lacked under-standing of the Union's aims and its preferred way of operating. Many of those who had joined the WSPU in 1907 had 'never seen the leaders of the movement', and it appeared that some of the newer branches had become 'a happy hunting ground for intriguers' who sought to 'change the general methods of work'.[4] The increased emphasis on employing district organisers would ensure that there were trusted officials in the regions, well-positioned to counter such rumblings in the future.

There were other obvious advantages to establishing more permanent bases for the WSPU, with organisers at the helm. The successes of itinerant campaigns could flounder within months of being left in the hands of local workers. No matter how enthusiastic they were, it was all too easy for their attempts to be thwarted by inexperience or lack of confidence, or for organisers to become fatally overstretched as they attempted to combine political activism with other demands of employment or housework that called on their time. It was much easier for a permanent organiser to follow initiatives through. Her presence also facilitated more gradual approaches to recruitment and encouraged links with existing local groups that might have a radical feminist membership, such as socialist groupings, trade unions or dissenting congregations. As the Union employed more organisers, the idea of longer term deployments became achievable. In building up to 'Women's Sunday', the mass demonstration in Hyde Park on 21 June 1908, Emmeline Pethick Lawrence had drawn on the talents of several recently appointed workers, including Nelly Crocker, Rachel Barret, Gertrude Conlan, Gladice Keevil, Edith New and Annot Robinson. These women worked flat out in a number of different centres to ensure that the attendance in Hyde Park was both as large and as regionally diverse as possible, and much of the success of Women's Sunday was attributed to their work. In her evaluation of the campaign, Emmeline acknowledged the success of the regional approach and declared that the WSPU ought to have 'an organiser in every great centre of the population'.[5] District initiatives, intended to capitalise on the mood at Hyde Park, commenced immediately. Mary Gawthorpe was sent to Manchester, and Nell Kenney returned to the Midlands with Gladice Keevil. The long-term deployment of district organisers had begun.

The earliest appointments were conceived as regional posts, with one organiser overseeing quite a large area. Annie Kenney, who became one of the longest serving of these workers, was originally put in charge of the 'West Country', a district that included Plymouth, Torquay and parts of south Wales. Mary Gawthorpe had the whole of Lancashire, while Gladice Keevil's work in the Midlands spanned Birmingham, Leicester, parts of Derbyshire and the Potteries. As it was unrealistic to expect a single official to work consistently across such a broad terrain, the first district organisers were encouraged to call in extra help. Annie Kenney was provided with a series of assistant organisers, including Aeta Lamb, Dorothy Pethick, and also Clara Codd and Mary Blathwayt whom she trained herself, while in Lancashire Mary Gawthorpe's workload was considerably lightened by the voluntary contribution of Edith Rigby, the *de facto* organiser of Preston WSPU, which had become 'one of the strongest [branches] in the country' by the time the Lancashire region was drawn up.[6] This policy continued when funding was available. Gladice Keevil was helped by Laura Ainsworth in the Midlands, and her successor, Dorothy Evans, was joined by Gladys Hazel for a time, while in Nottingham Nelly Crocker and Gladys Roberts worked together. As the use of district organisers evolved throughout 1908, cities became favoured as bases although regions could nominally remain attached as the WSPU's third Annual Report announced:

> One of the special developments ... has been the establishment in various districts of the country of centres of the National Organisation. From every one of these ... a national campaign is conducted throughout the surrounding district. The centre for London and the home counties is at 4 Clements Inn under the control of Mrs Drummond; the West of England is in [the] charge of Miss Annie Kenney with offices in Bristol and Torquay; Lancashire is being organised by Miss Mary Gawthorpe with headquarters in Manchester and offices in Preston and Rochdale; Birmingham and district by Miss Gladice Keevil, with headquarters in Birmingham; Leeds and Bradford by Miss Charlotte Marsh; Newcastle and district by Miss Edith New; Glasgow by Miss Conlan; Edinburgh by Miss Macaulay and Aberdeen by Miss Flatman.[7]

Being based in a town or city made the district organiser's job much more manageable. Although she was still expected to make visits into surrounding areas to build up meetings or work on particular protests, most organisers now spent their time working in much small areas. Cities were also preferred as they were more populous, with a greater number of potential recruits; they had more meeting halls and better open-air venues were available. 'You can't have a meeting in among the fields', Olive Bartels explained when describing the urban scope of her work in Chelmsford.[8] City bases offered the benefits of affordable lodgings and a good transport infrastructure, allowing the organiser to move around quickly and cheaply, and to come to London for meetings as needed. The trend towards smaller centres continued as the WSPU grew. Twenty three were listed in the Annual Report for 1910, with new centres in Southport, Derby, Nottingham, Northampton and Preston. The following year saw further expansion, raising the number of WSPU centres to seventy-four. Many of these were short-term ventures attempted during the two General Election campaigns of 1910, and a more realistic estimate, drawn from the regular district reports which organisers wrote for *VFW* and the *Suffragette*, suggests that the WSPU employed a district organiser in around

3   Flora Drummond (in scarf) welcomes Annie Kenney and a contingent of
Lancashire and Yorkshire women attending the third Women's Parliament,
February 1908

twenty-five areas between 1909 and 1914. Although the number of district
organisers thus remained stable, the profile of the actual districts was less
static with old centres closing and new ones opening right up to 1914.
At the outbreak of the First World War, the Union's network of district
organisers spread from Aberdeen to Hastings and Liverpool to Bristol, as
well as recently-created positions in Cork, Belfast and Dublin.

In theory, district organisers were employed by the WSPU's National
Committee. In practice, most knew that they were responsible to four
women: Christabel Pankhurst as the chief organiser; the treasurer Emmeline Pethick Lawrence, who technically controlled their salaries and was
responsible for their expenditure; Beatrice Sanders, the WSPU's financial
secretary who scrutinised the regional accounts; and Flora Drummond,
who Christabel placed in charge of organising local unions in November
1911.[9] After the departure of the Pethick Lawrences and Christabel's self-
imposed exile in France in 1912, organisers were still responsible to the
Union's headquarters at Kingsway where Emmeline Pankhurst now held

the purse strings. Communication with Christabel was more difficult and a sring of deputies, including Annie Kenney and Grace Roe, were often in prison or on the run as 'mice', making the co-ordination of district organisers more or less impossible. By this point, most district organisers had a good deal of experience in building and running campaigns, and were left largely to their own devices. In most cases this made very little difference as, outside of financial expenditure or major campaigns requiring provincial help, a district organiser enjoyed considerable autonomy and was fairly free to select her own campaigns and working practices within a broad, nationally devised agenda. What a district organiser did need was the consistent support of her branch. Her purpose was to lead others into higher levels of activity rather than single-handedly run every campaign herself. Without the support of her membership, a district organiser's life could be very difficult – and lonely – as will be seen.

Deployment saw the WSPU leadership at its most pro-active. Achieving the right match between an organiser and a branch or district was an important decision which had serious implications for the success of suffrage work in a given district and, by extension, nationally. Good personal skills were essential. While Christabel Pankhurst concerned herself largely with formulating policy, Emmeline Pethick Lawrence took upon herself the role of advising many new organisers. She reminded them that a good district organiser would oversee work in an area rather than 'attempting to do all the work [her]self'.[10] The 'secret of success' was to 'find out what people can do and let them do it'.[11] Personal charisma was vital. The WSPU's leaders were acutely aware of the personality quirks of many of their more active members and happily shared these with organisers, warning them off women who they perceived to be unsuited to certain jobs or were particularly problematical. Patricia Woodlock, a stalwart of the Liverpool WSPU was often publicly singled out for praise by the national leadership.[12] She was undoubtedly a bold activist, but, despite her heroic status, Christabel Pankhurst had misgivings about her ability to work in more controlled situations. She shared these with Jennie Baines who was planning to disrupt cabinet ministers' meetings in the north west in the autumn of 1907, warning that she had been 'told that Miss Woodlock … is not very suitable for this work so when you are making plans … do not rely upon her'.[13] Similarly, in Bath, the more experienced Aeta Lamb helped newly appointed Mary Blathwayt with her work, and explicitly forbade her from making one particular appointment, insisting that 'Miss Whittaker *must not* be allowed to become treasurer' of the newly inaugurated NWSPU branch in the city.[14] No records of the leaders' discussions about organisers' deployment have survived, but their levels of concern around who should take smaller positions make it inconceivable that less care would be taken over an appointment that could account for the success or failure of a whole region.

Particular qualities were required of district organisers that were not essential for effective work at headquarters or even in itinerant campaigns. Aeta Lamb went on to be one of the WSPU's longest-serving organisers at headquarters, but was said by her biographer to have 'failed utterly' at district work.[15] There were issues of personality as well. An effective organiser had to collect around her a group of willing and enthusiastic volunteers, who could be entrusted with time-consuming day-to-day tasks, leaving the organiser free to develop a wider strategic vision for her district. Members' enthusiasm had to be inspired and retained over quite lengthy periods, even when things were difficult. The fact that the WSPU recruited only women caused district organisers further difficulties as their members, especially those from working-class backgrounds, faced heavier demands on their time than did men. Organisers had to recognise that volunteers fitted in their suffrage work around a plethora of domestic tasks as well as full-time paid work in some instances. They might also suffer abuse. It was quickly apparent to all suffragettes who spoke or who sold newspapers in public that they had to face a continual barrage of criticism, much of which implied that they were neglecting their homes and somehow failing as women by giving up time to political work. While she was handing out leaflets to men arriving at Kings Cross station for the 1908 FA Cup Final, a man sneered at Minnie Baldock: ' It is a pity [these women] cannot look after their homes. I wonder what their places are like?'[16] In Ashton, Hannah Mitchell was constantly plagued by a local market trader who interrupted her meetings, shouting 'in a good strong market-trained voice: "Can any on ye bake a batch o'bread? Han yer mended the stockin's? Go whoam an mind yer babbies" and similar brainwaves'.[17]

Accusations of neglect of domestic duty were not restricted to married women. Jessie Stephenson recounted how the familiar criticisms would be adapted for the single suffragette campaigner. As hecklers 'couldn't tell her she ought to be at home minding her babies, they said no wonder *she* wasn't married'.[18] Molly Murphy, who was quite young when she started public speaking in Manchester also remembered men shouting at her: 'Gerr off hom and 'elp tha mother to look after t'kids.'[19] 'The way', Hannah Mitchell told a meeting in West Yorkshire in May 1907, 'such questions as "can you darn a stocking" were so often asked at [our] meetings by men, it seemed that the ability to do such things was regarded as a sufficient qualification for the franchise!'[20]

Catcalls and jeers reached all suffrage workers, but although their public profile meant that they received a greater share of unpleasantness than did volunteers, organisers were probably affected less by them. In most cases they were working in unfamiliar districts, away from the gaze of friends and family but buoyed up by the emotional support of other WSPU staff. Organisers also had more experience of the public platform and became skilled at turning hecklers' words against them. Annie Kenney recalled that she and her fellow-organisers 'were taught never to lose our tempers; to always to get the best of a joke, and to join in the laughter with the audience even if the joke was against us'.[21] Many organisers became 'quick witted, good at repartee'. When a man threw a cabbage at Mary Gawthorpe during a meeting in Manchester, she dodged it, quipping that she feared that he had lost his head, while in Derby Gladice Keevil silenced a man who suggested, during a Thursday meeting, that she ought to be doing her washing with the riposte that in her home, as in all respectable households, the washing was done and put away at the start of the week.[22]

Voluntary workers were more pressured. They often lacked the self-assurance of organisers, and were not able to conceive of their suffrage work in terms of a career, no matter how important it was to them individually. They also had to face the disapprobation of friends and neighbours. In Leeds, Leonora Cohen was fortunate in having a husband and young son who were completely behind her suffragette activity, but was aware that they suffered on her behalf, especially her husband who received hate mail and was snubbed by members at the Leeds and County Liberal Club where he had been an active member.[23] Mary Blathwayt, whose voluntary status meant that she organised mainly in and around her home, found that criticism was not reserved for her formal public appearances. Her diary recorded frequent low-level harassment even when she was not doing WSPU work, such as the time when someone rudely called out 'suffragette' at her when she walked to her local post office in January 1909.[24]

The pressure of public hostility weighed so heavily on rank and file suffragettes that they could go to extraordinary lengths to protect their domestic life from disruption. Grace Alderman from Preston WSPU recalled another local suffragette, Mrs Towler, who had four sons and a home which was 'always in order, so it was quite a thing for her to leave home and risk imprisonment. Anyway, she spent a whole week baking … she baked enough to keep the five of them going for a fortnight!'[25]

Domestic anxieties cut across class backgrounds, particularly where mothers were involved. When news reached her home city of York that

Nancy Seymour Pearson had become its first suffragette prisoner in January 1913, her WSPU friend Ada Robertson went straight off to visit Nancy's children and wrote to reassure Nancy that 'they both looked well and jolly'.[26] Myra Saad Brown, gaoled for her part in the WSPU's window-smashing raid of 1912, received letters from her three small children which 'were such a joy ... [she] wanted to kiss them all over'.[27] Organisers faced the difficult task of persuading their members to brave these painful separations. As few organisers had children themselves, the more imaginative had to demonstrate ways of conveying empathy with their members in such situations. In Liverpool, Ada Flatman encouraged Mrs Healis, an older suffragette, to look 'after the child of one of those who took part' in a deputation and subsequently went to prison.[28]

The extreme circumstances of prison facilitated co-operation, as they brought organisers many volunteers who were eager to do their bit without going quite so far. When other less dangerous tasks were required, organisers had to rely on the force of their own personalities to persuade and cajole. Local meetings, regular paper sales and small local demonstrations were much more important to retaining a regional structure than were acts of flamboyant militancy, but these could prove difficult to sustain. Even smaller actions, such as selling papers, could be unpleasant experiences in a suffragette's own town where she might be spotted by neighbours, relatives and friends. Margaret Haig 'tactfully, or at least timidly, dived down a side street', when selling *VFW* if she glimpsed her mother-in-law approaching.[29] The ability of a popular organiser to persuade her membership by appealing to their friendship as well as their political convictions was invaluable, and many worked hard to inspire an almost devotional following in their districts, which stayed with many of their members for years. In Preston, Edith Rigby was known for her powers of persuasion, which could induce even the most timid branch members to engage in bolder acts. One of her earliest recruits, Beth Hesmondhalgh, felt that much of Edith's success was due to her persuasiveness which meant that 'when [she] wanted you to undertake anything unpleasant or dangerous, she had a way of making you feel that *she* was doing *you* a favour!'[30]

Several district organisers shared Edith Rigby's talent. When Jessie Kenney considered the reasons for her sister Annie's success, she concluded that much of it was because Annie was 'one of the merriest organisers we had. She loved fun and she made friends wherever she went ... no one found so many friends and was so befriended as she was when she first became an organiser for the WSPU.'[31] Annie Kenney undoubtedly had a winning way with people which helped her to make many intense and enduring friendships in her organising work, but she was by no means unique in this. None of her members in the west of England would have hesitated in agreeing with Jessie's assessment of Annie, but other suffragettes would have made similar claims for their own district organisers. Despite being a Yorkshirewoman by birth, Mary Gawthorpe became extremely popular in her WSPU district of Lancashire. Edith Pepper and Dr Letitia Fairfield, both of whom worked alongside Mary in Manchester, recalled the vitality of her personality when interviewed some sixty years later. Dr Fairfield, whose sister, Rebecca West, penned an affectionate portrait of Mary in the *Daily Herald*, found her 'the most fascinating, magnetic person', while Edith Pepper confessed that the entire branch 'worshipped Mary ... we thought there was nobody like her'.[32] In Birmingham, Maude Smith 'adored', and was similarly inspired by, Dorothy Evans, who had a talent for building up her members' confidence in their own ability to undertake militant or public work.[33] Successful organisers instilled feelings of personal pride and possession amongst their membership, which contributed to a strong sense of collective identity and enhanced the work of the branch. When this did not happen, the life of a district organiser could become unbearable, as will be seen.

The main factors governing deployment were the national leaders' perception of an individual organiser's abilities and their view of the needs of a district. Like itinerant workers, district organisers were largely expected to go where they were sent, especially for a first posting. Such consultation as there was was usually initiated by headquarters. Grace Roe 'found' herself appointed East Anglian organiser after two years of voluntary work and campaigning.[34] Sometimes, unforeseen circumstances drove events. Jessie Stephenson had only just been taken on to the WSPU staff when, early in 1911, Christabel Pankhurst telegraphed her to go and 'fix things up for Manchester'.[35] Mary Gawthorpe was suffering from a serious illness, and it was evident that she would not be returning to her district in the near future. In the intensity of campaigns, such decisions could be hastily taken, and organisers were often less than content with the choices made. 'That is disposing of you without consultation with a vengeance', Helen Fraser wrote furiously to Isabel Seymour, to inform her of the current rumour that Emmeline Pethick Lawrence was about to dispatch her to organise in Scotland.[36] Annot Robinson was equally annoyed when whispers reached her during a spell in Holloway that she was to work in Dundee, despite her recent marriage to Sam Robinson of Manchester ILP. 'I am more astonished and vexed over this Dundee affair than I can say', she wrote to her husband; 'have I been appointed organiser [there] in my absence?'[37]

A little more care was exercised when organisers were being redeployed between districts. Unenthusiastic deportees from one region would not make effective organisers in another. Furthermore, they could leave groups of disenchanted supporters behind them who could make life difficult for the next incumbent. Annie Williams was moved from Newcastle, where she had worked well from 1909 to 1911, to Halifax and Huddersfield, a region with several long-established braches that had never had a paid organiser before. Miss Williams did not find the work there particularly inspiring after the larger Newcastle district, and she confided in the WSPU's demonstration secretary, Margaret Cameron, that she wanted another move.[38] When Annie Kenney assumed command after Christabel's departure to Paris, Miss Cameron passed on this information to her, and she was able to act. Rachel Barret was moved from her position in Wales at this point and Annie Williams was offered her district, a post that she happily accepted. Miss Williams had made a success of Newcastle, and as her new district was something of an experiment, she received a sympathetic hearing from her employers when things did not meet her expectations. Other organisers who requested moves for less apparent reasons found that the WSPU could be a somewhat inflexible employer. After ten months in Liverpool, Ada Flatman wrote to Emmeline Pethick Lawrence requesting a change. Miss Flatman had proved an effective and popular organiser. One of her great successes had been a WSPU shop which she had managed to get off the ground despite the misgivings of the treasurer. Unfortunately, she found shop work more congenial than organising, and was seeking a similar opening elsewhere. Emmeline Pethick Lawrence was immoveable, and wrote:

> I am afraid there is not an opening in our new shop in London, and I think it would be an immense mistake for you to change your work. You have just got hold of Liverpool ... [and] have made the campaign there a single success. A great deal of this would be thrown away if you were to change ...[39]

It was not until December 1910, after eight months of intense lobbying by Ada, that Mrs Pethick Lawrence finally informed her that 'Miss Pankhurst and I have ... fallen in with your wishes to go to a new place to found a centre', and she was moved to Cheltenham.[40] Dora Marsden found the leadership equally inflexible in accommodating her wishes as organiser. Before becoming an organiser, she had worked on campaigns in Huddersfield and Manchester, and found Southport a very different district. Emmeline Pethick Lawrence could not understand why 'a sale of one or two thousand copies' of *VFW* could not be achieved in the district, but

Dora had a different view.[41] She found the resort restrictive, and sought a larger field of action in which to work. Christabel acquiesced to a degree, but offered Blackburn in addition to Southport.[42] When Dora challenged this, saying that she would have preferred to take over Burnley, Christabel left her in no doubt that such decisions were a matter for the national leadership, in this case herself and Emmeline Pethick Lawrence, rather than for individual organisers. Dora was told: 'we selected Blackburn in preference to Burnley because it is a place of rather special importance, politically speaking ... Accrington and Burnley together would make a very good district for another organiser.'[43]

If organisers felt that they were dealt with in a rather high-handed manner, branch members received even less consultation as to who their organiser might be. Yet, with the exceptions of Ireland and some Scottish branches, which will be examined later, there is little evidence of dissent among the rank and file around the choice of organisers. Demand outweighed supply, and branch members were much more concerned with whether or not they would actually be given an organiser. Smaller districts could lose out when positions were shuffled. Annie Williams's move to Wales suited her, but it was not necessarily the best thing for the membership in Halifax and Huddersfield. The WSPU leaders were aware of this, and Rachel Barrett, the previous Welsh organiser, sought reassurances from Miss Williams before agreeing to the move:

> Do you think that ... members [in Halifax and Huddersfield] could carry out the work for about a month? We have several probationary organisers coming here for training ... but we cannot send one of them to the provinces until she has been in London for about a month ...[44]

In the event, Dr Helena Jones, an experienced WSPU worker, came forward as an honorary organiser for Halifax, which left Huddersfield adrift. As Huddersfield was quite small on its own, Annie Williams's position there was left unfilled. Even large districts could be left without organisers for lengthy periods. Manchester, despite its oft-vaunted status as the 'mother union', never had another organiser after Jessie Stephenson left in 1911, but had to manage with branch secretaries instead. The only leverage that districts appeared to have been able to deploy when requesting organisers was thier self-sufficiency in funding the post. This was not always helpful to organisers. Liverpool suffragettes established a separate organiser fund in February 1909, one month before the appointment of their first district organiser, Mary Phillips. Some years later she experienced the other side of self-funding when in July 1913 Christabel Pankhurst abruptly terminated her employment in Plymouth, declaring that 'if local people will provide neither money nor work it is impossible for headquarters to supply them with an organiser'.[45]

Once an organiser was assigned to a district, her first task was to find suitable accommodation. Many organisers stayed with friends or sympathisers, particularly when finding their feet in the early months. After this, they had a greater degree of flexibility than itinerant workers, and several organisers were able to rent flats, the ultimate symbol of female emancipation before the First World War. As with many other aspects of organising, the excitement occasioned by the freedom of moving beyond lodging rooms to a rented flat struck some interesting common chords between women of very different classes. Lady Constance Lytton had lived comfortably with her mother in a house on the family's estate at Knebworth, but was particularly thrilled that her salary 'enabled [her] to take a small flat in London near the Euston Road', which became entirely her own space.[46] Helen Craggs, whose first weekly wage was only 25 shillings, 'rented a room in Bloomsbury ... [and] employed a char who came in every morning and made her a cup of tea and washed her clothes'. In complete contrast to her previous life at home, when Helen had been forced to hide much of her suffragette work from her father, she was now free to 'lie in bed, read her mail, answer her correspondence and plan the day's activities ... before going out neatly dressed and totally prepared'.[47] Less affluent suffragettes also valued their independence. Jessie Kenney proudly remembered how her sister Annie was able to make 'a warm and cosy little home' of each of her flats.[48] Lettice Floyd who worked alongside Annie Williams as literature secretary in Newcastle, then Huddersfield and Wales, had worked as a nurse, but did not leave home until the age of 42, when she began suffrage work.[49] Organisers' ability to live as independent women boosted their self-confidence and reassured them that suffrage organising was valued and credible work.

Once accommodation was arranged, a new organiser had to establish herself and her work among the local membership as quickly as possible. This could be difficult. When Grace Roe was sent to Ipswich, 'there was only one member' for her to organise.[50] Similarly, on her arrival in Bristol, Annie Kenney had 'only the names of [two] veteran ladies ... as well as the name of one sympathiser who did not want the Vote, but was keen on prison reform'.[51] Like many new organisers, Annie and Grace tried to kick-start their campaigns with large public meetings, designed to introduce the organiser and the potential recruits to one another. Six weeks was the usual time allowed for working up such meetings, and, if there was no functioning branch, volunteers could be shaped into an embryonic structure during the planning period. Everything fell to the organiser in the early stages.

The first task was getting the hall. Annie Kenney tramped round all the halls in Bristol, taking notes on their suitability and acoustic quality.[52] Once a venue was chosen, it had to be hired, which was not always straightforward, as many local authorities used militancy as an excuse for refusing halls to suffragettes. Liverpool City Council denied the use of a library room to the WSPU for a meeting that aimed to explain 'militant methods' to the local population.[53] In other parts of the country, deputations from WSPU branches protested to local authorities at their exclusion from public buildings, but to little avail, most councils concurring with the Lord Mayor of Bath that they were not disposed to rent public buildings to 'ladies … [who] sallied forth and did thirty thousand pounds worth of damage' in orchestrated protests.[54] Local insurrection had further effects, even when the WSPU was its target rather than its instigator. Grace Roe was unable to get a suitable hall for her first meeting in Ipswich because the only previous WSPU meeting there had ended in a near riot. She finally secured the Corn Exchange, an unimposing and unattractive building, which she then had to spend hours decorating with flowers to make it more appealing.[55] If policing was deemed necessary, the organiser had to arrange it, often paying the cost as well. In Bath, Emily Blathwayt recorded that her daughter had secured two policemen from the local chief constable at a cost of half-a-crown each.[56] Such favours were worth courting, but took up a lot of an organiser's time without being obviously connected to the suffragette project.

Having secured both speaker and hall, the organiser then had to arrange for the printing and selling of tickets, and find cheap ways of advertising. Organisers reported innovative techniques in the local reports columns of *VFW* and the *Suffragette* for others to mimic. A variety of imaginative – and largely inexpensive – advertising techniques thus emerged. Perennial favourites were the house-to-house canvass and pavement-chalking, but there were original methods too. In Manchester, Mary Gawthorpe and her branch devised a 'human advertisement … composed of as many members as would represent each letter in the name Christabel Pankhurst', which they carried through the streets of the city.[57] The Manchester branch also had the idea of using a small group of fly-posters who used 'pillar boxes, barrack and prison walls' as a more effective (and cheaper) space than public hoardings.[58] In Birmingham, Dorothy Evans proudly reported that her modern scheme had literally 'electrified' the city:

The fact that Mrs Pankhurst was speaking in the Town Hall ... was brought to public notice by means of square lanterns fitted with electric lights which shone through throwing up the words ['] Mrs Pankhurst, Town Hall, November 15['] in strong relief.[59]

Once a branch was established, much of a district organiser's work was quite mundane. Molly Murphy, who worked in Sheffield, described how, when no large meeting or act of militancy was on the agenda, branches 'operated much as any other propaganda association or party, raising funds to help headquarters, holding meetings with their own local speakers ... distributing leaflets, selling Votes for Women pamphlets'.[60] The organiser was fairly free to choose her own routine, although she could expect that it would be punctuated from time to time by the demands of the movement. While there was no obligation to record the proceedings of branch meetings for headquarters, a district organiser was not free of paperwork. She was expected to keep a brief weekly diary of her work, and all organisers were given a sample diary which described the level of effort expected of them. The diary suggested a plan of work for a week in which a large public meeting was to take place, and outlined a plethora of activities which ranged from assessing the 'plan of appointing six hostesses to welcome strangers' to the branch 'At Home' on Monday afternoon, to directing the 'decoration of two private carriages and brake to advertise Friday's meeting'.

Although the model organiser in this example attended several private meetings during the week, much of the propaganda work was carried out by branch members, reinforcing the WSPU's priority for organisers to be organising rather than doing.[61] Nevertheless, her presence was required at many events, even if she was there only in a directing capacity. The diary suggested a punishing schedule. Meetings or activities were arranged for almost every morning, afternoon and evening. Sunday was a holiday, and the organiser also 'took afternoon and evening off' on Saturday, but reports of local activities in *VFW* suggest that such breaks were not universal.[62] The completed work diary was to be sent down to headquarters every week, although it was not necessarily read immediately. The WSPU leaders made no secret of this: Christabel Pankhurst once cautioned Mary Phillips about enclosing letters in with her diary (presumably done to save postage) 'as they may not be read so promptly as when sent in the usual way'.[63]

As there was no obligation to hold business meetings at branches, most district organisers favoured the format of the WSPU 'At Home' as the regular gathering of members and sympathisers. These meetings began in London shortly after the WSPU moved to Clements Inn. 'At

Homes' were less formal than public meetings, and could involve some business discussion. Most organisers used them, but there were variations between districts, reflecting some regional autonomy on the part of organisers and branches. Mary Gawthorpe, one of the first organisers to start At Home meetings outside of London, was an enthusiastic supporter of the initiative, which she felt offered a 'unique opportunity ... of bringing friends to meet and talk' with suffragettes, and made meetings as sociable as possible, with tea and biscuits served.[64] Mary was so convinced of the value of her At Homes that she encouraged women from other parts of the country to attend if they happened to be visiting Manchester on a Friday.[65]

One advantage of a regular district organiser was that she could always act as the main speaker at these meetings, saving the branch travel expenses. Having an organiser ensured that there was also always someone to publicise At Homes. VFW and the Suffragette were the main way of advertising them, but resourceful organisers developed other techniques, which were shared among the network of district workers by headquarters. Mary Phillips and Mary Gawthorpe ordered printed cards for their districts which carried the time and venue of the meeting with a contact name and address, and were headed with the name of the branch. Dates and speakers' names would be written in by hand. Recipients were expected to 'RSVP', presumably to help plan more effectively for the event, but also to promote attendance by encouraging a more formal approach. Emmeline Pethick Lawrence was so impressed with Phillips's card that she requested extra copies 'to set as a model to other organisers'.[66] They subsequently proved effective in other districts, particularly in Ipswich where Grace Roe gave small bundles out to her branch members and found that one member alone brought in thirty visitors through their use.[67]

Organisers were free to chose the day and time of their At Home meeting. In districts like Manchester, where the WSPU attracted a significant membership among working women, At Homes tended to be evening affairs, although other districts such as certain Midlands branches held them in the afternoons. The day had a bearing on attendance. Ada Flatman in 1909 switched the Aberdeen At Home day from Thursday, believing that Wednesday would be the better day to 'meet the wants of all classes' who wished to attend.[68] Although the WSPU restricted its membership to women, some organisers welcomed men to their At Homes and even invited occasional male speakers from sympathetic political groups or the local Men's League for Women's Suffrage. Other organisers, such as Edith New in Newcastle, felt that women-only meetings would be more successful, so arranged these for their branches.[69] When a local WSPU had no premises of its own, the venue chosen for At Homes could influence their success and again reflected a level of autonomy for organiser and branch. Some branches used members' homes – a cost-effective alternative, but one that could be restrictive as there were suggestions that working-class suffragettes might feel ill at ease in grand drawing rooms. Molly Murphy found some of the houses she visited as an organiser in Sheffield a world away from her home in Manchester.[70] In other districts, organisers hired rooms for At Homes, opting for venues that would be less intimidating to working-class women. The Liverpool branch held its At Homes at the local Engineers' Rooms until it had an office, while in Newcastle Edith New secured the local ILP rooms.[71]

While organisers enjoyed a degree of choice about the timing and frequency of events such as At Homes, other demands were more centralised. Much of a district organiser's time was taken up with finance. In London, Emmeline Pethick Lawrence raised phenomenal amounts from affluent supporters at large public meetings. Few local organisers could match this; instead they relied on raising several small donations from their district. Even if an organiser was blessed with some wealthy supporters in her branch, she could find them reluctant to make regular donations, despite their willingness to assist with other resources. Annie Kenney relied heavily on the Blathwayt family in Bath, and was so appreciative of them that they were almost the only local members she mentioned by name in her autobiography.[72] Throughout her five years incumbency in the west of England job, the Blathwayts were always on hand to drive her around, offer hospitality to overnight speakers, and even to tidy her clothes and have her stockings mended, yet they rarely gave money to the cause.[73] Even Mary Blathwayt, who actually worked as an assistant organiser for a year, kept her private income to herself, although she did begin selling her old clothes and passing the proceeds to the Union rather than giving them away as she had previously done.[74] In other districts organisers similarly found that wealthy supporters were more likely to offer cars or for meetings, drawing rooms than they were to give cash.[75]

District organisers engaged constantly in fundraising but a particular drive was expected for the WSPU's week of 'self-denial', an annual practice observed across the country. *VFW* and the *Suffragette* outlined productive schemes from different districts. Jumble sales and cake and produce sales predominated, although some organisers were more resourceful. Dorothy Pethick was particularly proud of the anonymous Birmingham member who 'cycled everywhere to save train fares' during self-denial week in 1910.[76] Elizabeth Grew used a 'surprise sale' where donated gifts were given numbers, which were sold, 'the joke [being] that [buyers] get what they do not want and put it back to be sold again'.[77] 'American teas' at which admission was dependent on both bringing something to buy and making a purchase were equally popular. While local reports were predictably upbeat in their accounts of fundraising initiatives, other sources are more forthcoming about the stresses that such initiatives could generate. Alice Milne's diary recorded the anxiety of a jumble sale in Manchester in October 1906. Despite careful planning, there were no tables on the day, necessitating 'a last minute rush' until a cleaner at a local 'ragged school' offered furniture. The sale comprised a 'mess of goods, much unsaleable', although at the appointed hour 'the great unwashed came trooping in ... [and] we reached five pounds in coppers', to Alice's surprise.[78]

As well as raising money, organisers had to account for each penny they received, a requirement that formed the basis for much of the communication between district organisers and London. An organiser had to submit careful accounts by post each week to Emmeline Pethick Lawrence or her assistants Beatrice Sanders and Mrs Knight. For women with no experience of book-keeping, this was a formidable task; even financially literate organisers found the work stressful. The need to appease the WSPU's treasurer before anything else remained one of the few things that Grace Roe could recall specifically about her work as a district organiser when interviewed decades years later.[79] Emmeline Pethick Lawrence frequently reminded organisers to 'take very seriously indeed their financial responsibilities'.[80] Annie Kenney recalled: 'The organisers with their petty cash books had to be careful of every penny entered'; mistakes 'had to come out of our own pockets'.[81] Petty cash could be sent out 'at one pound a time', but had to 'last for weeks unless there was the rent of the hall to pay for', in which case an advance would be made on the understanding that the collection at the meeting would cover this.[82] Annie Kenney was bullish about the overall effect of the constant emphasis on finance:

> That is why we did so much more with our money than Party politicians. Where hard work would tell, no money was spent on advertising. If a chair would be as suitable as a platform, why pay a few shillings for a trolley? If the weather was fine, why hire a hall? ... this went on for years.[83]

Other organisers were less enthusiastic. Concern over income was so inescapable that Mary Gawthorpe even sent her mother a collecting card to raise money on her behalf when she was off work on a prolonged sick leave.[84] Organisers who were not financially dependent on the WSPU were still worn down over the issue of finances. Although Mrs Mildred Mansel was the official organiser for Bath and district, she relied heavily on the unpaid work done by Mary Blathwayt, especially when it came to the accounts. The anxiety over money in Mary's diary is tangible. She sent constant receipts to London, kept the local accounts herself, and even dealt with Mrs Mansel's paying-in book, much to the concern of her mother Emily, who noted that, of all the worries about work her daughter experienced, 'it is anxiety in keeping the accounts which is worst. Mrs Mansel the organiser comes over and her expenses have to be paid and there is nothing to pay them with and M feels responsible even though she is not so.'[85] Mrs Mansel's implied inefficiencies were also costing Mary money, and on one occasion Mrs Sanders had to refund her £5 'as [she had] lent the union money and Mrs Mansel [had] not yet written for more'.[86]

For some organisers, the constant pressure to keep accurate and regular accounts proved too much. Dora Marsden, who developed into one of the WSPU's most problematical organisers, was constantly pestered by Emmeline Pethick Lawrence and Beatrice Sanders for her failure to produce regular accounts. Although several political and personal factors contributed to her eventual resignation, it was the suggestion of financial impropriety that followed her for several years after she left.[87] Rank and file suffragettes, who raised a large part of the WSPU's income, were extremely attuned to any suggestion of irregularity, and although the rumours that Dora had helped herself to some of her branch funds was completely unfounded, their spread between suffragettes in the north west suggests that Dora's financial inefficiency was fairly common knowledge among them.

Dora may have found finances particularly baffling, but even financially astute organisers could find themselves chastised by Mrs Pethick Lawrence if their districts did not raise the required money. In July 1909 she wrote to congratulate Mary Phillips on her work in Cornwall, saying that the district would 'take the first prize if you go on like you have been doing lately'.[88] The next month she was less confident, and reminded Phillips of the need to always take collections at public meetings: 'It seems to me that it ought to be possible to get quite a decent sum from the visitors on the beach, they are always rather lavish during the holiday."[89] By the time Mary moved to Bradford in the autumn she was receiving correspondence of a quite different tone. Some provincial meetings had begun to incur losses, and Mrs Pethick Lawrence was determined that this should not become a pattern, warning Mary that for her forthcoming large meeting she ought not to 'have any free seats at all ... I think you might have one or two rows of seats at two shillings or two and six for the really well-to-do ... if they do not go before the night you can fill them up with one shilling people'.[90] Again, Mrs Pethick Lawrence was eager to spread examples of best practice as widely as possible, and offered to 'show [Mary] the accounts of one or two other organisers showing that it is quite possible to make ends meet in every financial centre'.[91]

The financial anxiety of provincial organisers transformed into an emphasis on fundraising, which permeated most layers of branch activity. Many organisers found that using their own offices to serve as meeting rooms and shops alleviated some of this concern. The cost of weekly room hire could be considerable – Huddersfield Branch spent 1–2 shillings of its miniscule income on rent for a meeting room – making long-term renting a more economical option.[92] Taking premises also gave an organiser the opportunity to promote team spirit within her branch by giving everyone the chance to contribute to a project that was neither public nor illegally militant. In Birmingham, Gladice Keevil persuaded the comparatively affluent Bertha Brewster to contribute purple, white and green curtains for the shop, but expected all other members to contribute a single cup and saucer so that refreshments could be offered during the At Homes to be held there.[93] Premises could demand considerable outlay – Vera Wentworth found it impossible in Plymouth to secure 'a shop in a good position for less than seventy pounds per year' – but organisers' efforts could offset much of this. Annie Williams moved the Newcastle shop to larger premises when she was appointed district organiser, and opened a furnishing fund for 'a hundred chairs', offering ample opportunity for all to contribute.[94]

There were other opportunities to recoup the initial outlay for a shop. They sold a variety of goods, either made by local members or sourced from the WSPU's national commercial sources, including home-made jams, fancy goods, 'Votes for Women' china and tea, and numerous scarves, badges and propaganda postcards at varying prices. They were well supplied with literature, which was obtained at cost price from the Women's Press. A central shop also offered suffragettes the opportunity for free advertising space, and Mary Blathwayt was one of many organisers who 'cut ... out suffrage cuttings from the papers to put in the shop window' in her district.[95] Branch members were expected to staff local shops on a voluntary basis, although this could prove a little more arduous. Mary Blathwayt often ended up doing extra shifts in the Bath WSPU shop when members failed to turn up for their promised hours. She recorded ongoing petty abuse from the public in her diary, including the time when 'three girls shouted horrid things through the letter box' during one of her stints, and another occasion when 'a boy we helped several times by giving him work and sometimes money and food for nothing came [to the shop] ... and because we had nothing to give him spit [*sic*] into the shop several times through the letterbox'.[96]

The WSPU leaders were all too aware of the demands they placed on organisers, and did their best to compensate when appropriate. They were especially anxious that proper holidays should be taken. The pressure on district organisers was so great that they often felt unable to leave their posts, despite any official holiday entitlement. Emmeline Pethick Lawrence sometimes intervened directly, on one occasion taking Mary Gawthorpe and Annie Kenney on a continental trip to recuperate. When she was unable to act so directly, Emmeline Pethick Lawrence could be as strict about holidays as she was over financial matters. 'I want to talk to you about your holiday', she wrote to Mary Phillips in the summer of 1909. 'You went back to Cornwall almost immediately you were released from prison. Now dear, this is not a wise proceeding, it may seem alright to you now, but sooner or later you will find that your strength has run out.'[97] Mrs Pethick Lawrence's concern was pragmatic as well as personal. She continued:

> There are rumours of a General Election early in next year, well, if this happens we shall need to work furiously the last three months of this year, and we specially want *every one* of our organisers to be very fit, and to be able to help, everybody is taking a holiday and you must arrange to do the same. In a few days, not later than the first of September, you must knock off for a fortnight; go home to Scotland and take a thorough good rest. Do let me have a letter saying that this is all arranged. I know you are getting on well, and I know that it is a great temptation to disregard all other considerations and to stick to the work when it is so fascinating. But is does not do, we always find that sooner or later one has to pay for this kind of thing.[98]

Christabel Pankhurst tended to be less forgiving of her employees' personal limitations than Emmeline Pethick Lawrence, regarding many of them as rather irritating weaknesses. Her time in France altered this a little as she realised what demands she had placed on herself. Other organisers now found themselves pressured to take some breaks. Grace Roe had not taken a day off for two years prior to Christmas 1912 when 'Christabel sent word for [her] to leave for Switzerland for an immediate rest'.[99] Of course, the choice of Switzerland ensured that the rest was limited, as Grace was instructed to call into the Paris flat on her way back to England where she was informed of her new post as second in command to Annie Kenney. Yet despite Christabel's worries about the health of some of her friends, such concerns were always subordinate to the greater concern for the cause itself. Consequently, most district organisers remained with their branches even when the stress of their work bordered on being intolerable.

Although it offered some stability, working in a district was not an easy option for a WSPU organiser. Many organisers who spent lengthy periods in an area were themselves dissatisfied at certain points. The constant struggle to motivate those members who could be extremely difficult was not the sort of problem for which training could easily prepare. Issues in the branches could be exacerbated by the fact that many organisers were considerably younger than their volunteers. District organisers were also under constant financial pressure from their employers, and their worries about fundraising must have increased when they saw organisers being removed from unproductive districts. The slow but steady number of requests for a move to a slightly different district that arrived at Clements Inn from certain organisers also suggests that there were some problems with this more permanent model of deployment which encouraged organisers to identify with an area, but also inadvertently led them to blame many problems on their own district and feel that things would be better somewhere else.

Yet despite these problems, the position of district organiser could also be extremely rewarding. The district organiser became the personification of the WSPU for many local members all over Britain. Branches invested them with a degree of authority, which could sometimes exceed that which they actually possessed, and organisers could be idolised by their members. In the regions, it was the local organisers who shaped the campaigns, thus determining the experience of being a suffragette for the majority of the WSPU's members. Their collective role in progressing the campaign throughout Britain was thus arguably greater than that of the national leaders, although the Union's tendency to deploy its workers to districts other than those they would regard as home meant that in many instances their impact on the broader shape of local politics was more restricted.

Notes

1 Grace Roe, 'A suffragette's story', published by the Women's Kit, Ontario Institute for Studies in Education, 252 Bloor Street West, Toronto, Ontario, Canada M5S 1V6; copy in Nellie Hall Humpherson Papers.
2 *Women's Franchise*, 27 June 1907.
3 Emmeline Pankhurst to Miss Thompson, 17 September 1907, SFC.
4 Copy of 'Letter sent to enquirers from 4 Clements Inn', in 'Notes on the Formation of the Women's Freedom League', SFC.

5 *VFW*, 25 June 1908.
6 *Women's Franchise*, 4 July 1907.
7 WSPU Third Annual Report (to year ending February 1909), SFC.
8 Olive Bartels to Brian Harrison, 27 March 1976, Harrison Tapes.
9 Flora Drummond, circular to local WSPU secretaries, November 1911, SFC.
10 Emmeline Pethick Lawrence to Dora Marsden, 24 November 1909, Dora Marsden Papers.
11 Emmeline Pethick Lawrence to Mary Phillips, 1 December 1909, Mary Phillips Papers.
12 See for example, *VFW*, 2 April, 18 June 1909.
13 Christabel Pankhurst to Jennie Baines, 12 November 1907, Baines Papers.
14 Mary Blathwayt's diary, 2 May 1908, Blathwayt Diaries.
15 Anon., 'Notes on Aeta Lamb', SFC.
16 *VFW*, 30 April 1908.
17 Mitchell, *The Hard Way Up*, p. 155.
18 Stephenson, 'No other way', pp. 83–4.
19 Molly Murphy, typescript autobiography, p. 10, National Museum of Labour History, Manchester.
20 *Worker*, 4 May 1907.
21 Kenney, *Memories*, p. 104.
22 *Ibid.*, p. 103; E. M. Jackson to Brian Harrison, 30 March 1976, Harrison Tapes.
23 Leonora Cohen to Brian Harrison, 27 October 1974, Harrison Tapes.
24 Mary Blathwayt's diary, 1 January 1909, Blathwayt Diaries.
25 Hesketh, *My Aunt Edith*, p. 45.
26 Ada M. Robertson to Nancy Seymour Pearson, 30 January 1913, Mrs Seymour Pearson's WSPU scrapbook, Camellia Collection.
27 Undated smuggled letter from Myra Saad Brown to 'My three little darlings and Mlle', Autograph Letter Collection, Women's Library.
28 *VFW*, 2 July 1909.
29 Haig, *This Was My World*, p. 133.
30 Hesketh, *My Aunt Edith*, p. 35.
31 Jessie Kenney, 'The flame and the flood', fragment entitled 'Annie's weaknesses'.
32 Edith Pepper to Brian Harrison, 27 April 1975, Harrison Tapes.
33 Maude Kate Smith to Brian Harrison, 14 January 1975, Harrison Tapes.
34 Roe, 'A suffragette's story.'
35 Stephenson, 'No other way', p. 236; *VFW* dates this to January 1911.
36 Helen Fraser to Isabel Seymour, 6 September 1908, SFC.
37 Annot Robinson to Sam Robinson, 12 March 1908, 718/15, Annot Robinson Papers.
38 Annie Kenney to Annie Williams, 30 April 1912, SFC.
39 Emmeline Pethick Lawrence to Ada Flatman, 22 April 1910, SFC.
40 *Ibid.*, 14 December 1910, SFC.
41 Emmeline Pethick Lawrence to Dora Marsden, 8 December 1909, Dora Marsden Papers.
42 Christabel Pankhurst to Dora Marsden, 27 January 1910, Dora Marsden Papers.
43 *Ibid.*, 31 January 1910, Dora Marsden Papers.
44 Rachel Barrett to Annie Williams 3 May 1912, SFC.
45 Christabel Pankhurst to Mary Phillips, 9 July 1913, Mary Phillips Papers.

46 Lytton, *Prisons and Prisoners*, p. 311.

47 Walker, 'Helen Pethick Lawrence', p. 20.

48 J. Kenney, 'The flame and the flood', notes on 'Sylvia'.

49 Lettice Floyd to Edith How Martyn, 20 April 1932, SFC.

50 Roe, 'A suffragette's story'.

51 Kenney, *Memories*, pp. 123–4.

52 Mss notebook, in Annie Kenney's hand, describing things 'to be done' in Weymouth, Camellia Collection.

53 Krista Cowman, *'Mrs Brown is a Man and a Brother!' Women in Merseyside's Political Organisations 1890–1920* (Liverpool: Liverpool University Press, 2004), p. 92.

54 *Bath Herald*, 4 June 1912.

55 Grace Roe to Brian Harrison, 23 September 1974, Harrison Tapes.

56 Emily Blathwayt's diary, 31 March 1908, Blathwayt Diaries.

57 *VFW*, Manchester local report, 14 January 1909.

58 *Ibid.*

59 *VFW*, Birmingham local report, 18 November 1910.

60 Molly Murphy, typescript autobiography, National Museum of Labour History, p. 18.

61 Organiser's sample diary, Mary Phillips Papers.

62 *Ibid.*

63 Christabel Pankhurst to Mary Phillips, 31 January 1909, Mary Phillips Papers.

64 *VFW*, Manchester local report 24 September 1908; Edith Pepper to Brian Harrison, 27 April 1975, Harrison Tapes.

65 *VFW*, 17 September 1908.

66 Emmeline Pethick Lawrence to Mary Phillips, 1 December 1909, Mary Phillips Papers; for an example of the card, see Liverpool Women's Social and Political Union At Home, 1 December 1908, Mary Gawthorpe Papers.

67 *VFW*, Ipswich local report, 14 October 1910.

68 *VFW*, Aberdeen local report, 18 February 1909.

69 *VFW*, Newcastle local report, 29 October 1908.

70 Molly Murphy, autobiography, p. 18.

71 *VFW*, Newcastle report, 29 October 1908.

72 Kenney, *Memories*, p.120.

73 For more detail on the work that the Blathwayts did for the WSPU, see June Hannam, 'Suffragettes are splendid for any work: the Blathwayt diaries as a source for suffrage history', in Eustance, Ryan and Ugolini, (eds), *A Suffrage Reader*, pp. 53–68.

74 Mary Blathwayt's diary, 18 April 1908, Blathwayt Diaries.

75 For example, the car lent by Mrs Avery in Huyton, in 1910: Cowman, *Mrs Brown*, p. 87; also Mrs Hutchinson in East Nottingham: *Suffragette*, 26 April 1912.

76 *VFW*, 29 April 1910.

77 *Suffragette*, 28 February 1913.

78 Teresa Billington's notes on Alice Milne's diary, 17 October 1906, 397 A/6, TBG Papers.

79 Roe to Harrison, Harrison Tapes.

80 Emmeline Pethick Lawrence to Mary Phillips, 2 December 1909, Mary Phillips Papers.

81 Kenney, *Memories*, p. 82.

82 *Ibid.*, p. 124.

83 *Ibid.*, p. 83.
84 Mary Gawthorpe to Elizabeth Gawthorpe, 1 May 1910, Mary Gawthorpe Papers.
85 Emily Blathwayt's diary, 24 January 1911, Blathwayt Diaries.
86 Mary Blathwayt's diary, 3 January 1911, Blathwayt Diaries.
87 Theresa McGrath to Dora Marsden, 19 April 1912, Dora Marsden Papers.
88 Emmeline Pethick Lawrence to Mary Phillips, 30 July 1909, Mary Phillips Papers.
89 *Ibid.*, 23 August 1909, Mary Phillips Papers.
90 *Ibid.*, 7 December 1909, Mary Phillips Papers.
91 *Ibid.*, 2 December 1909, Mary Phillips Papers.
92 See Krista Cowman, '"Minutes of the last meeting passed": the Huddersfield WSPU minute book, January 1907–1909, a new source for suffrage history', *Twentieth-Century British History*, 13:3 (2002). pp. 298–315.
93 *VFW*, 17 September 1908.
94 *VFW*, 19 February 1909.
95 Emily Blathwayt's diary, 23 November 1910, Blathwayt Diaries.
96 Mary Blathwayt's diary, 17 January 1911; 12 November 1910, Blathwayt Diaries.
97 Emmeline Pethick Lawrence to Mary Phillips, 23 Aug 1909, Mary Phillips Papers.
98 *Ibid.*, 23 August 1909, Mary Phillips Papers.
99 Roe, 'The Suffragette's Story.'

4

Life at headquarters

F OR THE MOST PART, those who encountered the WSPU's officials met them in the provinces as they went about their work as itinerant or district organisers. Attempts to recover the experience of suffrage work at a local level have shifted attention to the importance of regional workers, and played down events at national level. Yet, while the majority of the WSPU's members worked outside of London and rarely if ever participated in events in the capital, they were reminded that they were members of a national organisation. All of the WSPU's itinerant and district organisers were employed and deployed throughout Britain from its national headquarters in London. 'Headquarters' came to be seen as the rather sinister centre of the WSPU's power, although its origins were quite innocent. Like all political organisations, the WSPU had to operate from an address that could send out propaganda and offer a contact point for responses. The need for an identifiable base grew as militancy and its attendant publicity increased. The full propaganda value of militant activities would be realised only if sympathisers among an increasingly aware public were able to contact the WSPU without difficulty. As the membership expanded, more staff (paid and voluntary) were required to oversee the daily running of the Union and to co-ordinate its national campaigns. These staff needed a base too. So, while the WSPU's first two official headquarters were sufficient to accommodate all of its small membership at once, these were swiftly outgrown as the organisation quickly expanded between 1906 and 1914, and its office space similarly enlarged.

The original WSPU had no money for premises but sent out its first propaganda from 62, Nelson Street, Manchester, the Pankhurst family home. Early committee meetings took place here, held round the dining-room table. After Annie Kenney's departure to London, the WSPU briefly operated out of Sylvia Pankhurst's lodgings at 45, Park Walk, Chelsea.

INFORMATION BUREAU, W.S.P.U.

4   The information bureau at WSPU headquarters, Clements Inn,
Aeta Lamb (extreme left) seated

Then, in September 1906, it moved to Clements Inn, starting with just two rooms but quickly expanding, taking over much of the first and second floor, as well as a few rooms in the building next door, and a separate base for certain departments in nearby Charing Cross Road.[1] In the autumn of 1912, coinciding with the split from the Pethick Lawrences, the WSPU removed to a large building at Lincolns Inn, Kingsway, bringing all of its departments together again under one roof. The Kingsway address was the WSPU's final official centre and remained its correspondence address, although other locations, including members' homes, were used towards the end of the militant campaign for preparing articles or laying other plans, as the police were increasingly present at Lincolns Inn.

Clements Inn was more than a new address for the WSPU, for the move here coincided with a shift in its internal structure. While previous addresses had been little more than that, first Clements, and then Lincolns Inn became the Union's national headquarters, frequently referenced with a capital 'H'. Outside observers certainly believed that its headquarters was indivisible from the WSPU. Mr Bodkin, the lawyer charged with summarising the case for the prosecution of Mabel Tuke, Christabel and Emmeline Pankhurst and the Pethick Lawrences in the conspiracy trial of March 1912, explained to the court that the women in the dock represented 'a highly organised union, the central office of which – the heart of which – was in 4, Clements Inn'.[2] Within a body as avowedly hierarchical as the WSPU, the word 'headquarters' swiftly became transformed into shorthand for a site of unbreachable power and centralised diktats. It also became a focus for the suspicions of those who dissented from the Union's autocracy, such as when the fact that all 'branches ... have to submit to dictation on all vital points from Clements Inn' became a major complaint of Teresa Billington Grieg during the split with the WFL.[3]

The behaviour of the WSPU's leaders based at headquarters furthered its presentation as the Union's real power centre to employees and members alike. Requests or orders emanating from headquarters were presented as indistinguishable from the voice and will of the WSPU itself. '[E]very part of the militant policy is thought out and controlled by headquarters as much as is humanly possible', Emmeline Pethick Lawrence explained to Mary Phillips when tactics were being discussed.[4] Actually, money matters were not widely discussed among central staff, but passed directly to Emmeline Pethick Lawrence's small treasury team, but her tendency to speak of 'Headquarters' in financial discussions implied that it was always the financial health of the entire Union that was at stake rather than the status of her own department. 'Every estimate must be submitted to Headquarters', she warned Dora Marsden during preparations for the ill-fated Southport Bazaar in December 1910. 'No arrangement must be made without our consent'.[5] Even Christabel Pankhurst, who seldom felt the need to mask her autocracy behind any claim of collectivism, used the word 'headquarters' to suggest that unpopular actions represented a consensus rather than her own personal whim. When Mary Phillips was dismissed from her post as a district organiser in the summer of 1913, Christabel Pankhurst countered Mary's protests at her sacking by claiming that she had implemented a collective decision, writing that she 'did not wish to hurt [Mary] needlessly by saying what has always been felt at headquarters that you are not effective as a district organiser ... such was the view held at headquarters'.[6]

Unsurprisingly, given the frequent usage of the term in this way, organisers who stepped out of line often felt that it was 'headquarters' rather than particular leaders pursuing them.[7] When Sylvia Pankhurst was summoned to Paris to defend the work of her East End suffragettes in 1914, her observation that 'the arrangements for [her] journey were made by Lincolns Inn House' emphasised her sense of individual powerlessness against the collective WSPU hierarchy.[8] This perception of headquarters as a dynamic force rather than a physical location also permeated discussions of more trivial matters among organisers. Mary Gawthorpe, who was largely absent from her post in 1910 because of a serious illness, wrote to apologise to her mother for a particularly unflattering photograph of herself which had been published during the summer: 'it was taken by command from headquarters ... and when the ... day came I was too poorly ... to take myself in hand so that I was just taken to the photographers and my hair dressed for me'.[9]

The presentation of the London headquarters as the nexus from which 'organisers and unpaid volunteers in the branches were directly controlled' has fuelled hostile and apprehensive interpretations of its work which link it with an 'inner circle' of the WSPU led by 'Christabelean authority'.[10] Further suspicions of its role have been aroused by accounts suggesting that the opening of a large London office was more political than practical, aimed at facilitating a shift in the WSPU's class base. Alice Milne, a young Manchester member, visited Clements Inn soon after the offices were opened, and found 'the place full of fashionable ladies in rustling silks and satins'.[11] Hannah Mitchell also recalled feeling 'shabby' and out of place at a reception when she visited London, although later she could not remember whether it had been held at Clements Inn or elsewhere.[12] Teresa Billington Grieg was particularly hurt by the changes, many of which occurred in her absence: 'Coming back, we ... [found] a smoothly organised and managed new machine ... from which the friendly faces of tired colleagues seemed to have disappeared. The old free and easy, hectic and responsive coming and going, sharing and innovating were gone.' Yet even this most regretful of commentators was forced to admit that some changes were necessary. Up to this point, administration had been haphazard, and 'record making and filing were crude and disorderly. Some papers of value were in private hands, some in the office in Manchester, some in London. Bills, receipts and subscribers' letters were where they happened to be left ... great democratic uprising could not continue on this chaotic way.'[13] Other suffragettes concurred that expansion required more efficient organisation. Many realised that a more effective headquarters did not mean that the national leaders would intrude unduly on the rank-and-file membership. Even in *The Suffragette Movement*, her second and less sympathetic version of WSPU history, Sylvia Pankhurst recognised that a degree of freedom existed between headquarters and the regional branches which were '[w]holly independent of headquarters, paying no fixed dues, and united to the Union only by sympathy with its policy'.[14]

This situation was not altered by the WSPU's reorganisation of 1907 although at this point most branches affiliated to the National Women's

Social and Political Union. An undue focus on the autocracy of head-quarters has detracted from attempts to consider the WSPU as a political organisation by overlooking the fact that central co-ordination is essential to any national political campaign. When the WSPU moved its headquarters to London, it aimed to build a thriving network of regional branches. Yet, despite the talents and abilities of district organisers, regional events required overall synchronisation and many required planning on a national rather than a regional scale. To regard headquarters as a restrictive site of control is to overlook much of the complexity and dynamism which characterised both the physical space of Clements and Lincolns Inn, and the working relationships which developed between women employed there. Headquarters brought together large groups of paid women workers, organisers and clerical support staff, as well as eager volunteers, most of whom were effectively full-time workers. Suffragettes discovered that working there offered them a collegiality missing from other forms of work available to women before the First World War. Some women who had tried district work found that headquarters also offered a welcome change from work in the regions where motivating volunteers was a constant struggle. While divisions could still emerge, most of the time the workforce at headquarters remained united, enticed by the prospect of working on a shared cause, at the nerve centre of its operation.

Number 4, Clements Inn became the WSPU's London base through a combination of personal connections and good fortune. In February 1906, Emmeline and Frederick Pethick Lawrence joined the Union. The couple had been interested to hear of the first militant disturbances in Manchester (which took place while they were on a prolonged visit to South Africa) and Emmeline in particular had determined to make the acquaintance of these new militant women as soon as possible. Their mutual friend Keir Hardie arranged an introduction to Mrs Pankhurst, but Emmeline initially declined her invitation to help to establish a base for the WSPU in London. She felt over-committed to a number of other projects, including the Espérance Working Girls' Club and the *Labour Record and Review*. A second approach by Annie Kenney proved more successful, as Emmeline was immediately drawn to the younger woman, finding 'something about [her] that touched my heart'.[15] She attended a meeting in Sylvia Pankhurst's rooms the next evening where the central London committee of the WSPU was formed. Sylvia was honorary secretary, and Emmeline Pethick Lawrence the honorary treasurer. The other members were Annie Kenney, Mary Neal (Emmeline's friend and co-worker at the Espérance Club), Mary Clarke (Mrs Pankhurst's sister), Mrs Row (Sylvia Pankhurst's landlady), Irene Fenwick Miller, daughter of the early suffragist Florence Fenwick Miller, and the Australian Nellie Martel.

While Emmeline Pethick Lawrence was not impervious to the charisma exerted by the powerful combinations of Annie Kenney and the Pankhurst women, she brought into the movement very particular qualities of her own which were associated with the less emotional world of business. She recognised that although each of her new colleagues 'possessed extraordinary qualities, they did not understand organisation, and they had absolutely no idea of finance. Theirs was the guerrilla method of political warfare. It became my business to give their genius a solid foundation.'[16] Emmeline recognised from the outset that if the WSPU was to achieve its aim of uniting women from across Britain behind the militant campaign, it needed a firm national base to direct them. When the Pethick Lawrences married in 1901, they took a house in Surrey and 'a simple flat in London'[17] – in Clements Inn, in a newly developed area 'recently … rebuilt for offices and flats … the front faced the new Law Courts [and] it backed on Old Wych Street … already in process of demolition to form Aldwych and Kingsway'.[18] The building was convenient for Frederick's political journalism, offering him easy access to both Parliament and Fleet Street; it also had the advantage of providing meals and other services for its tenants, leaving both Emmeline and Frederick completely free to devote themselves to work. Now, as a temporary measure, Emmeline offered the room previously occupied by her own secretary to the WSPU, along with the secretary herself who 'typed the business letters' for the Union.[19]

This was a short-term solution, but, with an early display of the prudence that characterised her tenure as treasurer, Emmeline was unwilling to seek more permanent premises until the WSPU's finances were more secure. By September 1906 the accounts looked hopeful. The Union had carried out some successful and high-profile activities, including large campaigns in Yorkshire and Scotland, and militant protests ending in arrests in London and Manchester. The national committee had expanded and re-aligned, shedding Sylvia Pankhurst but gaining Charlotte Despard and Edith How Martyn – and Christabel Pankhurst, who arrived in London in July armed with a first-class honours degree in law. Emmeline's confidence in the WSPU's ability to afford premises co-incided with the departure of the Land Registry from two rooms on the lower floor at Clements Inn, and the WSPU took them as its London headquarters, much to the relief of Frederick Pethick Lawrence who was able to 'recover undisputed possession' of his own flat.[20]

Clements Inn, with its proximity to national leaders of the press and the Government, was the ideal location for the WSPU, and for the next six years these offices were the hub of its activities. As the WSPU's national organisation grew so did its headquarters. The original 2 rooms expanded to over 20, making it 'the largest headquarters of any political party in London'.[21] Unlike other political parties, this was an almost exclusively female space (with the notable exception of Frederick Pethick Lawrence and a very few young office boys). Its feminised environment encouraged suffragettes to evolve a more domestic aspect to their headquarters, unique within contemporary politics. It was quickly apparent, for instance, that working at headquarters could put extreme strain on staff through excessive hours, especially during spells of militancy such as the raids on Parliament. Suffragettes devised the solution of keeping a small space available in the form of a garden flat on the roof, which had been a gift from Frederick to his wife on their first wedding anniversary, intended as her secret retreat.[22]

The flat offered quiet respite for some of the stressed workers of the WSPU, including Constance Lytton who referred to it in her account of headquarters as 'the upstairs rest room', and gratefully retired there when her poor physical health rendered her temporarily unfit.[23] It was also a wonderful hiding place for suffragettes during police raids on the WSPU headquarters. In October 1908 when Christabel and Emmeline Pankhurst and Flora Drummond were summonsed on a charge of incitement to riot, they frustrated police by deciding '[their] own time and place for arrest': they retired to the roof apartment where they remained undetected during a frantic police search of the building, laying plans for running the Union in their absence and finally coolly descending to the main office at 6pm to surrender before an eagerly assembled crowd of journalists.[24]

Descriptions of headquarters display a self-conscious pride in the overt modernity of the WSPU's premises, which outshone those of their political rivals. Offices were equipped with up-to-the-minute innovations, which both promoted savings of time (and, by inference, money) and the Union's young, fresh and modern image. Electricity, the very latest form of power, illuminated the work done by organisers at Clements Inn and enhanced its efficiency with electric clocks in every room, 'controlled from a central desk in [the general] office, thereby ensuring perfect time' was kept by all WSPU workers. Such modern novelties guaranteed that no organiser would 'waste ... valuable minutes in catching trains and keeping appointments'; no spare second of her day would be allowed to pass idly by if it could be directed towards the cause. Then there was the telephone, another recent device whose use effected 'an immense saving of time'. Clements Inn had three external lines, plus internal extensions

to each department. The switchboard, which employed several workers, was proudly displayed in the outer office where it proved 'a source
of great interest to visitors'.[25] Later reminiscences revealed that workers were well aware that the telephones were monitored by the police,
suggesting that the impression they conveyed was of more use to the
WSPU than the work they facilitated.[26] The palpable modernity that
permeated Clements Inn was surpassed by Lincolns Inn, whence headquarters moved in September 1912. By then the Union had taken over
'practically every floor of Clements Inn', but the key publishing department, the Women's Press, was still outhoused in Charing Cross Road.
Lincolns Inn was a new building on Kingsway, constructed 'with all the
conveniences of a business house', and large enough to accommodate all
the WSPU's central staff. That it had been 'suggested as suitable for "an
important Government office"' gives some indication of how the WSPU
now viewed its work. The new premises, with vaulted rooms, 'a fine tiled
staircase', and 'magnificent oak' panels, as well as 'an electric lift', were
chosen both for their size and because they constituted 'an actual proof
of the triumphant progress of the Union'.[27] Sylvia Pankhurst felt that Lincolns Inn made Clements Inn look 'dowdy and commonplace in comparison'.[28]

The modern building was impressive, but the mainstay of headquarters was always the organising staff. By 1908, 20 of the WSPU's 34 paid
employees were based there, providing a spectacle which the itinerant
worker Rosamund Massy found sufficient to 'inspire the most slack and
callous nature'.[29] There are no separate figures for later years, but the scope
of the work carried out in London suggests that headquarters continued
to account for an equally large proportion of the WSPU's overall staff.
Many of these workers were extremely skilled. Harriet Roberta Kerr was
brought in as general manager as soon as the premises began to expand.
Then in her mid-forties, Miss Kerr was somewhat older than many of the
WSPU's members and she claimed no interest in politics. She had run
her own business as a typist and knew the Pethick Lawrences through a
mutual friend, E. V. Lucas. Harriet Kerr was always diffident about her
work. While she downplayed the significance of her contribution, telling
the Suffragette Fellowship in 1928 that she did not 'want the press to be
interested in [her] suffrage career', her contemporaries were less reticent
about her importance, particularly Annie Kenney who remembered her
as 'a born businesswoman, the right person in the right place at Headquarters'.[30] Outsiders also recognised her as a key figure in the national
offices. She oversaw the general office and greeted any visitors, becoming
the public face of the WSPU for many new arrivals. As Francis Mulvey,

the 14–year-old lift boy at Lincolns Inn told the court during the 1913 conspiracy trial, she was omnipresent: 'everybody who called … saw Miss Kerr'.[31]

As well as greeting casual public visitors, Harriet Kerr was charged with overseeing the numerous voluntary workers who came to headquarters in the evening to offer some of their free time, once their full-time work was completed. Having run her own successful business, she was often exasperated by the excited young volunteers, and sometimes found it 'well-nigh impossible to impose upon them her excellent order, and to prevent a distracting babel of talk and laughter arising from their tables'.[32] Nevertheless, she realised the potential of the enthusiasm that drove women to sign up for what was in effect a second job with no reward other than the sense of being involved in the movement. Jessie Stephenson was one of several volunteers who ended up working full-time for the Union. She later described the pressure of effectively doing two jobs before coming on to the WSPU payroll, recalling how 'many were the calls from Christabel and innumerable the times I tore off hither and thither, sometimes necessitating my leaving [work] an hour or so earlier … Whatever engagement I had – theatre, friends coming – everything gave way to suffrage'.[33]

Harriet Kerr became particularly skilled at spotting suitable volunteers in her office.[34] Other leading suffragettes recognised her talents and relied on her ability to convince the less certain volunteers, offering them simple tasks as a means of bringing them into the movement more fully. Charlotte Marsh, who went on to become one of the WSPU's best-known organisers, was one of Harriet Kerr's discoveries. When she joined the WSPU, she was about to embark on a career as a sanitary inspector – quite an achievement, as she was one of the first women to train for the job. She was drawn to suffrage, but was uncertain which way to commit. The decision was forced when a friend took her to Clements Inn, where she 'went over to Miss Kerr and said keep an eye on that girl, don't let her go'.[35] Harriet Kerr smartly set her to the undemanding but time-consuming task of addressing envelopes, ensuring that Charlotte returned regularly to headquarters and so kept in contact with the WSPU's leaders. These tactics succeeded, and Charlotte gave up her prospective career and joined the WSPU's organising staff.

The work directed by Harriet Kerr typified the political approach of the WSPU. It combined campaigning with attention to practical detail, but took little account of the status of jobs that women were asked to do in its drive for financial stability. At headquarters, even the most mundane, subservient actions were transformed into an act of significance for the cause. When she realised that Christabel Pankhurst's single-minded attitude to her suffrage work might be endangering her health, Harriet charged the young office worker Esther Knowles with a very particular task. Esther later explained with pride how this had come about:

> When [Christabel] was engrossed in writing her leading articles ... she used to become so oblivious of anything else around her that she forgot all about her creature comforts. One cold winters morning Miss Kerr went into her room to find her literally blue with cold. The office was icy and the fire dead out. From that day it became my specific job to slip into CP's room at intervals and make up her fire as silently as I could and creep out again ...[36]

Like Harriet Kerr, several organisers were brought to work at headquarters because of specific skills that they had to offer the WSPU. With a weekly newspaper to fill, as well as innumerable pamphlets, leaflets and membership correspondence, typists were particularly welcome. Miss Nichols, an unknown supporter, 'arrived with a typewriter' one day, a gesture that instantly endeared her to the leaders.[37] Flora Drummond also used her previous work experience and 'offered to do all WSPU typing free' when she arrived in London.[38] She was quickly more involved with the political side of the work at headquarters but could still be sidetracked into typing at Clements Inn when particular deadlines approached.[39]

Nor were other skills overlooked. Mrs Sparboro, a working-class supporter who had been one of the first London prisoners, was taken on to the staff to take care of 'the domestic side' of office work, including supplying workers and visitors alike with innumerable cups of tea from a corner of the main office.[40] Her appointment made the office a much more pleasant place to be, but utilised skills that were not particularly difficult to source, which suggests that talent alone would not secure a position at headquarters. Workers needed dedication to the cause above all else. Many of the office staff, particularly those who did not need to type or supervise skilled clerical work as Miss Kerr did, were recruited because of their passion for suffrage, then given work to do which brought out the best of their abilities.

Aeta Lamb and Mary Home typified the enthusiastic paid worker for whom headquarters offered openings, allowing them to exploit abilities that were not necessarily suited to a district organiser. Aeta, 'a frail orphan, born in Demerara', was only 19 when she first went to work at Clements Inn.[41] She was extremely learned but, being mainly self-taught, was not well-qualified. Furthermore, although scholarly, she had 'no aptitude for teaching', which she had briefly attempted as an obvious career choice for a somewhat bookish young woman.[42] Aeta's devotion to the cause made her an obvious candidate for an organising post, but her attempt at working in a district floundered, so she was brought back to Clements Inn. There, more suitable work was found for her in the information department. Her new post was essentially a researcher's job, perfectly suited to 'a solitary soul ... tucked away in her office'.[43] Her friend Mary Gawthorpe believed that the time she spent at headquarters was the most satisfying of Aeta Lamb's life.[44] She was joined there by Mary Home, 'a pale young woman with a hare-lip who had been leading a claustrophobic existence in Kensington' with her widowed father. Mary had previously worked for the Women's Franchise Declaration Committee, and at Clements Inn was able to find further relief from her rather repressive home life.[45] In the information department she was appointed as clippings girl, and scanned the papers daily for relevant copy to cut and file.

There is no doubt that the staff at headquarters were devoted to their work, and not lacking in any of the aptitude or ability required for the tasks allocated to them. Nevertheless, as the Union's premises and its staff expanded, employment was clearly being offered to members for other reasons, which fuelled suggestions of cliquishness among workers who, like Teresa Billington Grieg, were now largely based outside London. Certain organisers were given posts at Clements Inn as a reward. Marguerite Sidley first worked for the WSPU on a voluntary basis, 'offer[ing] her services until [her] savings were gone'. She took part in a deputation to Parliament in March 1907 and was arrested and sentenced to twelve days' imprisonment. This compromised her employment but she 'was offered employment as shorthand typist and chief clerk in the WSPU office' a post she eagerly took up, although the WSPU later transferred her to the 'outdoor staff' on the advice of her doctor.[46] Helen Craggs was another keen voluntary worker who was saved for the Union by being taken on to the paid staff when her militancy caused her problems at home.[47]

Other offers of employment went to women who impressed individual WSPU leaders. Esther Knowles had been a member of Emmeline Pethick Lawrence's Espérance Club, and was a keen supporter of the WSPU who attended her first demonstration aged 13 against the wishes of her father.[48] She was a bright girl who had passed the civil service entrance exam, but was approached by Emmeline who 'asked if [she] would like to become one of the office girls in the WSPU instead'. Esther 'jumped at the chance', and became the WSPU's youngest employee.[49] Annie Kenney's sister Jessie was another young recruit suggested by Emmeline Pethick Lawrence. Jessie had left factory work and was employed as a secretary in Bingley, when Annie wrote informing her that she had been appointed Emmeline Pethick Lawrence's private secretary and should come to London. She was quickly poached by Christabel Pankhurst, and appointed organiser at the age of 19.[50] Jessie's first work involved planning and co-ordinating particular acts of militancy, such as the accosting or 'pestering' of cabinet ministers, assisted by fellow-office-based organiser Evelyn Hambling. This role expanded quickly and she was co-ordinator of the London branches by the age of 22.[51] She refuted any suggestion that her family connections had secured her this post, but explained: 'I had not been made an organiser because I was Annie Kenney's sister, but because I had shown initiative in every department of the work.'[52] As with Charlotte Marsh, the openings for work at Clements Inn provided an excellent opportunity to bring on young enthusiasts eager to do something for the cause.

The idea that a job at headquarters, which involved long hours, the risk of occasional police raids and modest rates of pay, was seen as a reward is indicative of the high regard in which much of the WSPU's membership held this place. They saw it as a site of glamour where suffragette 'stars' – familiar through their writings and the photographs which were widely available as postcards and badges, but becoming increasingly remote as the WSPU grew and demands from different regions increased – could be reached by the most ordinary member. In many autobiographical fragments, headquarters was associated with a first or early encounter with the WSPU leaders – most frequently Christabel Pankhurst or Emmeline Pethick Lawrence – and a subsequent change of life. Mary Gawthorpe was a keen supporter of the WSPU when Emmeline Pethick Lawrence called her to the offices. She arrived in London in August 1913, 'going straight to Clements Inn … [A]s I entered … Emmeline Pethick Lawrence … lifted her head and looked at me … it was a full moment. Nothing was said but I knew I was nearing a great decision.'[53] Mary Gawthorpe then left her post with the WLL and joined the WSPU staff. As Christabel Pankhurst actually lived at Clements Inn, she often invited new workers to meet her there. Frances Bartlett had met her at Clapham Women's Liberal Association when she intervened in Christabel's defence. In her memoir, this first meeting, the request to visit headquarters and the decision to join the WSPU became indivisible: '[Christabel] came to me and asked me to call and see her at Clements' Inn the following morning … I went up … and she told me they had opened up offices that week. She showed me around, and so I became one of its first members'.[54]

Other first visits to headquarters were even more arbitrary, but still marked a moment of conversion for women unaware of the strength of their suffrage belief. Mary Richardson wandered in almost accidentally, following Harry Pankhurst whom she had seen in the middle of a hostile crowd in Kingsway. On entering, she was 'suddenly face to face with a plump, pretty young woman ... she was Christabel, Mrs Pankhurst's daughter'. Christabel's cheerful assumption that Mary Richardson had come to help left her powerless in the face of the will of headquarters. She signed up, and altered the course of her life. Afterwards, she remembered feeling bewildered – 'my knees felt weak when I left Clements Inn to start my pilgrimage ... within a brief half hour I had turned my back on the literary work I was doing ... and for what?'[55]

The range of work on offer at headquarters coupled with the constant presence of many of the WSPU's leaders among a staff of like-minded and predominantly young women made for a unique working environment. Many visitors attested to the excitement of the atmosphere. Vida Goldstein, an Australian feminist campaigner, felt that ethos would serve as an example to women voters in Australia, and wrote of her visit that she wished that 'all members of the WPA [the Australian Women's Political Association] could be transhipped here so that they might learn what devotion to a great cause means. The spirit in these women is simply heroic.' The staff shared this view. Isabel Seymour, one of the first workers at headquarters, fondly recalled her time there as 'very happy-go-lucky – envelope addressing, and the almost daily tea party', despite the harrowing nature of some of her work with prisoners. Christabel Pankhurst, whose account of her work for the WSPU is generally quite dry, described Clements Inn as 'a hive seething with activity ... full of movement. As department was added to department, Clements Inn seemed always to have one more room to offer.'[56] Jessie Kenney remembered particularly the atmosphere in the general office: 'A lot of fun goes on in this office ... Vera Holme and Miss Douglas Smith are the very life and soul of this room if they get in there together.'[57] Sylvia Pankhurst, who was never particularly part of life at headquarters still managed to convey some of the enjoyment of the younger volunteers whose behaviour so exasperated Miss Kerr. They included: 'Young Jessie Spink a shop assistant ... who eventually changed her name to Vera Wentworth ... [and] Vera Holme ... a noisy, explosive young person, frequently rebuked by her elders for lack of dignity'.[58] Sylvia, who was prone to bouts of melancholy, was unsettled by the volunteers' enthusiasm and claimed that they 'were eliminated from the office', as soon as practicable.[59]

Other memories diverge on this point. Certainly, Vera Holme and Vera Wentworth were both taken onto the WSPU payroll and moved on, but other workers remained as volunteers for several years. Ethel Birnstingl, who offered to help in the banner department in January 1910, was still hard at work designing stencils in the art department in September 1911, described as 'a voluntary worker who devotes her time to the Union'.[60] Jessie Stephenson continued to put 'all [her] leisure ... after 6 pm' in the WSPU's hands, and remained 'a voluntary helper' until she lost her job after being imprisoned on Black Friday, in 1910.[61] Such women gave whatever time they could for many years and enjoyed the feelings of participation and importance that headquarters offered in return.

The paid staff, too, took pleasure in being based at headquarters. Many idealistic and dedicated young women found the combination of political activism and modern working conditions irresistible. The telegraphic switchboard and typing pool made good use of the clerical skills many girls now acquired as part of their education, and the sense of secrecy underpinning much of the work, augmented by frequent police raids, offered a frisson which was further enhanced by the shared sense of purpose. Esther Knowles, who was a keen recruit, 'had no hesitation in choosing to become an office girl at Clements Inn rather than a civil servant in Whitehall'.[62]

The excitement of being at headquarters remained with the workforce years later and coloured their memories even when the work got more difficult. Clements Inn experienced some police raids, and by the point at which Lincolns Inn was taken they were a regular occurrence. The police generally concentrated on gathering information on these raids, and often took van-loads of records away with them, but the staff were also personal risk. Harriet Kerr was among a group of office staff, mainly heads of departments, who were arrested in May 1913 and charged with conspiracy, a particular irony given that she had agreed to work for the Union only on condition that she would not personally be required to participate in militancy.[63] For her work as office manager, Miss Kerr received a sentence of 12 months, plus a further 12 months' supervision. Yet even at pressured times there was still a thrill to be derived from the work. Esther Knowles, who became 'the heroine of the hour' when she stowed the contents of the cashbox in her knickers during one raid, felt that 'it was great fun to us young folk – though not to our leaders ... we enjoyed the flitting from one secret hide out to yet another at that period as the police each time discovered our new whereabouts and we went on to the next secret temporary resting place ...'.[64]

From Esther's description, 'Headquarters' at this point in the campaign was becoming identified much more with a group of women rather than a particular location. Gertrude Harding's account, written with closer proximity to the events it describes than that of Esther Knowles, concurs with the suggestion that there was a shift from buildings to people when 'headquarters' was invoked, and also with Knowles's sense of excitement.

After attempts were made to suppress the *Suffragette* by threatening printers and distributors, Gertrude worked with Grace Roe, Cicely Hale and others to ensure that the paper appeared on schedule. She

> drove with the new printer to Maude Joachim's flat … [He] informed us we had enough material for an eight page paper. In the early afternoon the famous 'Raided' copy … had gone to press … Mrs Pankhurst looked transparent and terribly frail, and said … 'we won't be able to get the paper out for a few days' to which I replied 'We have already gone to press …'[65]

Despite the practical difficulties posed by increased police interference, the WSPU headquarters would remain intact as long as the suffragettes who made it were able to keep working.

The sense of fun and camaraderie, which permeates many organisers' memories of their time working at headquarters, can obscure its primary function as a workplace from where a large national campaign was devised and co-ordinated, yet ultimately this is what headquarters was for. Different forms of militancy were co-ordinated here, especially events such as the 'Women's Parliaments' and the two large window-smashing raids of 1911 and 1912. Other work done there was less obvious, but equally necessary to ensuring that the national organisation of the WSPU functioned effectively. As is so often the case, the allocation of office space was key to interpreting much of the work performed at headquarters. Although militancy remained at the heart of the Union's policy and campaigning, it had little space at headquarters. Rather, the designated areas within Clements and Lincolns Inn served as a reminder that the WSPU was primarily a political organisation, albeit one which carried out militancy on a large scale.

Clements and Lincolns Inn were dominated by Harriet Kerr's large general office. Beyond this, other organisers were designated space. Christabel Pankhurst had her own office from the start, in a room adjoining the general one. A single office was quickly provided for Mabel Tuke, the young widow befriended by Emmeline Pethick Lawrence on a voyage from South Africa in 1906, who became the national secretary. Mrs Tuke, known as 'Pansy' within the Union because of her large eyes and dark complexion, was socially well connected and 'regarded as a very charming emissary for the introduction as "a Suffragette" to the guests at a luncheon or dinner party in the hope of disarming their prejudices against "those dreadful militants"'.[66] She used her connections to expand the London 'At Home' meetings which were initially held in the offices, but moved to the

Portman Rooms and finally the Queen's Hall as their audience increased. 'People ought to know you, they don't realise what Mrs Pankhurst and the rest of you are like', she told Christabel Pankhurst, who later accredited the size and success of these gatherings to Mrs Tuke's behind-the-scenes work.[67]

On top of her general secretarial work, Pansy was particularly useful through her ability to ensure that the social niceties associated with a femininity the Union was keen to promote were attended to within its day-to-day work, and she was assiduous in her attention to 'the writing of letters of thanks and the paying of calls'.[68] Her office was not to remain entirely her own for long, however. While Christabel Pankhurst placed herself firmly at the helm of the WSPU's London base from her arrival in the capital, the position of her mother, the WSPU's founder, was a little less clear. Emmeline Pankhurst was at her best on the political platform, and made her key role that of an itinerant speaker, moving tirelessly around the country as required. This indefatigable approach to her work was not without its personal cost, emotionally as well as physically. Sylvia Pankhurst remembered that her mother 'felt herself almost an outsider' when she came to London, and 'often resented the position' into which her 'special mission in the country' forced her, while Jessie Kenney, observing from a more neutral position than that of a daughter, concurred that 'Mrs Pankhurst … must have naturally felt a little bit out of things at Clements Inn'.[69] As a solution, Christabel arranged for a desk to be 'placed for her [mother] in Mrs Tuke's room', and the two women worked quite closely together when Emmeline was in London, establishing a friendship that endured beyond the First World War.[70]

Other offices were allocated to suffragettes according to the importance of the work being done. Again, these offer some insight into the WSPU's priorities. Unsurprisingly, given the overriding concerns of Emmeline Pethick Lawrence, financial business was given much space. Beatrice Sanders, an early recruit from the ILP, was appointed financial secretary and worked closely with the treasurer in the treasury office, sometimes helped by Mrs Knight. Mrs Sanders remained in post when Emmeline Pankhurst replaced Emmeline Pethick Lawrence as treasurer in 1912. The financial organisers needed a separate space as their work included overseeing the weekly accounts of district organisers. They would call individual organisers to task when expenses or expenditure exceeded expectations, or would visit branches in person when they felt particularly concerned.[71] Separate offices allowed them to conduct delicate conversations with branch treasurers and provincial organisers with the necessary degree of privacy, but the status of any income-related work within the WSPU was the real reason for their allocation. Other departments, which had no need of confidentiality, were rewarded with space if they brought in money. The advertising department, which gained its own manager in 1909, had a separate office although one was not really necessary as much of its work took place away from headquarters. Kitty Marshall, who worked for this department, always managed to raise the required £250 each week by selling advertising slots to large stores.[72]

Some organisers were given space because of the scale of their jobs. There was also a packing department, initially housed with the Women's Press in Charing Cross Road, which despatched official merchandise, including badges, scarves, literature and *VFW* tea to WSPU shops and sales throughout the country. Separate office space was assigned for large one-off events such as the exhibitions and Christmas fairs that were organised from time to time, and there were more permanent arrangements in the form of a ticket office to provide for events such as Albert Hall meetings. Space remained a contentious issue among organisers throughout the WSPU's campaign. During a clandestine visit to Boulogne in April 1913, Beatrice Sanders was keener to tell Christabel of her disagreements with Annie Kenney over 'office accommodation' than she was to discuss financial business. Christabel advised her to discuss it directly with Annie, but, when the subject re-emerged, was forced to placate her by pointing out that 'editorial (my dept as it were) was being compressed into the smallest space limit'.[73]

The work done in offices arranging events or distributing tickets shows how much public display and campaigning of the kind labelled 'low-level' militancy benefited from central organisation. When the WSPU arranged its first 'monster' demonstration, for 'Women's Sunday' in Hyde Park in June 1908, two separate new offices were taken at Clements Inn to co-ordinate the planning. This was the largest event attempted by any political group. Even Mrs Tuke felt distinctly overtaken by the scale of disruption at Clements Inn, although she still found something hopeful in the general atmosphere as she wrote to Isabel Seymour: 'You would hardly know the office if you came into it now, a regular hive of busy people jostling ... I wish it were all safely over, everyone's nerves are more or less pained ... [but] you know how WSPUers tackle things, with smiling faces even through fear be knocking at their hearts'.[74]

At this demonstration, the WSPU abandoned its original colour scheme of black and white for a new one of purple, white and green, selected by Emmeline Pethick Lawrence to represent dignity, purity and hope. The new colours, and the large number of banners featuring them which were carried on the march, fixed the Union's visual identity firmly in the public consciousness. Branches were strongly encouraged to adopt the new colours, and headquarters stepped up the production of associated goods. In Huddersfield, members had been about to embark on the purchase of some black and white propaganda, but now wrote to ask how much it would cost them for 'scarves, badges and rosettes' in the new colours for the demonstration.[75]

In the weeks leading up to Women's Sunday, such items were produced under the auspices of the literature department, as part of the variety of ephemera available for general sale, but after the Hyde Park demonstration the planning rooms were handed over to a new department. Directed by a banner secretary, voluntary workers arrived daily to involve themselves with 'making and repairing and dispatching to various places' innumerable banners which were stored in Clements Inn between times.[76] This work was by no means restricted to the months before large national demonstrations. When Ethel Birnstingl wrote to Clements Inn volunteering her services for the General Election campaign of January 1910, Christabel Pankhurst did not send her to a district but replied that she would 'help … most by being at the office for the special purpose of making banners etc.'.[77] Attractive banners were loaned around the country and were in constant demand among district organisers.

While suffragettes were increasingly coupled in the public mind with the so-called 'argument of the stone', more traditional propagandising continued to underpin their claim to the vote. Literature was essential, although the WSPU's attitude to it differed from that taken by other political parties, which 'spen[t] large sums out of their general fund for the production and distribution of free literature', while the WSPU 'adopted the much healthier plan of selling its publications', propagandising without financial drain.[78] Frederick Pethick Lawrence set up the Women's Press in 1907. He intended it to combine 'a literature dept with a wholesale and retail side … entirely separate from the main accounts of the Union'. The enterprise began with a single desk at Clements Inn, but quickly expanded, with its own bookkeeper, Mrs Knight, and office space that finally outgrew headquarters and took the department round the corner to Charing Cross Road. By 1910, Frederick's experiment had grown into a business with a turnover annually of £10,000 through literature sales as well as pamphlets, badges, postcards and other fundraising ephemera.[79]

As well as producing WSPU literature, organisers at headquarters supported the Union's speakers through research. The information department widened to include Mary Home, Aeta Lamb, Cicely Hale, a typist, a general office girl named Lily and several volunteer or temporary staff, including Emily Davison.[80] Information department staff remained in the background compared with the high public profile of the WSPU's militant campaigners, but were responsible for shaping much of the campaign's presentation, selecting and supplying data to the leaders that formed the basis of their speeches. Cicely Hale, who joined the department on a part-time basis for a weekly salary of 10 shillings, explained that as well as scanning the press the information department was charged with 'supplying pithy material for speakers, verifying quotations, looking up facts in the British Museum ... if anyone wanted to know anything they asked us to find it for them'.[81] Mary Leigh, who had first-hand knowledge of their work, singled out Aeta Lamb and Mary Home as the real 'brains' behind some of Christabel Pankhurst's best-known rhetoric.[82]

Speakers and those engaged in similar forms of propaganda were encouraged to visit headquarters to consult material in the information department as required. Early in 1910, the WSPU's leaders persuaded Henry Nevinson to write several letters to the press complaining about the prison treatment of suffragettes. Nevinson recorded in his diary that he made a special visit to Clements Inn while preparing these letters, seeking out 'cuttings of Prison Commissioners and Gladstone's letter to Strangeways officials', to help him outline his case.[83] The information department also began to shape material for a suffragette archive while the campaign was still in process, with Aeta Lamb setting to work on a list of prisoners. During a police raid in March 1912 officers removed 'two cabloads and one dozen large packages' of papers, an indication of the extent of the department's work.[84] The prisoners' list survived, but was seized by the police in 1913, by which time it contained 'one thousand, two hundred documents containing particulars relating to the conviction of four hundred and fifty six suffragettes'.[85]

Although much of the work undertaken at headquarters was of a mundanely administrative kind, several employees there were more directly concerned with militancy. Edwardian London offered the WSPU many opportunities to stage encounters with prominent politicians, and no chance was wasted. Jessie Kenney, the organiser specifically charged with arranging such events, kept photographs of cabinet ministers and prominent MPs on her office mantelpiece so that suffragettes called to do more direct lobbying work might recognise them.[86] She also took full advantage of London's size, and its consequent membership resource. In December 1909, she wrote to London members prepared to disrupt ministers' meetings, informing them that she had arranged a special Welsh class, run by Mrs Davies of Fulham, so that they might tackle Lloyd George with 'appropriate sentences in Welsh'; a list of helpful 'words and syllables' was appended.[87] No public appearance by a prominent Liberal

MP could be allowed to pass without an interruption by suffragettes, so Jessie compiled lists of London teachers, women guardians and similar interest groups so that these protests were tightly targeted.

The lists helped her secure workers at a moment's notice, such as in July 1909 when she requested teacher Hannah Townsend to attend a Nurses' Congress at which Haldene was speaking. Jessie explained that she had chosen Hannah rather than a nurse, who might have been a more obvious choice, because 'I have got you down on my teachers' list and, as I understand that the L.C.C. schools are breaking up tomorrow, I thought you would most likely be able to go'.[88] Suffragettes also had to be prepared to capitalise on more private opportunities for protest and publicity presented by the London season. These too could appear at extremely short notice. In June 1909, headquarters received tickets for a Foreign Office reception to celebrate King Edward's birthday. The donor was the husband of a suffragette, who 'had persuaded him to pass on the tickets'. Theresa Garnett happened to be in Clements Inn when they arrived, and was pounced on by Christabel Pankhurst who felt that 'if anyone could get away with it, [she] could'. Theresa's complaint that she lacked a suitable outfit was waved away by Una Dugdale, who loaned her sister Daisy's gown, and also found Theresa a temporary 'husband' – 'a very nice young boy just down from Cambridge' – and together the young 'couple' slipped into the reception where Theresa delivered an impromptu speech before being hustled out by detectives.[89]

Organisers at headquarters also co-ordinated provincial volunteers in the national acts of militancy that took place in the capital. Although this work was administrative, militancy could not have reached the scale it did without it. The Metropolitan Police recognised this and were particularly interested in the activities of the hospitality department, the unit that put London sympathisers in touch with provincial volunteers. Sinister motives were imputed to the numerous 'active sympathisers' who corresponded with the hospitality secretary offering their willingness to 'put up one, two, three or more' women arriving in the capital intent on participating in 'the militant meetings'.[90]

In fact, suffragettes always regarded such support and hospitality as a form of militancy. Nancy Seymour Pearson was arrested in November 1912 for stone-throwing in London. She returned to the capital from her home in York in January 1913 to answer bail, and was put up by Dr M. Waller, head of a women's hospital, who lived in a large house with several medical student lodgers. One of them, an Irish girl named Miss O'Hague, loaned Mrs Seymour Pearson a bag to carry her personal effects to court, and was later said to be 'proud' and 'delighted to think her bag is in gaol for the Cause'.[91] Women like Miss O'Hague risked their university future if arrested, so while the loss of her bag was described with humour, it was her contribution to the militant campaign. Many other families in London took similar steps, offering hospitality and accommodation to volunteers in support of their actions when economic or social concerns precluded them from risking imprisonment themselves.

The work of the hospitality committee underpinned mass militancy, but it did not end when suffragettes were sentenced. Organisers involved with arranging hospitality soon found that their remit extended to over-seeing suffragette prisoners, as far as that could be done from outside prison. The prisoners' secretary became one of the most important posts at headquarters. Jessie Kenney was the first organiser to take on this job, which began in a rather casual manner to relieve some of the pressure on Christabel Pankhurst, who was becoming overwhelmed by the streams of worried parents who 'thronged offices … bewildered by [the] sudden imprisonment' of a daughter.[92] The post then passed to Isabel Seymour whose other role as hospitality secretary ensured that she had a list of women from outside of London who had volunteered for arrest. Olive Smith also did this job, then Joan Wickham, whose appointment Christabel approved from Paris in April 1913, and finally Nellie Hall in 1914.[93] Miss Hall later described how, by that point, the work of the prisoners' secretary was indivisible from actual acts of militancy:

> I was acting as Prisoners' Secretary with an office at the Headquarters, Lincolns Inn House in Kingsway … [but] my real job was organiser of militancy and in this capacity I was temporarily installed in the Maida Vale apartment of a friend. My job was to provide extra ammunition and to direct the women who would do major damage across the country if the petition [to the King in May 1914] was not delivered.[94]

The prisoners' secretary could do more mundane work. She arranged bail when necessary. Before 1913 bail was generally stood by Frederick Pethick Lawrence, and one of Isabel Seymour's first tasks following his departure from the WSPU was to arrange a pool of sympathisers, including the distinguished scientist Hertha Ayrton, who would be willing to stand as guarantors for suffragette bail if required.[95] Nellie Hall recalled that towards the end of the campaign there was also a move to pay fines, if they were offered in court, 'because frequent prison sentences disrupted the movement', and that her first day saw her 'sent out from court at 11 with a list of possible sympathisers and the job of getting £350 by 4 o'clock'.[96] Sometimes the number of WSPU prisoners overwhelmed the courts, as happened after the window-smashing raid of 1912. Isabel then returned to her role as hospitality secretary, and arranged further accommodation for provincial women returning to answer their bail. Headquarters arranged for food hampers to be sent in to suffragette prisoners on remand, and occasionally after trial, if permitted. The prisoners' secretary sometimes organised further militancy after sentencing had taken place. As the numbers of women going to prison increased, concerted defiance inside prison became part of the campaign. Tactics such as hunger-strikes were begun spontaneously, but the WSPU leadership quickly sanctioned them, and recognised that tight organisation was required if they were to be effective. Gladys Roberts, from Leeds, was sent to Holloway in June 1909 for her part in a deputation. She kept a secret shorthand diary in which she recorded how, by shouting from the windows, her fellow-prisoner Theresa Garnett managed to persuade a local woman whose garden adjoined the prison 'to send word to Clements Inn and the Press' that the first mass hunger-strike had begun. When the message was received, Christabel Pankhurst and Mabel Tuke headed to Holloway, then mounted a vigorous propaganda campaign around the strikers' exploits.[97]

Incarcerated suffragettes became adept at smuggling out letters which both kept the prisoners' secretary appraised of their circumstances and sought her advice on future courses of action. Central co-ordination was particularly necessary after large events when prisoners were held at several different locations. After the window-smashing raid of March 1912 Elsie Howey was sent to Aylesbury, where she penned a desperate note to Isabel Seymour seeking permission to initiate a hunger-strike:

> All of us who broke our windows are sentenced to 7 days solitary confinement … and had to lose our 'privileges' … Mrs Pankhurst doesn't know … and has told us not to hunger strike … will you take counsel and let us know on Monday? … We are bursting with rage, but of course must wait till Mrs Pankhurst knows and gives us permission to act.[98]

At the same time, Gladys Hazel complained of similar confusion in Holloway, writing that prisoners were 'getting all the time contradictory messages and rumours, first one thing and then another'. Her letter to headquarters also protested that some prisoners were campaigning against the idea of a hunger-strike: 'All the heart is being taken out of people, directly we have got them over Mrs Marshall gets them back … it looks as if there are only going to be about twenty of us hunger striking and some of these are not prepared to go right through with it'.[99] Gladys Hazel requested 'an authoritative message' from headquarters to be sent in via her cousin, a solicitor, who was due to visit that week. This letter may have been the catalyst that prompted the sanctioning of a hunger-strike in Aylesbury. With the help of covert suffragette communications, the action soon spread to Holloway. Janie Terrero, a prisoner there, noticed 'something electrical in the air … we heard [on 13 April] they were hunger-striking at Aylesbury and we immediately followed'.[100] This hunger-strike was quite brief, although women in Holloway required some persuasion that the demands in Aylesbury had been met. Janie Terrero was one of a group of about a dozen women who mistrusted a telegram, shown to them by officials, saying that the original strike had ended, and would only accept it when further evidence was offered.[101] At headquarters, Evelyn Sharp was given the job of ensuring that the telegrams had been understood and that the efforts remained co-ordinated and directed.[102]

As well as organising resistance in prison, the prisoners' secretary was the main receptacle for much useful information. By 1912, the police were attending most WSPU meetings and monitoring work at Clements Inn. Fears spread that there were spies among the prisoners, attempting to glean information about future acts of militancy and with a view to undermining prison protests. New volunteers were still coming forward for militant action at this stage – indeed, for the window-smashing raids they were encouraged in the hope that first offenders would attract shorter prison sentences – so the notion that the authorities might hide a mole among the prisoners was not too improbable. Janie Terrero alerted her husband to the activities of two of her fellow-prisoners:

> There are two people here I do not like at all and I wish you could give them a hint at Clements Inn … One … never talks much but listens to everything. She told me she was a member of the WSPU and then told someone else she was not a member … I may be wrong but I have been suspicious from the very first. I never tell either of these ladies anything but others are not as careful.[103]

Other smuggled letters contained personal messages for headquarters to pass on. Liaising with prisoners' families was an important part of the prisoners' secretary's role, exemplifying the WSPU's ability to underpin politics with more personal touches. Janie Terrero went to prison in March 1912 against her husband Manuel's wishes, although as he was a member of the Men's Political Union she must have been fairly certain of his ultimate support. She left a letter with her WSPU friend Muriel Thompson, explaining that, although she knew he would be upset, she felt her 'honour, as a woman, at stake' and begged him not to pay her fine 'but let me go through with it properly'.[104] Many of the letters she smuggled out of Holloway attested to the work that organisers at headquarters could do for prisoners' families. When Manuel was denied a visitor's permit, she wrote that he could 'always get news if there is any at Clements Inn'.[105] After conviction prisoners were allowed to receive a set number of letters, which could be as small as one per fortnight. To ensure that as many messages as possible were passed on to convicted suffragettes, the prisoners' secretary would complete 'one long letter giving everybody's messages' together, provided they were first sent to her at headquarters.[106]

It was also the job of the prisoners' secretary to offer prisoners' relatives as much information as possible about the health and well-being of their convicted wives or daughters. This was something of a two-way process. *VFW* warned families that 'the prison authorities will only give information with regards to [release dates] to [prisoners'] relatives', and requested that such information should be forwarded to the prisoners' secretary.[107] Relatives contacted headquarters even if they were familiar with the WSPU's local power structures. When Dr Alice Ker was in Holloway in the spring of 1912, her daughters Margaret and Mary, both suffragette suporters, enquired at Clements Inn rather than the local WSPU offices in Liverpool. Dr Ker gently reminded them that this was not necessary:

> I had a visitor yesterday. A Miss Wright came in response to your request to Clements Inn. It was awfully good of her and it shows how well HQ looks after us all, but, as I said before, don't bother them again, for I'll get on alright.[108]

A letter sent from or via the prisoners' secretary might sometimes be the first a family knew of a daughter's decision to go to prison. Constance Lytton, who sent one such letter to her mother, recalled that collecting and posting this correspondence was one of the jobs given to the organisers who met with deputation members just before the Women's Parliament convened.[109] Helen Watts, who travelled from Nottingham to the Women's Parliament of February 1909, slipped a note to a suffragette at the Police Court, acknowledging that her parents would have 'a great shock ... to see [her] name in the paper' that evening.[110] Gertrude Watts, who approved her daughter's action, contacted Clements Inn and Isabel Seymour immediately appraised her of the appropriate procedures:

> As [Helen was] sentenced to the second division I am afraid it would be impossible to send her your letter. The only way you could get any news in ... would be by writing to the Governor ... [She] will not be allowed to received any newspapers or flowers or anything else, but if you were to send books ... she would probably get them ... You might get a permit to see Miss Watts from the Home Secretary ... [She] will be out on March 24th.[111]

These communications represented more than mere courtesy. Many suffragettes were arrested for offences that carried the option of a fine instead of a prison sentence, and their fines could be paid any time during a sentence without their consent. Newspapers, which suggested that certain women had never been serious about their undertaking, would gleefully report early releases.[112] To maintain the Union's prison policy, organisers had to become adept at pacifying anxious relatives. The information they had to send was not always pleasant. Among the more difficult letters that Isabel Seymour had to write was one to the sister of May Billinghurst, a suffragette arrested in her wheelchair in December 1912, informing her of the progress of May's hunger-strike: 'I am grieved to say that we have heard that your sister is being forcibly fed with a cup, I need not tell you how we feel for you and your mother.'[113] Headquarters' main role here was to calm the nerves of anxious relatives and ensure that everything possible was done for suffragette prisoners, as well as keeping them firmly in the public eye. This also continued after release. From the time of the earliest London imprisonments, it became customary for headquarters to organise a welcome breakfast for released suffragettes at which speeches would be given and appropriate presentations made. These occasions were so successful in attracting wide press coverage that the authorities could go to great pains to contain them, releasing prisoners earlier than expected, which at least avoided clamour in the streets around Holloway. Prisoners' welcomes also united supporting families, invited by the prisoners' secretary. Their sense of ceremony created an important rite of passage for suffragettes as they ended their sentences and returned to the world of active campaigning.

The WSPU's headquarters was always more than a central set of offices. It was the heart of the Union's campaign, an ultra-modern space in which dozens of young women came together to share the comradeship of suffrage work, helped by state-of-the-art equipment. The constant presence of the national leaders and the increasingly frequent police raids brought a sense of urgent excitement to their work there, which was heightened by the impression that workers at headquarters were closer to the leaders of the Union – and by implication to their decisions – than the provincial employees who had to consult or wait for directives. Such feelings intensified as police interference and state clampdowns meant that by the end of the WSPU's militant campaign 'headquarters' as a source of power or decision-making was actually a group of organisers rather than a physical location. They have also helped fuel the impression that there was something sinister in the way that headquarters operated.

Yet to dwell on headquarters as a site of control is to miss the rather obvious point that the WSPU was organising a national campaign. Most large political organisations experience tension between local and national leaderships at some point. Branch members can feel overlooked while national workers become exasperated as their attempts to maintain cohesion are threatened. The WSPU was no different from other bodies in this respect. Demonstrations and campaigns had to be planned, militancy co-ordinated, prisoners helped and the membership serviced by its own organisation. What remains most striking about headquarters is that all of the work there was done by women, who consistently sought a more feminised way of doing things. This, together with an awareness that they were at the epicentre of the campaign, explains the sense of excitement that is almost universal among organisers' recollections of their time at Clements and Lincolns Inn.

Notes

1 In sources contemporary with the events referred to here, mentions of Clements and Lincolns Inn are found both with and without the apostrophe. I omit it throughout.
2 *VFW*, 22 March 1912.
3 Rosen, *Rise Up Women*, p. 91.
4 Emmeline Pethick Lawrence to Mary Phillips, 21 Sept 1909, Mary Phillips Papers.
5 Emmeline Pethick Lawrence to Dora Marsden, 2 December 1910, Dora Marsden Papers.
6 Christabel Pankhurst to Mary Phillips, 1 August 1913, Mary Phillips Papers.
7 See, for instance, Dora Marsden to Emmeline Pethick Lawrence, 9 January 1911, Dora Marsden Papers.
8 E. S. Pankhurst, *The Suffragette Movement*, p. 516.
9 Mary Gawthorpe to Anne Gawthorpe, 9 September 1910, Mary Gawthorpe Papers.
10 David Mitchell, *Queen Christabel: A Biography of Christabel Pankhurst* (London: Macdonald & Janes, 1977), p. 108; Morley with Stanley, *Life and Death of Emily Wilding Davison*, pp. 82, 92; Rosen, *Rise Up Women*, pp. 88, 89.
11 Teresa Billington's notes on Alice Milne's diary, 21 October 1906, Box 397 A/6, TBG Papers.
12 Mitchell, *The Hard Way Up*, p. 159.
13 Theresa Billington Grieg, untitled fragment, Box 397 A/6, TBG Papers.
14 E. S. Pankhurst, *The Suffragette Movement*, p. 266.
15 E. Pethick Lawrence, *My Part*, p. 147.
16 *Ibid.*, p. 152.
17 Pethick Lawrence, *Fate*, p. 59.
18 *Ibid.*
19 E. Pethick Lawrence, *My Part*, p. 152.
20 F. Pethick Lawrence, *Fate*, p. 71.
21 E. Pethick Lawrence, *My Part*, p. 130.
22 *Ibid.*, p. 131.
23 Lytton, *Prisons and Prisoners*, p. 35.

24 C. Pankhurst, *Unshackled*, p. 105.
25 Frederick Pethick Lawrence, 'The home of the WSPU', *VFW*, 6 September 1911.
26 An item in the *Standard*, 7 March 1912, demonstrates the ease with which Scotland Yard were able to get WSPU's telephones tapped while searching for Christabel Pankhurst.
27 *VFW*, 20 September 1912.
28 E. S. Pankhurst, *The Suffragette Movement*, p. 411.
29 *VFW*, January 1908.
30 Kenney, *Memories*, p. 82.
31 *Suffragette*, 23 May 1913.
32 E. S. Pankhurst, *The Suffragette Movement*, p. 224.
33 Stephenson, 'No other way', pp. 97, 100.
34 E. S. Pankhurst, *The Suffragette Movement*, pp. 224–5.
35 Notes on Charlotte Marsh, Camellia Collection.
36 Esther Knowles, 'Born under a lucky star', *Calling All Women*, 1971.
37 C. Pankhurst, *Unshackled* p. 71; unfortunately she died of pneumonia shortly after beginning work.
38 Teresa Billington Grieg to David Mitchell, 12 September 1964, Mitchell Collection.
39 C. Pankhurst, *Unshackled*, p. 71.
40 F. Pethick Lawrence, *Fate*, p. 71; E. S. Pankhurst, *The Suffragette Movement*, p. 224.
41 E. S. Pankhurst, *The Suffragette Movement*, p. 224.
42 Mitchell, *Queen Christabel*, p. 93; Atea Lamb, profile, *VFW*, June 1908; *VFW*, January 1908.
43 Hale, *A Good Long Time*, p. 52.
44 Gawthorpe, *Uphill to Holloway*, pp. 238–9.
45 Mitchell, *Queen Christabel*, p. 93; E. S. Pankhurst, *The Suffragette Movement*, p. 224.
46 Scrap notes on Marguerite Anne Sidley, SFC.
47 Walker, 'Helen Pethick Lawrence', p. 19.
48 Raeburn, *The Militant Suffragettes*, pp. 145–6.
49 Knowles, 'Born under a lucky star'.
50 Kenney, 'The flame and the flood', notes for Book 2.
51 C. Pankhurst, *Unshackled*, pp. 77–8; E .S. Pankhurst, *The Suffragette*, pp. 322–3.
52 Kenney, 'The flame and the flood', notes for Book 2.
53 Gawthorpe, *Uphill to Holloway*, p. 227.
54 Frances Bartlett, memoir, SFC.
55 Richardson, *Laugh a Defiance*, pp. 1, 2.
56 C. Pankhurst, *Unshackled*, pp. 77–8.
57 Kenney, 'The flame and the flood', ch. 3
58 E. S. Pankhurst, *The Suffragette Movement*, pp. 224–5.
59 *Ibid.*, p. 225.
60 *VFW*, 8 September 1911.
61 Stephenson, 'No other way'.
62 Knowles, 'Born under a lucky star'.
63 See Harriet R. Kerr to Edith How Martyn, 22 January 1928, SFC; also letter from Kerr's niece to David Mitchell, 27 July 1975, Mitchell Collection.
64 Knowles, 'Born under a lucky star'; also *Radio Times'* 'Shoulder to Shoulder' commemorative supplement.
65 Wilson, *With All Her Might*, pp. 113–15.

66 E. S. Pankhurst, *The Suffragette Movement*, p. 267.
67 C. Pankhurst, *Unshackled*, p. 77.
68 E. S. Pankhurst, *The Suffragette Movement*, p. 267.
69 *Ibid.*, p. 266; Kenney, 'The flame and the flood', untitled fragment.
70 Mrs Tuke worked with Emmeline and Christabel in their short-lived tea-shop enterprise in the south of France in 1925: Purvis, *Emmeline Pankhurst*, pp. 337–8.
71 For example, Emmeline Pethick Lawrence to Dora Marsden, 2 November 1910, Dora Marsden Papers, which informs Marsden that Mrs Sanders is being sent to her district to talk over financial matters; Mary Blathwayt's diary for 20 March 1911 mentions a similar visit by Mrs Sanders to Bath.
72 E. Katharine Willoughby Marshall, 'Suffragette escapes and adventures', typescript autobiography, September 1947, p. 36, SFC.
73 Christabel Pankhurst to Harriet Kerr, n.d. (April 1913) and 24 April 1913, TNA, DPP 1/19, Exhibit 33.
74 Mabel Tuke to Isabel Seymour, 11 June 1908, SFC.
75 Huddersfield WSPU Minute Book, 19 May 1908, Key Papers, West Yorkshire Archives.
76 *VFW*, 8 September 1911.
77 Christabel Pankhurst to Ethel Birnstingl, 11 December 1909, SFC.
78 Frederick Pethick Lawrence, 'The romance of the Women's Press', *VFW*, 15 September 1911.
79 *Ibid.*
80 Hale, *A Good Long Time*, p. 52.
81 *Ibid.*, p. 49
82 Mary Leigh, interview with David Mitchell, 21 March 1965, Mitchell Collection.
83 Henry Nevinson's diary, 4 January 1910, Bodleian Library , Oxford.
84 *VFW*, 8 March 1912.
85 *The Times*, 16 May 1913.
86 Jessie Kenney interview with David Mitchell, 24 March 1964, Mitchell Collection.
87 Jessie Kenney, circular letter, 7 December 1909, SFC.
88 Jessie Kenney to Miss Townsend, SFC.
89 Raeburn, *The Militant Suffragettes*, p. 102.
90 See report of conspiracy trial, *VFW*, 22 March 1912
91 Nancy Seymour Pearson, undated letter (written on toilet paper) to her husband; postcard from Dr M. Waller to Isabel Seymour Pearson, Mrs Seymour Pearson's scrapbook, Camellia Collection.
92 Jessie Kenney interview with David Mitchell, 24 March 1964, Mitchell Collection.
93 Christabel Pankhurst to Harriet Kerr, 21 April 1913, TNA, DPP 1/19, Exhibit 33.
94 Undated notes from talk on WSPU history, 1996 E2 16, Nellie Hall Humpherson Papers.
95 Hertha Ayrton to Isabel Seymour, 14 June 1913, SFC.
96 Cutting from *Canadian Weekly*, 16 October 1965, Nellie Hall Humpherson Papers.
97 Raeburn, *The Militant Suffragettes*, p. 108; E. S. Pankhurst, *Suffragette*, p. 393.
98 Elsie Howey to Isabel Seymour, n.d., smuggled letter, SFC.
99 Gladys Hazel to Isabel Seymour, n.d., SFC.
100 Janie Terrero, notes on prison experiences, SFC.
101 *Ibid.*
102 Henry Nevinson's diary, 7 April 1912.

103 Janie Terrero, smuggled letter, 17 May 1912, Camellia Collection.
104 Janie Terrero to Manuel Terrero, March 1912, Camellia Collection.
105 *Ibid.*, 6 March 1912, Camellia Collection.
106 Christabel Pankhurst to Annot Robinson, 9 November 1906, M220/1/1/3, Robinson Papers; see also, for example, Isabel Seymour to Mrs Watts, 26 February 1909, Watts Papers.
107 *VFW*, 5 March 1912.
108 Alice Ker to her daughters, 16 March 1912, Autograph Letter Collection, Women's Library.
109 Lytton, *Prisons and Prisoners*, p. 35.
110 Helen Watts to 'My dear mother and father and all', 24 February 1909, Watts Papers
111 Isabel Seymour to Mrs Watts, 26 February 1909, Watts Papers.
112 See, for example, 'Tired of prison and wants to go home', *Daily Mail*, 27 March 1907.
113 Isabel Seymour to Miss Billinghurst, 14 January 1913, Billinghurst Papers, Women's Library.

5

'I urge you not to run the risk of arrest':[1] organisers and militancy

ORE THAN ANY OTHER ISSUE, the question of militancy fired contemporary debates about the efficacy of the WSPU's campaign. Once Mrs Pankhurst had, in 1905, made her 'tremendous and irrevocable decision' to 'put herself behind militancy', supporters and opponents of women's suffrage centred much of their discussion on the appropriateness and utility of such tactics.[2] Suffragettes drew on a longstanding radical heritage to justify their actions. They were, it was repeatedly argued, only following 'the methods which men had used to get the vote'.[3] Sylvia Pankhurst was quick to remind supporters of the symbolism of the site of Christabel and Annie Kenney's first militant protest when they 'fought for votes as their forefathers had done, upon the site of Peterloo'.[4] Opponents, meanwhile, had much to say about the inappropriateness of such behaviours for women: 'Do these amazons who shriek and fight and "roll in the mud" with policemen ... really think they are proving their fitness to manage the affairs of the nation?', wrote one observer of a militant demonstration to the *Daily News*; 'I am ashamed of my sex'.[5]

Historians' engagement with the WSPU's campaign has centred largely on the theme of militancy, 'fetishising' the act 'at the expense of the political rationale', as one has put it.[6] Yet while the intensity of such debates testifies to the capacity of women's militancy to provoke, even a century later, the focus on outcome and action above process and mechanism misses the subtlety that characterised much WSPU militancy and overlooks the role of paid workers in furthering the militant campaign. While all suffragettes who engaged in militancy did so at some degree of personal risk, organisers were in a position of particular difficulty, which intensified as the pace of militancy increased. For although they were often ordered to remain on the sidelines when militant demonstrations were taking place, a large part of their work effectively involved persuading other women to commit risky, often illegal, actions, and that could prove an dicomforting role for an organiser to embrace.

This was not obvious at the start of the militant campaign, which began in an extremely small way. On 20 February 1904, four months after the WSPU's formation, Christabel Pankhurst went to the Free Trade Hall, Manchester, to hear Winston Churchill speak for the Free Trade League. She had drawn one of the random allocation of platform tickets reserved for women at Edwardian political meetings. Facing the audience, she attempted what she later described as 'the first militant step' for suffrage. As Churchill moved a resolution on free trade, she asked 'to be allowed to move an amendment with regard to Woman Suffrage ... The Chairman said he was afraid he could not permit [her to do so] ... Miss Pankhurst seemed loth [sic] to give way, but finally, amid loud cries of "Chair", she retired'.[7] Over the next decade, suffragette militancy would intensify. Buildings would be burned, bombs would be planted, property defaced and destroyed. Yet in her autobiography Christabel Pankhurst remembered this first step as being:

> The hardest ... because it *was* the first. To move from my place on the platform to the speakers' table in the teeth of the astonishment and opposition of will of that immense throng, those civic and county leaders ... was the most difficult thing that I have ever done.[8]

This reflection offers a clear vision of suffragette militancy. For Christabel, militancy was defined not by the violence or illegality of an action, but by the transgressive potential of that action and the perceptions of, and reactions to, it by contemporary observers. This was more than a staged interruption. Jon Lawrence's investigation into the gendering of Edwardian political occasions noted that women were deliberately elevated to the platform to protect them from the 'bear-pit of partisan masculinity' that comprised the main body of the meeting. In return for their protected status they had to refrain from speaking 'unless ... on behalf of an absent or incapacitated male relative'.[9] Read against this, Christabel Pankhurst's defiance did more than challenge the authority of the chairman: it demanded inclusion in a participatory political tradition which remained overwhelmingly gendered as male despite the increasing presence of women in municipal political life. The 'astonishment' and 'opposition' that she met with came from an audience who recognised this immediately. After the meeting, apart from the brief report in the *Manchester Guardian*, quoted above, the first militant action was quickly forgotten. Christabel ascribed this to the fact that her boldness 'did not result in imprisonment' and determined that future militant protests would not be so easily ignored.[10] Nor were they. Inspired by her leadership over the next decade the WSPU devised innumerable manifestations of militancy, which were deployed in support of its claim to the vote. While not all resulted in prison sentences, each action seized public attention and the WSPU was rarely off the front pages.

Despite the prominence of militancy within historical accounts of the WSPU, surprisingly little attention is paid to its variety, or to continuities in its many forms. Rather, there has been a tendency to view militancy as an escalating phenomenon in which violent forms had displaced non-violent or 'early' militancy by about 1912, the year when Emmeline and Frederick Pethick Lawrence were expelled from the WSPU. This overlooks the emphasis that the Union placed on expanding rather than supplanting its range of militant tactics. Admittedly Christabel Pankhurst, in exile by this point, suggested a hierarchy of militancy that elevated daring exploits above less physical actions, which she believed were ultimately more submissive, but her mother who remained in England was more aware of how the campaign was shaped and urged her members to a more nuanced variety of activities:

> Be militant in your own way. Those of you who can express your militancy by going to the House of Commons and refusing to leave ... as we did in the early days – do so. Those of you who can express your militancy by facing Cabinet Ministers' meetings – do so ... those of you who can still further attack the sacred idol of property ... do so.[11]

Emmeline Pankhurst's reference here to tactics dating from the first years of the WSPU's campaign acknowledged that for most suffragettes, early manifestations of militancy did not disappear when more extreme tactics were adopted. Continuities abounded, particularly in collectively-organised militancy. In the iconographic image of Emmeline's arrest at Buckingham Palace in May 1914 we see both defiance of the police and the crime of obstruction, the same offence for which she was arrested in February 1908, November 1911 and November 1912. Acknowledging continuity amid diverse forms of militancy problematises attempts to impose chronological distinctions between 'early' and 'later' militancy or to distinguish a progression in the level of violence committed or the fiscal value of damage done. There is also the inescapable fact that only a small minority of WSPU members participated in stone-throwing or arson, while all would have described themselves as being militant. A more useful conception of militancy recognises three distinct but not necessarily separate types of action, each of which rested on a commitment on the part of the perpetrator to contravene the expected gendered behaviours of the

Edwardian period. Thus for some women, like the upper-class heroine of Gertrude Colmore's novel *Suffragette Sally*, the disapprobation attracted by wearing a badge or a scarf in the WSPU's colours may have been as far as they felt able to go in militancy.[12] Other women felt more confident in undertaking behaviours that would lead to their imprisonment. This was more overtly transgressive but again covered a wide spectrum as a significant proportion of suffragette prisoners were imprisoned for refusal to pay a fine rather than for committing an action that carried an automatic custodial sentence. The third type of militancy comprised actions that were clearly illegal such as arson, bombing and criminal damage.

Normative expectations of behaviour are not fixed, but are themselves cleaved by other social signifiers such as class, age, race and even geographical location. The WSPU's retention of a range of militant actions allowed each individual in its eclectic membership to chose a level with which they felt comfortable, which might vary depending on the social, economic or familial circumstances of the perpetrator. Perpetuating older tactics alongside innovations allowed suffragettes to alter their choices if their personal circumstances (or opinions) shifted. Furthermore, it encouraged a situation in which individual and collective, and locally based and nationally co-ordinated acts of militancy combined and complemented each other in building what was described as a 'truly national' movement.[13] Much of the work that was done by the WSPU's full-time workers was connected to the first type of militancy: demonstrations, paper sales, advertising and emphasising the Union's presence in various regional centres were daily tasks for district organisers, while the national headquarters in London arranged similar activities in the capital. It was the second and third types of militancy, those which carried the threat of arrest, that were to become problematical for organisers as the campaign progressed.

Militancy would have been neither as widespread nor as diverse without full-time organisers, particularly at the start of the WSPU's national campaign when a handful of staff had to lead by example. Organisers' weekly £2 salaries freed them from fear of losing their livelihoods were they to be imprisoned, but also placed a higher expectation on their determination to see actions through. Organisers' positions undoubtedly made militancy less daunting for them. Their leadership status militated against the penalties of social ostracism that attended deviant behaviour as for their co-workers and fellow-suffragettes they became elevated to the status of heroines. In spite of this, the pressure on organisers to put themselves at the forefront of militancy lessened as the number of suffragette prisoners increased. There was concern in the

WSPU that it was becoming over-reliant on organisers' willingness to go to prison. Its structure was changing too. In January 1906, not long after the first arrests, suffragettes completed their first General Election campaign, having had some success in irritating, if not persuading, leading Liberal politicians electioneering in the north. Following the Election, government returned to Westminster and Christabel Pankhurst realised that, if the WSPU's campaign was to maintain its momentum, it had to follow. This provided the impetus for the Union's move to London, which brought it a national headquarters and a network of branches throughout Britain. There was no longer any need to keep militancy to the north.

Although London was the WSPU's administrative centre, the capital city also offered an appropriate backdrop for staging acts of militancy which emphasised the Union's proximity to the heart of the Edwardian political establishment. In June 1906 the WSPU initiated direct militancy in London, demonstrating outside Asquith's house in Cavendish Square. Four arrests ensued, consideration of which reveals some of the tensions inherent in switching the role of prisoner from organisers to voluntary workers. The four apprehended women were Annie Kenney, Teresa Billington, Adelaide Knight and Jane Sparboro. Although they were jailed for similar offences at the same place, their actions were rooted in different social and cultural contexts. Teresa Billington and Annie Kenney were full-time organisers who saw agitation as an accepted part of their work. They had been political workers before joining the WSPU, Annie for a trade union and Teresa for the ILP. They shared personal circumstances too: Annie Kenney's mother had recently died, while Teresa Billington was estranged from her family. Both women had found a sympathetic mother figure in Emmeline Pankhurst, and her strong approval of their actions removed any sense of shame or social stigma. Arrest thus augmented rather than diminished Annie and Teresa's status in the eyes of their friends and their employers. Mrs Sparboro and Mrs Knight braved militancy from a different position. Both women were involved with socialism, but as activists rather than as officials; and both were married with family responsibilities. Mrs Knight worried about leaving her children – the youngest of whom was only 18 months old – to go to prison, while the elderly Mrs Sparboro fretted about her worrying husband and was desperate to let him know that she was free from fleas and flies.[14] Dora Montefiore, who knew them personally, remarked that the stigma of prison was greater for them and others like them, as their immediate neighbours, lacking 'the idealism that inspired ... militant women', would be inclined to 'gibe and ... point out the jail birds or to persecute their children'.[15] The four women received similar sentences, but the cost to the volunteers was far higher.

In February 1907, the WSPU unveiled its strategy for future militant actions in London. It would target Parliament, as the key site of power, but also as an arena in which women had 'no share', from which they were excluded except on the invitation of men.[16] The first Women's Parliament was held in 1907 – one of ten such meetings between then and 1911. Women's Parliaments, which met close to Westminster, were timed to co-incide with key political events, such as openings of new parliamentary sessions or debates around Private Members' Bills on suffrage, thus accentuating the hopelessness of women relying on the 'Men's Parliament' to effect change on their behalf. Delegates would listen to a series of speeches and await news from Westminster. When reports reached Caxton Hall of further setbacks, such as the omission of any mention of suffrage from the King's Speech, a set reaction was precipitated. A broad, condemnatory resolution would be passed. Successive small deputations would then leave the Hall to carry the resolution to Parliament. The police would try to block them, the deputies would attempt to pass through police lines and increasing numbers of arrests would follow. Emmeline Pethick Lawrence described how, by the second Women's Parliament, of March 1907, the imprisonment of women on these deputations had become 'almost a matter of routine', while Sylvia Pankhurst, who acquired retrospective disapproval for the initiative despite her enthusiastic participation in the first Parliament of February 1907, described them as 'really a rallying ground for those who were to march up to the House of Commons and get themselves arrested'.[17]

Women's Parliaments brought suffragette militancy on a large scale to the streets of London. The WSPU leaders did not seek to bring out large numbers of women as an end in itself. In order to represent the scale of women's exclusion from the apparatus of the State, Women's Parliaments had to be presented as being as inclusive as possible and to bring in fresh waves of delegates from throughout the country each time they met. Demonstrations which resulted in the same women getting arrested would no longer work. Furthermore, now that the WSPU was a national organisation, its district organisers made up a valuable resource which could not be spared lightly, particularly as London magistrates were now imposing more severe sentences on repeat offenders, 'to give everyone warning' to avoid being 'convicted ... on more than one occasion'.[18] Arrest was now forbidden to most district organisers attending London deputations except on very rare occasions. Even Annie Kenney, the first suffragette prisoner, was refused permission to participate in the fourth Parliament in June 1908.[19]

The prohibition was not as rigidly applied to all of the WSPU's workers. District organisers who worked closely with their branches appreciated what an undertaking it was for many rank and file members to go to prison. When Annie Kenney was charged with recruiting women for one of the first deputations to the Prime Minister, she made a point of explaining that this time there were no plans for arrests. The local WSPU contact was advised: 'Bring as many as possible ... tell the women not to be afraid and to follow us ... The women will not get into any trouble so they have no occasion to be nervous.'[20] No such undertaking could be given to participants in the Women's Parliaments. During arrangements for the third parliament, in February 1908, Annie Kenney and Adela Pankhurst sent a circular letter to volunteers in Yorkshire and Lancashire which explained the travel arrangements which had been made on their behalf, and reassured them: 'fear not, we shall look after you when you get to Manchester'. In a private note to Annot Robinson who was co-ordinating the arrivals at Manchester, Annie admitted that she and Adela were 'almost frantic with people drawing back' at the last minute.[21]

No matter how pragmatic the reasons were for keeping organisers out of prison, the members found it difficult to appreciate why they were being asked to go further than their leaders. Any organiser who had been imprisoned would have found it easier to persuade other women to follow her example. The short biographical statements which prisoners gave to *VFW* often cited this influence, such as the testimony of Hannah Sheppard, a young mill worker arrested on a demonstration in Rochdale, who claimed she had 'volunteered for militant service as a mark of appreciation of the services of Mrs Leigh, also a working woman'.[22] Recognising this, the WSPU was careful to ensure that some organisers appeared in the lists of women arrested in London, although they tended to be clerical workers at headquarters or were drawn from a small pool of nationally deployed workers who spent most of their time engaged in militant acts. New organisers who had not yet been in prison often served a period of detention at the very start of their training, as happened to Rona Robinson and Dora Marsden, who resigned their teaching posts to attend the seventh Women's Parliament, in March 1909, and announced their new careers on their release from prison.

For district organisers, the main engagement with the militancy of Women's Parliaments centred not on achieving their own arrests but on planning and co-ordination. The WSPU's drive for broad representation gave district organisers a special role in preparing volunteers. Sometimes certain constituencies would be targeted. Adela Pankhurst made special visits to meetings of ILP women while she was organising in Leeds in

February 1908, in the hope that these would produce 'at least one repre-sentative … at the Women's Parliament', and three Leeds women were subsequently arrested.[23] District organisers also had to check that volun-teers were suitable. Delegates attending the Women's Parliaments could be chosen at regional meetings or might simply hand in their names to the local organiser or directly to Clements Inn.

There was to be no shadow of doubt about what they volunteered for. Florence Haig, who was arrested in February 1908, recognised the level of responsibility the WSPU placed on individual members' deci-sions, and explained that only those women who had actually given in their names and said they were willing to be arrested would be sent out of Caxton Hall.[24] District organisers used their local knowledge to discour-age any potential prisoners who they felt might not be up to the ordeal. Mary Blathwayt was one activist who attended the Women's Parliaments without volunteering for arrest. She received a personal approach from the WSPU leadership in June 1909 to see if she would be prepared to go to prison, but was unable to commit herself to this action, fearing the reaction of her father. Mary was strongly supported by Annie Kenney, her district organiser, who was aware that her health would probably not withstand a prison sentence.[25]

Such compassion from a district organiser was often highly prag-matic, for young and unfit women prisoners provoked heavy criticism of the WSPU. The Women's Parliament of March 1907, which was largely comprised of delegates from the textile districts of Lancashire and Yorkshire, attracted widespread hostile comment concerning the arrest of two young girls, Annie Evelyn Armstrong, from Blackpool, whose age was variously given as 15 and 17, and Dora Thewlis, a mill worker from Huddersfield, who was 16. Not all of the press coverage was unsympa-thetic. The *Daily Chronicle* informed readers that Annie Armstrong's par-ents were unlikely to comply with the magistrate's wish that they would come for her during her time on remand, 'as the father is an invalid, and has been in bed for three years, and her mother has to work hard to sup-port him and the family by company housekeeping', while Annie herself had worked since the age of 13.[26]

Dora Thewlis's family were more directly involved in their daugh-ters' defence, writing to explain to the magistrate that she was acting with their consent and approval in standing up for her political rights. While they agreed with his comment that Dora 'ought to be at school … girls of Dora's age in her station of life are … compelled by their thousands to spend ten hours per day in health destroying factories'.[27] Other com-mentators were less sanguine, and had a strong sense of where they would place the blame for the worrying new phenomenon of juvenile suffrage militants. 'The whole circumstances', the presiding magistrate informed Dora Thewlis, 'reflect the gravest discredit on all concerned with bringing you up to London'.[28] Others in the press were even more direct in apportioning responsibility. One paper noted that to girls like Dora and

> to other agitators of [this] class and age the exchange of dull employ-
> ment for excitement and notoriety is a delightful piece of fortune. The
> dangers to which they may be exposed, the difficulty they may experi-
> ence in getting back to work after they have given their little services, do
> not occur to them. To the leaders of the movement these things must
> have occurred, and it is they who are responsible ...[29]

Families hostile to the cause who paid the fines, thereby releasing prisoners against their will, could also bring adverse publicity. Even the most active suffragettes could face this problem. In an early meeting with Emily Blathwayt, the future organiser Vera Wentworth confided that during her time in prison 'her brother came to ask if he should pay the fine. She sent back a message to him to mind his own business.'[30] All of these risks had to be calculated by a local organiser when selecting volunteers, the possible serious consequences of errors making this a formidable responsibility.

Once volunteers were secured, a huge amount of planning and co-ordinating went into Women's Parliaments. Accommodation was arranged by district organisers liasing with the hospitality department at Clements Inn. As police violence against suffragettes increased, precautions became necessary. Several suffragettes recalled being fitted out with cardboard armour which they wore beneath their clothes 'so that the thumping of the policemen would not be so painful', another task for the organisers.[31] Intermediaries, too, were needed to liaise between arrested women and their families. Once the pattern of violence and arrests at Women's Parliaments was established, friends and relatives of delegates faced hours of anxiety awaiting telegrams and press reports. Emily Blathwayt spent 'a very anxious time' on 29 June 1909, 'the terrible night when Mrs Pankhurst is going to lead a deputation from Caxton Hall which Asquith says he will not receive'.[32] Organisers in London had an important role in alleviating the worst of such anxiety experienced by the relatives and friends of volunteers for militant action.

Outside of London, provincial organisers were expected to make as much use as they could of any arrests at Women's Parliaments. Heavy emphasis was laid on the connection between a particular region and its arrested women. District organisers would arrange flamboyant departures for delegates with bands and processions to local stations. Organisers worked to promote a sense of ownership of local protesters amongst their branch and its supporters. This was made easier when volunteers clearly expected arrest as they were both responding and acting on behalf of other members. Mary Blathwayt recorded that she had joined members of the Bath branch and accompanied Clara Codd 'to the station to see her off' for London in October 1908, the air of ceremony necessitated as 'Miss Codd … is probably going to prison'.[33] Huddersfield suffragettes accompanied their delegates by train as far as Manchester in March 1907, where 'boquets [sic] were presented to the women who were journeying to do and dare for the vote'.[34]

Similar scenes occurred throughout the country. The newsworthiness of suffragette prisoners remained high in the provinces even after arrests on demonstrations had become commonplace and were not attracting the coverage in the national press that they once did. Local organisers were able to make much of this in their own reports, and found that revivals of interest paid dividends in terms of membership. Elizabeth Redfern, reporting on the previous year's work in the Midlands in December 1908, remarked on a turning-point in the fortunes of the Birmingham branch which she linked directly to militancy that had taken place elsewhere: 'In February of this year Birmingham sent a deputation of women to the Caxton Hall, London, when every member was arrested and imprisoned and from that date the number of sympathisers and supporters has daily increased.'[35]

When prisoners were released, there were further opportunities for organisers to arrange local publicity. The first prisoners' welcome was arranged for Christabel Pankhurst and Annie Kenney in October 1905, and this ceremony came to serve as the model for how the WSPU marked the end of a suffragette's time in jail.[36] Here, speeches – often combined with a breakfast – and a parade capitalised on the press interest in suffragette prisoners. These welcomes remained in use until the militant campaign ended in August 1914, and organisers put a great amount of time and energy into arranging them. When Patricia Woodlock was released in June 1909 after serving the longest sentence to date passed on a suffragette, Mary Gawthorpe organised separate welcome ceremonies for her in London, Manchester and Liverpool. More than forty suffragettes acted as 'horses' in the London parade, which saw Miss Woodlock drawn through the streets in an open carriage, while in Manchester a separate press cart was arranged to report on the procession which included three banners, the WSPU Drum and Fife Band and a large number of carriages.[37] Such endeavours ensured that the effects of metropolitan militancy were carried to the provinces.

As the Liberal Government remained the main target of suffragette militancy, most of its manifestations took place in London, but when the Government, embodied in the persons of cabinet ministers, progressed around the country, the WSPU followed it with grim determination. Disruptive militant protests were arranged whenever ministers were scheduled to speak. The term used for these protests was 'pestering', following the advice given to suffragettes by Sir Henry Campbell Bannerman in early 1906 that women would have to go on 'pestering' if anti-suffrage feeling in government was to be won over. Both district and itinerant organisers were expected to orchestrate these protests. Rachel Bartlett recalled going from London, 'up and down the country following Cabinet Ministers about and making myself a nuisance to them wherever they went. We never knew what was in store for us, but we braved the fury and sometimes extreme violence.'[38]

Such uncertainty was compounded, because, unlike Women's Parliaments, regional protests had no set location. Cabinet ministers had to be found and as pestering increased, they took increasingly evasive action. Entry to public political meetings was restricted to women holding tickets, distribution of which was tightly controlled. In Leeds, Mrs Pankhurst told an amused and sympathetic crowd that Mr Asquith and his supporters dared not have a 'public meeting' in the city; instead, 'it was a ticket meeting, and no woman's ticket could be got for less than 3s 6d. And then the name and address had to be given, and a detective was sent to see if the woman was a suffragette.'[39]

Against such precautions, some suffragette workers disguised themselves sufficiently to get in at halls. This was easiest in areas where they would not be recognised, and a band of organisers was kept ready for this work. One, Evelyn Sharp, recalled:

> It was very nerve-racking to travel down to some provincial town, to mingle with the crowd … and speculate as to whether 'any of those dreadful women will get in this time', to sail past the scrutineers at the entrance door, with or without a forged ticket, often quite easily because, like the crowd, they expected the dreadful women to look like nothing on earth.[40]

Evelyn Sharp volunteered for this work because she feared going to prison, but it was by no means an easy option. Most of the suffragettes who were ejected from 'closed' meetings were thrown out violently, their uninvited presence ensuring that they gained little sympathy from the onlooking crowd.

When restricting access to ticket holders failed to exclude all suffragette hecklers, some ministers refused to address meetings with any
women in the audience. Faced with diminishing opportunities to tackle
the enemy face to face, suffragettes were forced to determine ever more
original ways of ensuring that their voices were heard. Organisers now
had to hide in halls overnight to avoid detection. Vera Holme and Elsie
Howey crept into Colston Hall, Bristol, on the afternoon of Augustine
Birrell's meeting in May 1909, and hid behind the tops of the organ pipes,
from where they had a good view of the subsequent security search.
When the meeting began, some three hours later, the women interrupted
Birrell's speech repeatedly, avoiding detection for a ten minutes.[41] Mary
Phillips repeated this tactic when Birrell spoke, with Lord Crew, at St
George's Hall, Liverpool. This time security had been tightened even
more, and Mary had to go into the hall the night before, slipping in while
the organist practised, and concealing herself in the dusty space behind
the organ for over twenty-four hours.[42] As halls were closed earlier by
bodyguards and Liberal workers, suffragettes hid earlier still to avoid
being detected. Adela Pankhurst and Maud Joachim hid for two days
and nights to interrupt Churchill's meetings at Kinnaird Hall, Dundee,
in October 1909. They were arrested along with Helen Archdale and two
other women, but only after a significant disturbance had occurred.

Another way of ensuring that cabinet ministers did not escape suffragette pressure was to move protests beyond the confines of political meetings. Any vaguely public appearance by a cabinet minister now attracted
a suffragette presence. Asquith was 'pestered' on a number of occasions
during his holidays, including leaving a church service and while playing golf with Gladstone. When this tactic was criticised for its failure to
distinguish between ministers' personal and public roles, Christabel Pankhurst defended the development in *VFW*:

> The absurdity of arguing that Mr Asquith's holiday must not be marred
> by Suffragette protests is apparent … If he had left to us the choice of
> battle-ground we should elect to pursue the conflict with him at great
> public meetings … but since he refuses to meet us at these, the appro-
> priate places, we are compelled, and we are resolved, to meet him at any
> other place in which he could be found.[43]

Other organisers duly sought out ministers in places, which, while not
wholly private, were less obvious – and less well guarded – than public
political meetings. Adela Pankhurst, Helen Archdale and other local
suffragettes acquired a car, which they parked opposite a house where
Churchill was attending a private garden party in Dundee in October

1909. Alice Paul and Amelia Brown disguised themselves as kitchen maids to enter the London Guildhall in November 1910. They managed to avoid attention, 'hiding all day under some benches [until] they finally emerged when the guests were seated', and caused great consternation by smashing one of the stained-glass windows in a protest aimed at Asquith, Churchill and Haldane, the Secretary of State for War.[44] Chance encounters, a not uncommon feature of Edwardian political life, were also exploited. Jessie Kenney hopped on a tramcar in pursuit of John Burns, forcing him to dodge 'from side to side' in the carriage in a futile attempt to avoid her, eventually escaping by jumping off the footboard while the tram was at full speed.[45]

Most of the WSPU's regional protests made use of an itinerant work-force who might be dispatched into districts at least a week before a protest was planned 'for the purpose of spying around and making preliminary plans and arrangements'.[46] In high-profile protests this would happen even if a district organiser was already in situ. Although this was in part to avoid overloading or hampering district organisers' usual work, it also facilitated some militant actions that may have been compromised had the district organiser been left to act alone. A district organiser regularly liaised with local authorities and police, and engaged in regular public speaking, quickly becoming a familiar figure, which made for great difficulty in any work where anonymity was required.

Again, less recognisable women were needed. Elsa Gye was despatched from London to Sheffield in October 1909, several weeks before a demonstration 'to see about taking any necessary premises ... before people begin to suspect'.[47] Similarly, when Annie Kenney was detailed with organising the protest against Birrell at Colston Hall, Bristol, headquarters sent Minnie Baldock, Elsie Howey and Vera Holme to help her. District organisers generally welcomed extra help, although sometimes they worried that workers from London were treading on their toes. Murmurings against incomers were severely stamped on by the WSPU's leaders. Christabel Pankhurst advised Jennie Baines, whose main deployment as an organiser consisted of working up pestering campaigns in various centres, that London should be informed immediately of any friction she encountered:

> If you get any complaints from other organisers please tell them to write at once to me and I will deal with the matter ... you are such an expert in militant work that your help and presence in any protest centre must be an advantage even if another organiser is on the spot.[48]

As when planning for Women's Parliaments, organisers were expected to bring on numbers of local volunteers for regional militant work. This often proved even more difficult as the bolder, more active women would be recognised and arrested before a protest had even taken place, thus negating its impact. Conversely, less well-known local members could be more fearful of arrest in the face of family and friends. Dora Marsden, the Southport organiser, was expected to organise a protest against cabinet ministers visiting the town during the General Election of 1910, but complained to Christabel Pankhurst:

> You asked me if I had secured volunteers for militant action. I have done my best ... but Southport is the last resort of degenerates and I have only got one definite promise from a Southport dweller ... I have two wobblers though who might, if they could go outside Southport to do the deeds.[49]

Although exasperated and desperate for help, Dora was not unsympathetic as to why her volunteers should be so uncertain. The reasons were frequently economic. Of her two 'wobblers', one kept 'a boarding house and the other goes out as a sort of help to invalid ladies'. Both jobs could be compromised if an unsuitable act were to be committed by women in full view of their friends, neighbours and employers.[50] The names of volunteers willing to undertake the more risky forms of militancy away from their homes were collated at Clements Inn, sent in either by district organisers or, in the case of areas without official WSPU representation, by individual suffragettes and circulated to organisers when protests were about to begin. Local protests might have appeared opportunistic or spontaneous, but arose from lengthy and complicated planning between local and national organisers.

Planning by organisers became more elaborate as the Government's security increased. The Newcastle protest of December 1909 involved no fewer than three co-ordinators; the local organiser Annie Williams, Jennie Baines as an itinerant organiser with a wealth of experience in such protests, and Christabel Pankhurst who travelled up with protester Constance Lytton to address a meeting the day before the protest but also to run through events with the volunteers.[51] Christabel was particularly concerned about this event, as it was the first since forcible feeding had been introduced, and she was keen to develop the use of the hunger-strike, believing that the WSPU stood 'to beat the government on this point'.[52] She also suspected the Home Office was attempting to restrict contact between suffragette prisoners and legal representatives, and supplied Jennie Baines with slips of paper carrying the names and addresses of appropriate solicitors to be distributed to the protesters before they went out.[53] Volunteers' names were circulated to Mrs Baines and Miss Williams, and their actions carefully considered and co-ordinated through-out the day. Constance Lytton was particularly struck by the efficiency of the arrangements, although unaware that six weeks of planning had gone into them:

> All was hurry and determination ... The organiser ... was sending each [protester] to a different place. She said 'There is a stone wants to be put through the door of the Palace Theatre ... It must be done at once or the gang of detectives will have become too thick ... this job will have to be done alone – two would be detected at once'.[54]

While itinerant workers were in the front line, district organisers charged with arranging regional protests were still expected to avoid arrest themselves. As militancy progressed, the WSPU faced mounting criticism that it paid volunteers to break the law. This was a very difficult issue for suffragettes. On the one hand, they wished their protests to appear principled, motivated by political beliefs rather then economic gain. On the other hand, representative demonstrations needed to recruit from a cross-section of the population, including working women. The Union had paid the fare of participants in early Women's Parliaments, but the discovery of this arrangement caused outrage in the popular press which accused suffragettes of employing 'rent-a-mob' tactics and failing to represent genuine concerns. 'One has been led to believe', commented the *Daily Telegraph*,

> that so anxious were the women of England to assert their rights that they were willing to incur the expense of undertaking a journey to London in order to voice their demands within the walls of the Legislature. The secret is out ... the fact is the expenses are paid for them. Mrs Jenkins, the wife of an elector in Mr S. Evans' constituency, frankly admitted that it was Miss Pankhurst who brought her to London, and that the 'association' paid the expenses.[55]

Organisers attempted different tactics to counter this accusation, such as getting the branch to club together to fund one or two delegates, or arranging practical help in terms of child care or domestic work for prisoners. Accusations of payment still remained common, and were used by cabinet ministers in an attempt to undermine the WSPU. Lloyd George, interrupted by suffragettes at Swansea,

> taunted the women. 'I wonder how much she has been paid for coming here', he called as one was being dragged away ... Mrs Pethick Lawrence wrote ... to protest against his suggestion that the women who interrupted cabinet ministers did so as a 'profession' ... she forwarded him a copy of [the WSPU] Annual Report. He replied by repeating his

insinuations and calling attention to the fact that the Report showed considerable sums of money to have been dispensed in 'salaries', 'travelling expenses' and 'special board and lodging'.[56]

Mrs Pethick Lawrence countered that although the WSPU had some paid staff, like any other political organisation, its organisers would rarely engage in protests at ministers' meetings, these being carried out largely by unpaid volunteers. Meanwhile, behind the scenes, the pressure remained on organisers to stay out of prison themselves whenever possible. Olive Bartels, who worked as both a district and a national organiser, believed that this policy was intended to protect the integrity of militant actions against accusations that women were motivated by payment rather than principle.[57] Joining deputations, harassing cabinet ministers and other militancies of these kinds required no special expertise and were best left to the rank and file, if they could be persuaded. Although she was very much a back-room worker, in the WSPU's literature department, Christabel Pankhurst tried to dissuade Ethel Birnstingl when she put her name forward for a deputation in December 1910, writing that she thought that

> the matter had better be discussed between Mrs Knight [the department's head] and yourself, and decided by both of you. Personally, I am very anxious that those upon whom the burden of organisation rests should, as far as possible, remain at their posts when militant action takes place; otherwise, the sacrifice made by members of the deputation does not have its full effect.[58]

What amounted to a prohibition on involvement in militancy created a paradox for many organisers. In most cases they had been recruited from the rank and file themselves, but had come to the attention of the leadership because of their dedication to the cause, including their willingness to go to prison. From having been celebrated for their bravery, many organisers now found themselves transformed into administrators while their members took centre stage at prisoners' welcomes. Jealousy over the attention given to other suffragettes' militancy was not uncommon, and could run deep. In 1905, Mrs Pankhurst forbade Teresa Billington from joining Annie Kenney and Christabel Pankhurst in the first suffragette arrests. Teresa went to extreme lengths to ensure she was arrested herself as soon as was practicable, slapping and kicking a policeman in Cavendish Square the following June, but almost sixty years later she still looked back on the decision to exclude her from the first arrests with 'a mixed sense of relief and regret'.[59] Mary Phillips was another organiser who found it hard to accept that she needed to keep out of prison.

Although she had served three sentences – including one of three months as a repeat offender – and had been forcibly fed, she was keen to undergo more. Christabel Pankhurst expressly forbade her, fearing that her search for personal heroism threatened to undermine her district work:

> You speak of getting arrested. Nothing would be more mistaken at the present time. On no account run the risk of it, as the work you have being doing recently would all go to pieces. It will be necessary to get your volunteer workers to make the protest which of course you will organise ...[60]

Dora Marsden, who had also been in jail twice, received equally explicit instructions from Emmeline Pethick Lawrence when planning the Southport protest of December 1909:

> I want to urge upon you not to run the risk of arrest. We simply cannot afford to lose our organisers in this way. The movement cannot go on and grow without effective and constant leadership in every part of the country. It is not only that imprisonment robs us of the organiser's services, it is the undermining of her health and the impossibility of getting into any regular fruitful line of action. I assure you that you are not serving the best interests of the Union in exposing yourself to more imprisonment.[61]

While Mary Phillips accepted the decisions, Dora was soon to quit as organiser, complaining of her treatment from Clements Inn, which she felt did not allow her sufficient autonomy. District organisers were free to arrange any amount of pestering but no longer free to determine their own militant involvement irrespective of any talent they felt they had in this direction.

Other organisers may well have taken similar steps, had it not been for a new development in militancy in 1911. A truce the previous year, while an all-party group drew up women's suffrage legislation known as the Conciliation Bill, had ended with a Women's Parliament where unprecedented violence was used against the suffragettes. The deaths of two women were later attributed to injuries gained on what became known as 'Black Friday'. This, and the authorities' refusal to sanction a public enquiry, brought a marked change in the attitudes of many suffragettes towards more violent protests. Emmeline Pethick Lawrence found that 'women who had never approved of breaking windows adopted the method now saying it was better to break a pane of glass than have the bodies of women broken as they had been on Black Friday'.[62]

When a second Conciliation Bill was proposed, Christabel Pankhurst reluctantly agreed to another truce, but admitted that she was planning for an immediate resumption of militancy at any point, and that organisers were occupied 'with recruiting for militant action in case of need. Volunteers were many.'[63] When Asquith scuppered the second Bill, militancy resumed immediately. The WSPU's actions were conceived as reactive, both to the continued snubs of the Government and also to the violence meted out to suffragettes on Black Friday. Emmeline Pethick Lawrence led out a deputation from the Women's Parliament. Meanwhile, another group of women was told to report to 'the Women's Press Shop ... at 7 pm' – dressed 'as quietly as possible', wearing no badges and bearing an enclosed ticket of admittance – to 'be given full instructions' for the protest.[64] Smaller groups then went out from the shop and other arranged venues, armed with hammers and small black bags full of stones, and broke numerous windows both of government buildings and of Liberal premises and commercial shops. Over 200 women were arrested and imprisoned for their part in this protest. Similar numbers were detained after another mass window-smashing the following March.

Volunteers for deputations had risked arrest, but for window-smashers arrest was certain. Persuading sufficient numbers to come forward was a formidable task. Even the charismatic Mrs Pankhurst confided to Ethel Smyth how wearing she found the excuses of

> all these women who come to me with their pros and cons, their families, their claims. If I could only let out at them I should not feel it so much but that's just what I can't do. I have just to listen and bear it ... One said to me on Wednesday 'you make us feel like curs' as if she had a grievance against me for it. All I could say was 'of course that's what I want to do'. All this is far more trying than doing the thing itself.[65]

Less glamorous organisers faced an even more difficult task. Jennie Baines 'tramped for miles' but secured only two volunteers from Rossendale Valley, although she was 'assured' that with a little more time and effort she would 'be able to get together a band of Women ready for anything'.[66] It was not only arrest that concerned potential volunteers. Lilias Mitchell, who was working up a new district some distance from London, found the fare 'so heavy that few could afford to come even if they would'. Paying for them was not an option in her district as her branch contained 'still one or two mischief making members who might make out that we are paying people to go'.[67]

District organisers worked flat out in the regions to get as many recruits as possible. They also explained the protest wherever the opportunity arose so that the political significance of breaking windows was not lost in broader discussions about the levels of damage done. In Newcastle, Laura Ainsworth sought invitations 'to address meetings among ... Unions, co-operative guilds, ILP, Liberal Associations, Trades Unions, Labour Leagues etc. ...'. Miss Billing, in Kent, hit on the idea of 'house to house selling of *Votes for Women* so that the public ... know the truth about what is going on at this critical time'.[68] National and district organisers liaised to ensure that everything went smoothly. Miss Hambling, at Clements Inn, sent circulars to all participants containing advice about appropriate clothing and reminding them to take to court 'a HANDBAG containing night things and a change of clothing' in anticipation of a prison sentence.[69] Volunteers able to get to London before the actual date of the protest were sent to secret addresses to receive further instruction from Bertha Brewster and Marion Wallace Dunlop.[70] Accommodation was arranged on a scale exceeding anything done for the Women's Parliaments and also for longer, as the numbers of prisoners overwhelmed the courts and many women had lengthy periods on bail. Window-smashing offered more obvious organising tasks too. When Mary Leigh and Edith New broke the first windows at 10 Downing Street in June 1908 they slipped into St James's Park to grab suitable stones. In the West End raids, window-smashing 'was now carefully organised. Motors were driven at dusk to quiet country lanes where flints could be obtained. Would-be window-breakers met ... trusted members of the WSPU at somebody's flat, and were furnished with hammers or black bags'.[71] Organisers procured the hammers, made the bags, and stored them and the stones until they were required.

Frustrated district organisers were soon allowed to join these large-scale militant protests, although they were instructed 'not to inform the police on their arrest that they are organisers for the Union' as this would increase their sentences.[72] Charlotte Marsh, working in Portsmouth, 'volunteered ... to smash windows' in March 1912, and made sure she publicised what was to happen as much as she could before leaving her base.[73] She was joined by co-organiser Vera Wentworth. Alice Davis, the Liverpool organiser, left her district to join the same protest after undertaking careful planning to ensure that her work did not suffer during her absence. Lilias Mitchell was also given permission to participate after promising to make 'arrangements ... for the work to be carried out' while she was away.[74] Members were told via the local reports column of *VFW* three days before the protest took place that 'during the absence of the organiser, Mrs Abraham and Miss Martin have most kindly agreed to take charge of the office'.[75]

After the second mass window-smashing, suffragette violence

5   Mary Leigh and Edith New, welcomed by Lilias Hall, and Sylvia and Christabel Pankhurst, on their release from prison for window-smashing, August 1908

expanded to include arson and other attacks on property. Annie Kenney explained this development in spatial terms:

> The first part of the Movement was the genuine constructive part ...
> The structure was [now] complete, but the tower was lacking. The tower
> was built by the extreme Militants. They had a building upon which to
> work, but their task was more dangerous than that of the hundreds and
> thousands of women who had been employed in making the structure
> grand and imposing ...[76]

Her tower metaphor reminds us that far fewer suffragettes undertook the work done by 'extreme militants'. In considering them as a group, several accounts have given great weight to the role played by so-called 'freelance' workers. The term implies that certain acts of militancy came from women who were beyond the control of both the State and their own leaders, 'who would not always confine themselves to the policy guidelines issued from Clements Inn', but it has also been usefully deployed by feminist historians in attempts to reappraise the WSPU's function as a political organisation.[77] For writers engaging with hostile accounts of the Union which suggest that it comprised an autocratic leadership whose diktats were followed blindly by a bovinely compliant membership, the concept of the freelance militant offered a means of retaining agency for suffragette activists.[78]

Those acts which have been described as 'freelance' (or 'roving' as David Mitchell also described the work of Mary Leigh) were often the more extreme manifestations of militancy at the time and were initiated by individual independently-minded suffragettes who acted without first seeking the sanction of the WSPU leadership.[79] Mary Leigh's and Edith New's first act of stone-throwing fits neatly into this category; so too does the first attack on a pillar box by Emily Wilding Davison, carried out in December 1911 'entirely on [her] own responsibility'.[80] Ellen Pitfield, a nurse severely injured on Black Friday, was the first suffragette to use arson as a means of drawing attention to her plight, and tried to burn down the General Post Office in London.[81] Yet while each of these actions demonstrated the freedom of individual suffragettes, and the capacity of women to act on their own initiative, they were all embraced retrospectively by the WSPU leadership.[82]

Freelance militancy thus brought all organisers back to the forefront of the militant campaign. Rather than reflecting a membership that was out of control, this type of militancy required intense co-ordination. The planning was lesser in scope than that required for deputations, as the fewer women who knew about attacks the better, but those who held the plans had to work with utmost secrecy. Preparation was vital, as property only was the target. The WSPU determined that no lives would be at risk (excepting those of its own members), and Christabel Pankhurst kept a watchful eye on proceedings from her exile in Paris, demanding reassurance from organisers if she perceived that actions had gone too far.

Organisers and volunteers were well aware that they were not to act independently. Lillian Lenton, who on her own admission was responsible for 'the real serious fires in this country', recalled how her work was facilitated by 'a certain amount of organisation going on all the time'. Lillian's recollections acknowledge the importance of district organisers in the arson campaign, but suggest that it was co-ordinated at a national level. She herself volunteered for arson and was put in touch with another member at the London headquarters who had made the same request.[83] Gertrude Harding, who joined Lillian Lenton's attack on the Orchid House at Kew, also recalled being sent to headquarters, where certain precautions were taken; 'I ... was interviewed by Annie Kenney ... after deciding that I wasn't a spy from Scotland Yard, Miss Kenney asked me if I would go on an assignment with another girl the following day'.[84]

The final phase of militancy may have involved smaller numbers than the London spectacles, but this did not make it less demanding for the organisers who were charged with co-ordinating it: women participating in arson and property damage had to be moved around the country and accommodated in total secrecy. Interestingly, it was often the flouting of conventions which this involved that created as much outrage as the deeds themselves. Kitty Marion recalled how, during her trial for arson, it was the behaviour of Mrs Casey, who had given lodgings to Kitty and her co-accused Clara Giveen, that most astonished the court:

> [F]or one to trust a mere acquaintance who had never previously been to her home with a latch key and to bring in another, an utter stranger. Neither court nor counsels could grasp the idea. 'She was a suffragette', said Mrs Casey, 'that was quite good enough for us.'[85]

District organisers were generally charged with co-ordinating the movements of personnel and equipment involved in acts of arson and criminal damage. They handed out passwords and directions, and ensured that explosives and corrosive agents, often manufactured by local members with scientific training, were ready for collection when required. Maude Kate Smith, a Birmingham suffragette who fired both pillar boxes and post offices, was adamant that in her district no protests could have occurred without the efforts of Dorothy Evans, the local organiser: 'She told me to get [the explosives] from there, she gave me the name, and address, and the password'.[86] Other district organisers were more directly involved. Clara Giveen, who had been working as district organiser in Norwich and on the south-east coast since she joined the WSPU in late 1910, was also sent on a series of arson attacks, including a football stadium in Leeds and the fire laid with Kitty Marion, mentioned above, to mark the death of Emily Wilding Davison.[87] Lillias Mitchell was the Birmingham organiser when she and Mary Richardson placed a bomb in a local railway station. Olive Bartels, who was emphatic in her recollection that no organiser could be arrested, also remembered being in charge of an incendiary device herself. 'I was on top of a bus with this bally thing on my lap and it began to buzz. And I was terrified ... I quickly got off the bus with this beastly thing in my hand ...'.[88] Olive's memories are not as contradictory as they first appear. In arson and extreme criminal damage, organisers were again expected to lead from the front, just as they had been in the first arrests a few years previously.

The shift towards covert militant actions made it easier for district organisers to participate. The intention was that militants would maximise the disruption they could cause while not getting caught, as their crimes, and the ensuing sentences, were more severe. This overturned the previous emphasis on prison as an important part of the activity which had run through deputations and 'pestering' protests. Branches did not automatically suffer if their organisers participated in this sort of militancy. Indeed, some gained organisers through this work. Arabella Scott was jailed in May 1913 after attempting to burn Kelso Racecourse. Released under the Cat and Mouse Act, she absconded in August, and worked as a WSPU organiser in Brighton under the name of Catherine Reid.[89]

There were other reasons for the change in the WSPU leaders' view of the limits of their district organisers' deployment. All the officials were now at great personal risk, no matter what work they were charged with. The State had previously made small attempts to curb the challenge which the WSPU posed to its authority, such as the 1909 prosecution of Christabel and Mrs Pankhurst and Flora Drummond for incitement to 'rush the House of Commons', but their sentences were not particularly severe, and in general the responsibility for militant action lay with the individual who had committed them. This shifted as arson and criminal damage became included within the WSPU's definition of militancy.

As these tactics spread, responsibility for them was perceived as resting collectively with officials of the Union. While Christabel Pankhurst managed to escape to Paris, other organisers faced criminal charges for overseeing the campaign in Britain. Annie Kenney, Beatrice Sanders, Harriet Kerr, Rachel Barrett, Geraldine Lennox, Agnes Lake and Flora Drummond were arrested in April 1913, following a police raid on WSPU headquarters. Although Flora Drummond and Annie Kenney had worked directly in regions and branches, the remaining five women had positions that were largely administrative. Harriet Kerr had actually 'made it a condition of her employment [by the WSPU] that her work was entirely industrial', something which did not save her from a twelvemonth prison sentence.[90] In this climate it was unrealistic to expect willing organisers to desist from participation in the more extreme actions, as they were liable to be arrested anyway for their association with those actions, regardless of how far their involvement actually went. Indeed, many may have preferred to be sentenced for actually *doing* something.

The position of a district organiser within her area may also have made it easier for her to undertake arson without detection. The need for secrecy was greater than at any other point in the suffragette campaign.

When Edith Rigby, the honorary organiser in Preston, set out to place a bomb in the Liverpool stock exchange, she allowed only one close WSPU colleague, Beth Hesmondhalgh, to help her procure the device and set up their meetings under strict codes which dictated that the friends 'were never seen to meet, and never corresponded. All their fellow members and their families were kept in the dark.'[91] The nature of district organiser's work forced them to remain somewhat aloof from their membership, while their regional patterns of deployment kept them at a physical distance from other close friends and family. Secrecy was much easier for women in this position who could leave home at odd hours of the night without arousing immediate curiosity.

The Prisoners' Temporary Discharge for Ill Health Bill of 1913, the Cat and Mouse Act alluded to above, offered suffrage organisers a further dimension for militant work, particularly if they were not deployed as district workers. 'Mice' out on licence were moved around the country and hidden in safe houses, in increasingly ingenious ways. Disguises were employed, and decoys used to smuggle prisoners with expired licences out of the reach of the authorities, who increasingly guarded 'known' suffragette addresses. As ever, careful planning and co-ordination underpinned this work. Under the direction of Grace Roe, a special bodyguard was formed 'to protect Mrs Pankhurst from the rough treatment by the police that she often had to endure while being arrested'. WSPU organiser Gertrude Harding was put in charge and was instructed by Grace Roe that the bodyguard could be armed. This led to some misapprehension, as Gertrude recalled:

> All volunteers had to be carefully selected. They must be completely trustworthy, in good physical shape, and be ready at a moments notice to do battle with the police in defence of Mrs Pankhurst ... after some thirty recruits had been accepted, they were notified to come to Lincolns Inn House for our first evening meeting, when the weapons would be distributed. They all turned up full of curiosity ... it was somewhat of an anticlimax when each member of the bodyguard was handed a neat little Indian club with instructions to tie this around her waist.[92]

Those who felt unable to become bodyguards had ample opportunity for involvement in the many escapes and disguises which the 'mice' precipitated, ensuring that militancy continued to offer suffragettes a variety of opportunities for participation until the end of the WSPU's campaign.

When suffragette militancy is revisited from the perspective of the WSPU's paid organisers, it appears a much more controlled phenomenon than a brief perusal of its manifestations might suggest. Organisers were vital to the spread and momentum of militancy. The Union's approach to arranging its protests at national and local level also suggests that, paradoxically, it was the large, flamboyant, militant demonstrations in London that women found it easier to participate in, as these offered greater potential for anonymity.

A further paradox lies in the approach that the WSPU took to organisers' own militant activities. While national organisers were sometimes deployed on protests with the specific aim of achieving their own arrests, district organisers were expected to remain at their posts and encourage branch members to take the greater risks. This caused friction between several organisers and their employers, and might have led to a crisis in the internal structure of the WSPU had not a new form of militancy been embraced in 1911. The change in attitude which led to suffragettes avoiding rather than courting arrest returned organisers to the forefront of militant work, the position they had taken at the very start of the campaign.

Notes

1 Emmeline Pethick Lawrence to Dora Marsden, 1 December 1909, Dora Marsden Papers.
2 C. Pankhurst, *Unshackled*, p. 49.
3 Mrs Swales of Leeds WSPU, quoted in the *Worker*, 8 August 1908.
4 E. S. Pankhurst, *The Suffragette*, p. 29.
5 Helen G. Brodie to the *Daily News*, 18 February 1907.
6 Laura E. Nym Mayhall, *The Militant Suffrage Movement*, p. 135. Brian Harrison has offered a nuanced reading of militancy that does attempt to recover some of its meanings for participants in 'The act of militancy'. For a more hostile view, see Pugh, *The March of the Women*, ch. 8, 'The anatomy of militancy'.
7 *Manchester Guardian*, quoted in C. Pankhurst, *Unshackled*, p. 46.
8 C. Pankhurst, *Unshackled*, p. 46.
9 Jon Lawrence, 'Contesting the male polity: the suffragettes and the politics of disruption in Edwardian Britain', in Amanda Vickery (ed.), *Women, Privilege and Power: British Politics, 1750 to the Present* (Stanford, CA: Stanford University Press, 2001), pp. 201–26, at p. 203.
10 C. Pankhurst, *Unshackled*, p. 46.
11 Christabel Pankhurst 'Why the Union is strong', *Suffragette*, 29 December 1912; Emmeline Pankhurst, speech at the Albert Hall, *Suffragette*, 25 October 1912.
12 Gertrude Colmore, *Suffragette Sally* (London: Stanley Paul, 1911), reprinted as *Suffragettes: A Story of Three Women* (London: Pandora, 1984).
13 Leah Leneman, 'A truly national movement: the view from outside London', in Maroula Joannou and June Purvis, (eds), *The Women's Suffrage Movement: New Feminist Perspectives* (Manchester: Manchester University Press, 1998), pp. 37–50.
14 Mrs Sparboro to Mrs Baldock, cited in Raeburn, *The Militant Suffragettes*, p. 22.
15 Dora B. Montefiore, *From a Victorian to a Modern* (London: E. Archer, 1927), p. 52.

16   C. Pankhurst, *Unshackled*, p. 75.
17   E. Pethick Lawrence, *My Part*, p. 174; E. S. Pankhurst, *The Suffragette Movement*, p. 252.
18   Mr Horace Smith, JP, to Patricia Woodlock, *Guardian*, 22 March 1907.
19   Emily Blathwayt's diary, 26 June 1908, Blathwayt Diaries.
20   Annie Kenney to Mrs Rowe, 4 March 1906, quoted by Rosen, *Rise Up Women!*, p. 64.
21   Annie Kenney to Annot Robinson, 31 January 1908, Annot Robinson Papers.
22   *VFW*, 29 October 1909.
23   *VFW*, February 1908.
24   Florence Haig, SFC.
25   Mary Blathwayt's diary, 15 June 1909, Blathwayt Diaries.
26   *Daily Chronicle*, 22 March 1907.
27   *Daily News*, 28 March 1907.
28   *Daily Mail*, 22 March 1907.
29   Unidentified press cutting, c. March 1907, Maude Arncliffe Sennett Collection, British Library.
30   Emily Blathwayt's diary, 21 March 1908, Blathwayt Diaries.
31   E. Katherine Willoughby Marshall, 'Suffragette escapes', typescript, SFC; see also Cohen to Harrison, Harrison Tapes.
32   Emily Blathwayt's diary, 29 June 1909, Blathwayt Diaries.
33   Mary Blathwayt's diary, 9 and 12 October 1908, Blathwayt Diaries.
34   *Worker*, 23 March 1907.
35   *VFW*, 24 December 1908.
36   Christabel Pankhurst, *Unshackled*, p. 55; E. Sylvia Pankhurst, *The Suffragette*, p. 35.
37   Miscellaneous handbills and notes concerning Patricia Woodlock's welcome processions, Mary Gawthorpe Papers.
38   Rachel Bartlett, quoted in Raeburn, *The Militant Suffragettes*, p. 44.
39   *Worker*, 3 October 1908.
40   Sharp, *Unfinished Adventure*, p. 138.
41   Raeburn, *The Militant Suffragettes*, p. 98; E. S. Pankhurst, *The Suffragette*, p. 376.
42   E. S. Pankhurst, *The Suffragette*, p. 376; E. Pethick Lawrence, *My Part*, p. 228.
43   Raeburn, *The Militant Suffragettes*, p. 114–15.
44   *Ibid.*, p 131
45   *VFW*, 1 October 1909.
46   *Ibid.*, p. 97; Christabel Pankhurst to Jennie Baines, 22 November 1909, Baines Papers.
47   Christabel Pankhurst to Jennie Baines, 1 October 1909, Baines Papers.
48   *Ibid.*, 4 December 1909, Baines Papers.
49   Dora Marsden to Christabel Pankhurst, 28 November 1909, Baines Papers.
50   *Ibid.*
51   Lytton, *Prisons and Prisoners*, p. 204.
52   Christabel Pankhurst to Jennie Baines, 29 September 1909, Baines Papers.
53   *Ibid.*, 1 October 1909, Baines Papers.
54   Lytton, *Prisons and Prisoners*, p. 207.
55   *Daily Telegraph*, 22 March 1907.
56   E. S. Pankhurst, *The Suffragette*, p. 259.
57   Bartels to Harrison, Harrison Tapes.
58   Christabel Pankhurst to Miss Birnstingl, 13 December 1910, SFC.

59 Police report on disturbances at Cavendish Square, 21 June 1906, TNA, MEPOL 2/1016; Teresa Billington Grieg, *Guardian*, 11 May 1960.
60 Christabel Pankhurst to Mary Phillips, 26 November 1909, Mary Phillips Papers.
61 Emmeline Pethick Lawrence to Dora Marsden, 1 December 1909, Dora Marsden Papers.
62 E. Pethick Lawrence, *My Part*, p. 250.
63 F. Pethick Lawrence, *Fate*, p. 88; C. Pankhurst, *Unshackled*, p. 178.
64 Circular from Miss Hambling, 18 November 1911, National Library of Scotland Suffrage Collection, DEP 176, Box 2.
65 Emmeline Pankhurst to Ethel Smyth, undated (April 1912), TNA, DPP 1/19, Exhibit 135.
66 Jennie Baines to Christabel Pankhurst, n.d. [February 1912] TNA, DPP 1/19, Exhibit 137.
67 Lilias Mitchell to Miss Pankhurst, 16 February 1912. TNA, DPP 1/19, Exhibit 141.
68 *VFW*, 17 November 1911.
69 Circular from A. Hambling, 21 November 1911, Maude Arncliffe Sennett Papers.
70 WSPU Circulars, TNA, DPP 1/19, Exhibits 90 and 133.
71 E. S. Pankhurst, *The Suffragette Movement*, p. 359.
72 Unsigned letter concerning conduct of WSPU organisers on forthcoming deputation, sent to Dorothy Evans, 27 Feb 1912, TNA, DPP 1/19, Exhibit 137.
73 Charlotte Marsh, interview with Lady Jessie Street, London, 1960, SFC.
74 Lilias Mitchell to Miss Pankhurst, 16 February 1912, TNA, DPP 1/19, Exhibit 141a.
75 *VFW*, 1 March 1912.
76 Kenney, *Memories of a Militant*, p. 190.
77 Les Garner, *A Brave and Beautiful Spirit: Dora Marsden, 1882–1960* (Aldershot: Avebury, 1990) p. 37; see also Morley with Stanley, *Emily Wilding Davison*, particularly chs 4 and 5.
78 Purvis, *Emmeline Pankhurst*, p. 109.
79 David Mitchell, notes on Mary Leigh, Mitchell Collection; see also Mitchell, *Queen Christabel*, p. 321.
80 Gertrude Colmore, *The Life of Emily Davison*, republished (London: Women's Press, 1988), p. 41.
81 Raeburn, *The Militant Suffragettes*, p. 177.
82 See Harrison, 'The act of militancy', pp. 50–2.
83 Lillian Lenton, interview with Lady Jessie Street at the White House, Albany Street, March 1960, SFC.
84 Gertrude Harding, unpublished memoir, quoted in Wilson, *With All Her Might*, p. 96.
85 Kitty Marion, unpublished typescript autobiography, SFC, p. 242.
86 Maude Kate Smith to Brian Harrison, 14 January 1975, Harrison Tapes.
87 Jenny Overton and Joan Mant, *A Suffragette Nest: Peaslake, 1910 and After* (Guildford: Hazeltree Publishing, 1998), pp. 41–4; Kitty Marion, typescript autobiography, SFC.
88 Bartels to Harrison, Harrison Tapes.
89 Elizabeth Crawford, 'The Scott family', in *The Women's Suffrage Movement: A Reference Guide, 1866–1928* (London: Taylor & Francis, 2005), pp. 620–1; Leah Leneman, *Martyrs in Our Midst: Dundee, Perth and the Forcible Feeding of Suffragettes* (Dundee: Abertay Historical Society, 1993), pp. 21–2.

90 Letter from Harriet Kerr's niece to David Mitchell, 27 July 1975, Mitchell Collection.
91 Hesketh, *My Aunt Edith*, p. 68.
92 Gertrude Harding, memoir, quoted in Wilson, *With All Her Might*, p. 131.

6

'There is [no] person living who, as an organiser, would entirely satisfy some people':[1] Organisers and dissent

THE WSPU'S UNAPOLOGETICALLY autocratic structure provided little or no space for open discussion of policy or tactics among its organisers. Her Union, Emmeline Pankhurst frequently explained, was 'purely a volunteer army ... no one [was] obliged to remain in it', but those who chose to do so were expected to follow the decisions made by its leaders.[2] The loyalty that many suffragettes displayed in the face of ridicule, prosecution and personal privation suggests that members were, for the most part, happy with Emmeline's structuring of the WSPU and that they remained willing to fall in with decisions made further up the chain of command. Members were also aware that they were not expected to be passive followers in all situations: certainly, within the branches, a more active approach was required of them. Here, regional variations in working practices and activities plus the persistence of a variety of forms of militancy, enabled members to exercise a degree of control over their actions and offered a freedom of choice obscured in later accounts of the campaign. Employees too benefited from this. 'Our organisers', wrote Christabel Pankhurst, 'found our leadership perfectly compatible with their own freedom to develop their activities, and ... they often astonished themselves and their friends by their ability and initiative. They knew "where they were" and to whom they were account-able'.[3]

This generally worked well, and the Union functioned relatively smoothly, given that it was a large political organisation whose dispersed membership came from a variety of social backgrounds and who brought different party-political perspectives to their work. Anyone who did not like the way it was arranged was free to leave. Yet despite the criticism levelled at the Pankhursts' autocratic style, both by their contemporaries and in subsequent historical assessments, few took this option. Admit-tedly, it is difficult to reconstruct attitudes among the WSPU's rank-and-file membership, as many of them remain anonymous, although studies of individual branches suggest continuity in membership.[4] What can be more confidently stated is that among the organisers, who, as front line workers, were more vulnerable to the negative effects of campaigning, dissent was comparatively rare. Organisers who did give up official work during the campaign were often burnt out rather than disenchanted, and some, like Ada Flatman and Minnie Baldock, remained WSPU activists after resigning as employees. Others were organisers throughout the campaign. Of the large group recruited as part of the Union's expansion in 1908–9, Dorothy Evans, Arabella Scott, Gladys Hazel, and Charlotte Marsh were still in post in 1914, while other workers in the national office, such as Harriet Kerr and Aeta Lamb, had been on the Union's payroll for even longer.

This is not to say that relationships between WSPU organisers and their employers always ran smoothly. Organisers, almost by definition, were distinctive individuals who required strong personalities to succeed at their work, to inspire an uncertain membership or to withstand ongoing public criticism. The very qualities that made women good organisers could make them equally difficult employees if they found themselves in conflict with the national leadership. Militancy was not the only source of conflict. Although schism and factionalism were comparatively rare within the Union, there were two highly publicised splits in 1907 and 1912 when disgruntled members grouped around dissenting organisers. In addition, some organisers resigned because of disillusion with WSPU policy, and a few more were eventually dismissed. Furthermore, all of these situations had to be managed in some way that minimised the effect of disagreements on the rank-and-file membership, and consequently on the overall campaign.

Dissent was not restricted to the relationship between the WSPU leaders and their employees. District organisers could become embroiled in conflict with their own members who saw them as a convenient focus for the irritated discontent that eventually permeates most political campaigns. Such circumstances were infrequent, but when they erupted they could make organisers' lives extremely unpleasant. Branch quarrels also worried the Union's leaders, who feared the effect that a group of disenchanted members might have on a national campaign, so organisers who became the target of whispering campaigns within their own branches could generally rely on the support of their employers. Ada Flatman faced an unhappy time during her first official organising job in Aberdeen. The local branch had been pursuing a fairly independent pathway, with closer links to the local Liberal movement than the WSPU leaders may have wished.[5] Certain members suspected that the decision to send them an organiser was intended to bring them into line with national policy. The arrival of the comparatively inexperienced Ada Flatman, accompanied by Sylvia Pankhurst, heralded 'a thoroughly messy bout of faction-fighting and mud-slinging'.[6] Ann McRobie, a local member, sent the secretary Caroline Phillips a depressing report of one meeting:

> Our friends were out in full war paint. I was glad you were not present, and yet I regret that you missed the show … there was something irresistibly funny in the solemnity with which the enormities of our Secretary were reeled off … After mauling you beyond all recognition, they lashed out against Helen Ogston, gave Constance Ogston a kick in passing, and as a grand finale, wiped up the floor with Sylvia Pankhurst.[7]

Unsurprisingly, the new officials made little headway against the opposition. Caroline Phillips soon reported the 'faction … re-established [and] in full favour' – and within less than three months Ada Flatman had returned to England.[8] Helen Ogston, who had supported her, was deployed on itinerant campaigns in southern England. Less predictably, but more frustratingly, the dissenting members did not continue in a maverick branch, but abandoned the Union once they had got their way. So complete was this desertion that when the next organiser, Lilias Mitchell, was sent to Abderdeen in 1911, she was unaware that a branch had once existed there.[9]

That Sylvia Pankhurst and Ada Flatman were English formed no part of the unhappy members' platform of complaint. Leah Leneman's extensive study of the women's suffrage movement in Scotland similarly found that 'for the most part Scottish WSPU branches did not object' on principle to the presence of English organisers.[10] Nevertheless, Englishness was the excuse put forward when the Edinburgh members fell out with their organiser, Mary Allen, in the spring of 1914. When Glasgow organiser Janie Allan raised this with Christabel Pankhurst, Christabel left her in no doubt as to her opinion of rank-and-file members who behaved in this manner towards the WSPU's officials:

> You refer to the position of affairs in Edinburgh. There is in Edinburgh a small handful of people who are decidedly cantankerous, and the person who is organising for the time being is made to feel the effect of this. These people criticise Miss Mary Allen at the present time, but profess to have had a great admiration for a previous organiser, Miss Lucy Burns. As a matter of fact, Miss Lucy Burns was virtually driven away from Edinburgh, so unhappy was she because of the attitude of a few members. The ostensible reason [for] the trouble was the stand she made with regard to a certain Miss Gorrie, who does not now seem to

possess the confidence of the very people who were her champions at the time in question. I doubt whether there is any person living who, as an organiser, would entirely satisfy some people! The fact is that their attitude towards organisers is a wrong and false one, and we are determined to protect organisers from unfair and unreasonable criticism.[11]

Wisely, Christabel added that such difficulties did arise 'every now and again in the course of organising work', but, in her opinion, 'it often happens that things are all the better and calmer after the storm'.[12] She recognised that a volunteer membership could be demanding and difficult to please, and believed that organisers were not to be sacrificed to their whim, no matter how vociferous they were in their discontent.

Fortunately for most organisers such unpleasantness was rare. More common, but still by no means prevalent, were disagreements between organisers and their employers about the direction of the militant campaign. The first schism in the WSPU's ranks centred around one of the earliest organisers, Teresa Billington, now Mrs Billington-Grieg. The origins of the Women's Freedom League, which emerged from this split, may well have been rooted in deeper political differences among the WSPU's increasing membership.[13] Teresa's own motives, on the other hand, were largely personal. As one of the first recruits, she had enjoyed a close relationship with Emmeline Pankhurst, who had become something of a mother figure to the young Manchester teacher.

Teresa's relationship with Emmeline's natural daughters was more complicated. She could tolerate the younger Adela, but the older sisters were a different matter. Teresa later claimed that in her early years in the WSPU she did not see Christabel 'more than half a dozen times. She was studying … Sylvia I never saw until 1905 when down in London for Parliament and no more until early 1906.'[14] Actually, although Sylvia was studying art in London from the autumn of 1904, Christabel was living at the family home in Manchester and was also, with Teresa, one of the very small number of speakers on whom the embryonic Union could depend. The two women worked closely together at meetings in and around Manchester. Teresa's selective memory probably reflects the fact that Christabel was now much closer to Annie Kenney, who virtually lived with the Pankhursts after joining the Union in 1905. Teresa interpreted Annie's presence as a threat to her position within her surrogate family, which was heightened by her intimacy with Mrs Pankhurst's favourite daughter.

When the WSPU set up a base in London Teresa was somewhat appeased. She was sent to follow Annie Kenney and oversee the work in the capital where Annie deferred to her as the senior WSPU member. This changed when Christabel joined them. Teresa worked closely with

Christabel throughout 1906 in a number of propaganda tours, including the much-discussed Cockermouth by-election, where the two organisers launched the WSPU's new policy of opposition to all political parties, to the disgust of many of their fellow-ILP members. Yet she was feeling less important within the WSPU. The Union was changing, rapid expansion removing the sense of intimacy of its first three years of work. Organisers were 'scattered to "rouse the country"', while Christabel and the Pethick Lawrences remained in London.[15] On her visits to London, Teresa felt excluded, and was stung to find that more formalised arrangements for access to the WSPU's offices should extend to one such as herself who 'had left London supposed to be a member of the [executive committee] and ... had been mainly responsible for the application of policy in practical ways'.[16] There were also changes in Teresa's personal life. In February 1907, she married Frederick Grieg, a Scotsman, and moved permanently to Glasgow. She ceased her official work as organiser at this point, but continued in a voluntary capacity.[17]

This freed Teresa to be more openly critical of the Union's workings, and she was soon accusing all her earlier allies of various failings towards herself or the organisation. Even Emmeline Pankhurst did not escape her complaints: she believed that at the Aberdeen by-election in 1907, Mrs Pankhurst had reneged on an earlier decision to put Teresa in charge, assuming command herself instead.[18] Teresa conflated her anger at her perceived marginalisation within the WSPU with resentment at what she felt was the increasing autocracy of the Union, and encouraged the Scottish branches to lobby Clements Inn in favour of a more democratic system with elected leaders. Resolutions were sent in complaining about the preference afforded to paid organisers in the Union's hierarchy.[19] Protests were also filed about the decision to oppose all candidates at by-elections, which officially distanced the WSPU from the Labour Party, although Teresa had happily complied with the new policy at the Cockermouth by-election.

Amid this antagonism, Sylvia Pankhurst suspected that political discontents were being used to mask a situation which was better understood in terms of 'questions of personality ... [and] a clashing of temperaments'.[20] Meanwhile, Christabel and Emmeline Pankhurst, together with the Pethick Lawrences, sought to combat the growing opposition. Their correspondence reveals how far the deepening antipathy between Teresa Billington-Grieg and her former friends had poisoned the atmosphere of the Union. Emmeline Pankhurst repeatedly paused her propaganda tours to fret about these internal tensions, with which other more loyal members kept her informed by letter. She wrote to Sam Robinson from the Jarrow by-election in June 1909:

> I want to ask you to let me have that letter you showed me [in] Manchester to use discretely. I can't tell you the details but the same disloyalty that preoccupied the letter is at work in other directions ... I want the Committee to understand what is going on. I don't mind open opposition of a fair and straightforward kind but these whisperings and suggestions are not fair fighting.[21]

The exact nature of the previous disloyalty remains unknown, but in a note to her daughter Sylvia the same day Emmeline was more open about its source, and identified the troublemakers by name:

> I have just written to J[ames] K[eir] H[ardie] about Teresa BG. He promised he would help with Mrs C[obden] S[anderson] if it became necessary, and judging from what I hear the time has come to act ... As for the TBG affair, we have just to face her and put her in her place. She has gone too far this time.[22]

Emmeline was worn down by such incidents, but Christabel attempted to assess the scale of the damage. 'I wonder', she asked Sylvia, 'if you can discover exactly what Mrs Wells had heard and what she thinks is brewing. I feel as though some of us would have to round on the enemy ... T.B. is a wrecker ...'.[23] Dissent was also discussed beyond the immediate family circle. Jennie Baines sent further information to Christabel, who felt 'very sad that such a spirit as you tell me of should be gaining ground in the Union'.[24]

Fearing that dissenters would use the planned conference of the WSPU in September to overthrow its leaders, Emmeline determined to act. After a brief discussion, she bravely decided to cancel the conference and 'tear up the constitution' drawn up in the Union's early days. Emmeline Pethick Lawrence, who later experienced the downside of such boldness, felt that at this point Mrs Pankhurst's actions typified her strongest points, showing how 'when apparently hemmed in by difficulties [she] always cut her way through them'.[25] A new committee was presented to the WSPU membership, consisting of Emmeline Pankhurst, Mrs Tuke, Emmeline Pethick Lawrence, Christabel Pankhurst, Elizabeth Robins, Mary Gawthorpe, Nellie Martel and Mary Neal. Little consultation had occurred. Mary Gawthorpe, who was ill with appendicitis, later suggested that the committee had not really functioned as a decision-making body. The dissenting members, led by Teresa Billington-Grieg and Charlotte Despard, indignantly resigned along with some others, declaring their intention to hold the conference anyway. Within weeks they were leading a new organisation, the Women's Freedom League.

While many later accounts have taken Teresa Billington-Grieg's version at its word, Mrs Pankhurst was not without her supporters at the time. The 'so-called autocratic action', Elizabeth Wolstenholme Elmy wrote to Harriet McIlquham, was unavoidable, the entire business being 'London intrigue of the worst kind all over'.[26] Others agreed with Sylvia Pankhurst that the party-political dimensions of the affair, which was presented as a left–right split, were seriously overplayed. Teresa Billington-Grieg herself declared that the idea that the WFL was seeking stronger links with the Labour Party was 'completely disproved' by 1910, while conversely several members of the WSPU continued their socialist activities within the branches.[27]

The split had some repercussions for the WSPU's organisation and, consequently, for its organisers. Christabel Pankhurst was undoubtedly concerned for her own position, but she also feared the effects of any lingering resentment at 'the running of candidate against candidate for the committee … Unity, harmony, enthusiasm, earnestness and happiness prevailed in our ranks. No one was obliged to join … or to stay in … if she did not so wish.'[28] This enviable situation differed from the bitter in-fighting in some ILP branches that Christabel was all too familiar with, and which she now feared was awakening in her Union. A circular sent out to branches from Clements Inn sympathised with any seceders who had genuine political differences, but warned members that the majority of opposition came from 'disappointed place-seekers and … every dissatisfied and disappointed person'.

Christabel was determined that no factionalism would threaten the equilibrium of her organisation. In forcing the split she did not completely succeed in this. There was much confusion within the branches, especially over the initial attempts by the WFL to retain control of the name WSPU. Further correspondence was sent out by both sides. Huddersfield WSPU held a special meeting to decide its allegiance, where letters from Mrs Despard, Mrs How Martyn and Mrs Pankhurst were debated, before members voted to 'express their confidence in Mrs Pankhurst and the women working with her; and pledge themselves to strive to secure Votes for Women by the methods laid down in the constitution'.[29]

Other branches were more inclined to wait and see what developed on both sides, and 31 out of 52 attended the conference.[30] Some valued activists were lost. Several Scottish workers stayed loyal to Teresa Billington-Grieg, although Leah Leneman has concluded that 'the major … WSPU branches remained intact' afterwards.[31] Emma Sproson, the secretary of Wolverhampton WSPU, went too, although most of her branch stuck with the WSPU. One organiser, Marguerite Sidley, did join the WFL the following year, but most key workers did not waver. Mary Phillips wrote to Mrs Pankhurst assuring her of her full support and suggesting a more public rebuttal of the seceders, which Emmeline graciously refused.[32] Such letters boosted Emmeline's confidence: 'All our best workers are with us', she assured Elizabeth Robins.[33] Andrew Rosen estimated that less than 20 per cent of the WSPU went into the WFL, and certainly the older society did not find its arrangements compromised by this new challenge, but continued to expand its network of branches.[34]

The decision to drop the parts of the constitution dealing with organisational structure affected organisers much more than ordinary members. In an attempt to ensure that no further challenge could be posed to the tenure of the Union's leaders, a vertical structure was imposed on all members, including organisers. With no further national conferences, organisers had no official channels through which they could raise concerns relating to their work. Instead, as Emmeline Pethick Lawrence described, 'any organiser ... who had a difficulty or a grievance came to one or other of those responsible at Headquarters, and we talked the matter over as friends and smoothed out complications'. She felt that this system promoted 'an atmosphere of comradeship, confidence and happiness was maintained between members and organisers'.[35] Sylvia Pankhurst was less sure, and worried that without a policy-making forum, organisers could now be 'dismissed as readily as an employer discharges her cook. There was no democratic procedure'.[36]

This may have been so, but the dismissal of organisers was rare between 1907 and 1912. Rather, as the case of one dissenting organiser, Dora Marsden, illustrates, the WSPU's leaders made great efforts to support organisers who got into difficulties and to retain their services for the cause. The events that culminated in Dora Marsden's resignation from the WSPU at the beginning of 1911 also illuminate a common paradox that affected full-time suffrage workers. Dora was appointed because the WSPU's leaders were impressed by her commitment to the cause, displayed through her bravery and a tendency towards flamboyant acts of daring militancy, which made for excellent headlines. Regrettably, those same qualities made her unsuited to the position of organiser. Never a team player, she found it difficult to settle down to the tedious clerical duties that took up most of a district organiser's time. Although Dora Marsden was prepared to sacrifice all of her time, and her health, to the Union she loved, her economic circumstances meant that she could do this only if she were paid, and the Union had good reasons for not paying women to engage purely in militancy. Dora soon found that the job that she was given as a reward for her bold actions ironically curbed her behaviour, and transformed her from an activist into an administrator.

Dora Marsden's biographer suggested that she enjoyed a rapid rise through the WSPU's ranks, but in fact she was not made an organiser until about a year after she became active, a not atypical trajectory for many of the organisers recruited between 1908 and 1909.[37] Nor was she isolated by her new work. Many district organisers moved far away from their homes, and some also faced the disapprobation of their families. Dora did neither. After attending Owens' College, Manchester, on a Queen's Scholarship, she took a post at Altrincham Pupil Teacher Centre in 1904. Several future suffragettes were among her fellow-students, and the group of young Manchester teachers she was part of included Adela Pankhurst, Teresa Billington, Hilda and Jessie Russell, Katie Wallwork and Rona Robinson, all early members of the local WSPU.

Friendships were important to Dora, and as well as Rona Robinson, who taught in the same school, she became close to Mary Gawthorpe, with whom she shared much experience. They had both been pupil teach-ers, encouraged by their mothers but let down by fathers who were now absent from their family homes. Consequently, both women now sup-ported their mothers financially, and the friendship soon grew to include them, with Mary calling Dora's mother her 'Mammy Marsden'.[38] Later, through her WSPU work, Dora formed another important friendship with Grace Jardine whom she took with her when she went to work in Southport in 1909. This network of friends and family became indispen-sable to Dora as she began her organising work and she looked to them to for support in her efforts and her militancy. They fostered in her a self-assurance which eluded many part-time activists and encouraged her when work became difficult.

In December 1908, Dora deputed for Mary, who was ill, in a debate at the Athanaeum.[39] It was not uncommon for organisers to be trained up by volunteering alongside more experienced workers, and this may have been in Mary's mind when she asked her friend to cover for her. Certainly by the following March, Dora had made a decision: she and Rona Robinson volunteered for the Lancashire contingent to the seventh Women's Parliament. Although arrest was on their agenda, that would not necessarily have ended their teaching careers. Hilda Kean's study of suffragette teachers found that those who were among arrested suffra-gettes might return to work afterwards with no problem.[40] 'I kept the authorities informed daily of my whereabouts', suffragette prisoner and teacher Frances Creaton informed readers of *VFW* in March 1912, 'as well as acquainting them fully with the motives that led me to adopt this pro-test'.[41] Other teachers timed their arrest to fit in with school holidays or used assumed names when imprisoned.[42]

Yet Dora and Rona chose to resign from Altrincham before leaving for London. Dora had probably been contemplating this step for some time. A condition of her scholarship was that she teach for five years after graduation, but this had expired in October 1908, while her WSPU work had steadily increased. The WSPU's northern campaign was about to expand, and Rona and Dora were exactly the type of worker – young, bright, articulate and dependable –needed by Mary Gawthorpe. When they got on the train to London they had probably already been offered organiser posts. With a dependent mother, Dora would not have walked lightly away from the £130 that Altrincham paid her annually had she not been sure of employment elsewhere. Rona certainly knew, as on the day of her release from Holloway Mrs Pankhurst announced that she had given up her teaching career and 'was now about to throw her talents and energies into the enfranchisement of the women of her profession'.[43]

Rona and Dora began their new careers as stars of the WSPU. Dora, particularly, had been singled out by the press for her part in the deputation. At only 4ft 6ins in height, 'looking exactly like a Florentine angel' beneath the WSPU's tricolour, she made perfect copy for the newspapers.[44] Once the celebrations surrounding their release had abated, both women settled down to their new work. For much of May, they deputised for Mary Gawthorpe in Manchester while she worked on the WSPU's large exhibition at the Princes Skating Rink in London. Emmeline Pethick Lawrence later ascribed many of Dora's problems to the fact that she had returned to Manchester immediately after her appointment, and thus had not had 'an opportunity' of learning many of the practicalities which were impressed upon organisers 'who are trained in London'.[45] While this was true, it was not unprecedented, and Dora and Rona did have the advantage of returning to their own branches rather than being sent to districts where they knew nobody. What was lacking in Dora's case was any desire to master the more mundane necessities of an organiser's job. Taking full advantage of her current standing in the WSPU she persuaded well-known speakers such as Gladice Keevil, the Midlands organiser, and Evelyn Sharp to address her branch. She also organised a spectacular action at a Manchester Free Trade Hall meeting in May when Florence Clarkson and Helen Tolson, two local members, 'crouched for hours behind a screen' to interrupt Winston Churchill's speech.[46] The Manchester branch, the oldest in the country, was packed with volunteers, yet Dora opted to bring two other organisers, Laura Ainsworth and Charlotte Marsh in to help with the disruption. Clearly she now saw herself as a leader, and preferred to work with other suffragette celebrities rather than the rank and file.

When Mary Gawthorpe returned, Dora spent a hectic few months campaigning wherever the Union sent her, working as far afield as London and Dumfries. She also managed to fit in two further arrests in Manchester itself. The first occurred at a protest against Augustine Birrell's meeting at White City in September. For the second, Dora, Mary and Rona, dressed in academic robes, 'advanced down the central aisle of the Whitworth Hall of the [Victoria University]' when Lord Morley was about to open a prestigious new laboratory, crying out, 'My Lord, our women are in prison', a reference to the suffragettes currently detained in Birmingham.[47] The three protesters were released to much press interest, when the vice-chancellor and the chief constable realised that charges 'of disorderly conduct and abusive language ... could not be substantiated'.[48] The flamboyant protests favoured by Dora were at odds with what the WSPU leaders required from their organisers. Thus, when she was sent to Southport in November to open up her own district, it was with the expectation common to all district organisers that she would persuade others rather than lead from the front.

Dora did not have to break new ground in Southport. A WSPU branch formed earlier that year was enjoying reasonable success, with regular At Homes and a stall in its name at the Princes Skating Rink exhibition. There was a small but devoted band of local workers, and they had a focus: Winston Churchill was touring Lancashire preparing for the forthcoming General Election, and the WSPU was dogging his steps. With several protests each day, Christabel Pankhurst advised organisers to look to imaginative strategies that would maximise impact while minimising the number of arrests. Arrest was no longer to be an objective in itself, and members were to be assured that 'if it should happen that protesters are not sent to prison it is rather an advantage than otherwise because they are able to go somewhere else and make another protest'.[49] Laying siege to a minister should have been the sort of protest at which Dora excelled, yet she hit problems immediately. The lack of local volunteers for militant action made her endeavour like 'making bricks without mortar', particularly as Jennie Baines had mopped up most of the likely recruits for her Rossendale Valley campaign.[50] Dora asked Christabel Pankhurst if she could bring her former prison friends Helen Tolson, Florence Clarkson and Emily Davison over from Manchester? Emily, being well-known to the police, 'could take another name' while the other two women 'do not speak much and I think could be spared'.[51] Deployment of other WSPU employees exceeded the remit of a district organiser, but Dora did not stop there. Her letter also stated her determination to 'run the risk of arrest' herself in any forthcoming protest, flying in the face of current policy for organisers.[52]

The initial recipient of the letter (probably Mabel Tuke, who opened most of the WSPU's correspondence) was so worried by its contents that she passed it to Emmeline Pethick Lawrence, who replied immediately in Christabel's absence. She firmly reminded Dora that organisers could not be spared. The WSPU was in the midst of a demanding General Election campaign, and Dora was 'not serving the best interests of the Union in exposing [herself] to more imprisonment'. Emphatically, Dora was told 'you must not send for Miss Davison. We cannot have Miss Davison arrested again … it would be a great mistake for Miss Tolson or Miss Clarkson to be arrested either'. Persistent protest was required, not flamboyant gestures.[53] There were other worrying signs in Dora's letter. She clearly craved the limelight, seeking her own arrest rather than attempting to motivate others as an organiser was expected to do. Then there was the way in which she was positioning herself in the Union. Dora forged alliances with certain organisers, including Emily Wilding Davison, who were gaining a reputation for unpredictability, and set herself in opposition to, for example, Jennie Baines, failing to appreciate that Mrs Baines's work in the Rossendale Valley was also part of the Lancashire campaign. The similarities with Teresa Billington's behaviour two years earlier are marked.

Dora ignored the instructions and carried out a daring roof-top protest with the help of Mary Gawthorpe. Helen Tolson did accompany her, and both women were arrested, despite the WSPU's prohibition. As if this were not enough, Dora then hired a legal representative, neither consulting her employers nor clearing the ensuing expenditure. The women's counsel got the charges against them dropped, and that put the WSPU leadership in a tricky position. Emmeline Pethick Lawrence took a dim view of Dora's disobedience and her unauthorised expenditure. Conversely, her protest had been a success, disrupting Churchill and attracting national publicity without taking any workers out of the field. The public reprimanding of a successful organiser was out of the question in the midst of the election campaign. Dora's popularity with other organisers also suggested that she had the potential to do some harm if crossed too overtly. And she was inexperienced. For all these reasons, her employers were prepared to be lenient. Emmeline Pethick Lawrence gave her a warning about incurring expenditure without approval, while taking care to praise the women's courage in a protest which offered 'a story worthy of one of the nation's great battlefields'.[54]

As we have seen, it was difficult for the WSPU leaders to criticise its organisers for being too militant, even when they had failed to grasp the fundamental point about remaining at their posts. Dora's actions were also hard to control because of her distance from London. District organisers had to be trusted to work in ways suited to their local conditions. Policing them with other organisers was both expensive and pointless, given that the network of district organisers was intended to promote efficient national co-ordination. Christabel Pankhurst forbade Dora from taking part in a further militant demonstration planned for London in June 1910, but she had less control over her disobedience on her own patch.[55]

Organisers' administrative failings and financial mismanagement were different matters. These were always treated as private issues and were dealt with internally, and it was here that the leadership was able to exercise a little more control over wayward employees. Although she was an imaginative protester, Dora's administrative abilities left much to be desired. Her record keeping was poor, often late or incomplete; and her accounting was even worse – book-keeping was almost non-existent. Her repeated failure to produce accounts for the Union's end of year audit forced the financial secretary Beatrice Sanders to make a special visit to Southport to 'explain … the whole financial system of the Union'.[56] When Dora did her accounts, she failed to differentiate between political and personal expenditure.[57] She replaced the local literature secretary Miss Henry with her friend Grace Jardine who she proposed to pay as a general secretary. Janie Whittaker and her mother, two stalwart local members, complained to the national treasurer about the way that Southport money was being spent. Emmeline Pethick Lawrence pleaded with Dora to discuss her decisions as 'when the … financial secretary comes to me and asks if I have sanctioned [changes] … it is well for me to be in a position to give an affirmative answer'. Without good communication from organisers, Emmeline explained, she could not 'follow every change and keep track of every development [and] I am apt to find that I have lost touch with the position as it stands at the moment'.[58]

Matters came to a head over Dora's plans to hold a large bazaar in Southport. She wanted something along the lines of the WSPU's large exhibition at the Princes Skating Rink in London, in May 1909. Her employers had no problem with endorsing a fundraising event, but the scale of Dora's plans alarmed them, particularly when she did little in the way of concrete preparation, such as acquiring goods for sale, expending most of her energy on dreaming up ways to expand the spectacle with banners and well-known speakers. By November, the bazaar, already postponed once, was still under-prepared, and Christabel Pankhurst finally ran out of patience. She wrote tersely:

I have consulted others, and we adhere to the decision that a political shooting gallery is not desirable, and must not be undertaken.

It will be quite useless to write and ask the Countess De La Warr to open the Bazaar as she certainly will not do this.

I have also discussed the carnival idea with Mrs Pankhurst and Mrs Pethick Lawrence and they agree with me in saying that it would be a great mistake[59]

Furious at this rebuke, Dora attempted to rally support among her friends. Mary Gawthorpe, who had been away from Manchester since the spring, was at this point seriously ill at the Merton home of Rose Larmatine Yates, her friend from Wimbledon WSPU. From such a distance it was impossible for Mary and Rose to appreciate the gaps in Dora's administrative ability or the mistakes that were being made over the bazaar. Trusting Dora's version of events, they supported her attempts to override headquarters, and suggested that she should act on her instincts and deliver a *fait accompli* as she had done with the Churchill demonstration. Mary wrote:

> R[ose] L[armatine] Y[ates] hopes you will think twice about asking permission [from headquarters] re Queens Hall; if you get no it would be awkward. Why not take it as a matter of course? I see your point of view clearly and perhaps it would be better to give notice; but do this latter rather than ask a refusal.[60]

Encouraged, Dora sent out her publicity without submitting it to Clements Inn for approval. This made things extremely awkward for headquarters, particularly when Mrs Sykes, who had been loaned to Southport to help with the plans, reported that things were far from ready. A seething Emmeline Pethick Lawrence wrote to Dora:

> [Y]ou have placed us in a very serious position of publicly repudiating your actions if we did not go on with it. It is not the first time that you have acted on your own authority and placed us in a somewhat similar position. In every case we have stepped in and backed you up as far as the public is concerned but because we have done this you will be very much mistaken if you come to the conclusion that we regard this action of yours lightly ... There is no other organiser in the Union who would assume the responsibility that you assume ...[61]

As Dora's employer, Emmeline was not being unreasonable. The WSPU valued Dora's work and appreciated that she lacked experience. She had been handled leniently and her previous insubordination had been overlooked, but this was too much. Dora, set on a collision course, ignored her own errors, writing an angry letter in reply. She felt that the committee was not affording her the respect she deserved. Rather, they had 'sent... an educated, talented, and thoughtful woman a lecture couched in tones which the meekest standards of self-respect could only consider intolerable'.[62] Ignoring the fact that she had not secured sufficient goods or helpers for the bazaar, despite almost a year of planning, she claimed to have 'won success in every venture' since her appointment. No mention was made of scaling down her plans.[63] At this outburst, all indulgence ceased and the committee, irritated as much by the 'improper tone' of her letter as her refusal to comply, cancelled the bazaar.[64] Dora petulantly resigned, refusing a conciliatory gesture of two months' salary, and cut all ties with Clements Inn.[65]

The WSPU's official reaction to Dora Marsden's resignation shows that hard lessons had been learned from the split with the WFL. Now, when alternative power bases were suspected, swift action was taken, regardless of how effectual or popular an organiser was. Rona Robinson, who with Dora's encouragement had complained of her workload in Manchester, was summoned to London for discussions with Christabel Pankhurst.[66] The committee also attempted to remove Grace Jardine from Dora's orbit, writing that they thought it best 'for Miss Jardine to come to London for a time. She has never ... had any experience of the work at Headquarters ... she would find this both useful and interesting'.[67]

Suspicions of Dora's motives were not wholly unfounded. On her departure she did briefly work for the WFL, but found its authoritarian stance equally hard to stomach. She used her next venture, the *Freewoman*, to mount vituperative attacks on her former employers, which drew accusations from other WSPU members that the editors were acting as a second Teresa Billington Grieg.[68] Yet although some commentators have suggested that a group of 'Lancashire militants associated with Mary Gawthorpe' were becoming 'difficult to control', Dora's resignation does not support the notion of any organised plotting among them.[69] Mary Gawthorpe was ill, and absent from Manchester at the time. If she was guilty of encouraging Dora in dissent, this was due to her misunderstanding of the situation rather than a desire to form a rival group of organisers. Both of Dora's remaining allies, Grace Jardine and Rona Robinson, left the WSPU with her, but did not take other workers with them, as the instigators of the WFL had done. They were not looking for a new society but were simply worn out – in Dora's own words, 'sick of the unending donkey-work of the gutter and pavement'.[70] Dora's admission that such women had formed 'a tiny group' among the most 'faithful of the faithful' suffragettes, who called themselves SOS for 'sick of suffrage', emphasises the paradox that faced organisers.[71] Many, like her, had been recruited for their militant prowess, but were then set to work on a variety of administrative tasks which demanded none of the daring of emboldened militants. A new organiser, Jessie Stephenson, was quickly dispatched to Manchester to rectify the situation.

Dora's unhappy departure offers a flavour of the climate that could develop between workers within the WSPU. The decision to deal with any complaints personally rather than through a committee structure streamlined operations and removed the problem of elections, but placed undue importance on personalities. All political organisations attract their share of intrigue and personality clashes, and the WSPU, which self-consciously created and promoted its own heroines, was no exception. In such a climate, with no official channels for open discussion, gossip and innuendo could flourish, often routed through the same close friendship networks that supported suffragettes in their work. Dora Marsden had been a target for northern members prior to her resignation. An unidentified 'incident concerning … Kate Wallwork', a longstanding member of the Manchester branch, had been brought to the attention of Clements Inn, although Dora had emerged unscathed, with 'the charges… from Headquarters… disproved'.[72]

Following her resignation the rumours concerning her undoubted financial incompetence persisted. Theresa McGrath, who remained in touch with both sides, disingenuously informed Dora in 1912 that the Manchester suffragette Lillian Williamson had told her that Dora had resigned over an unexplained deficit in the Southport accounts.[73] Other former colleagues complained that Dora had placed undue pressure on Mary Gawthorpe to join her at the *Freewoman* at a time when she had been too ill to make a decision. Actually, this was more or less true, but Dora was stung by the accusation and wrote Mary a letter that gives a wonderful flavour of the way rumours could spread through the movement:

> Rona has been in and she tells me that Miss Mabel Atkinson met her in the street and told her that she had been to see you, and that 'a girl from Manchester' – I presume that will be Hilda R[ussell] – 1) told her that I had got you onto my paper & 2) that you had been very much worse since, 3) that you were constantly writing … *Tales told in this spirit will have a very damning influence. I wish you would give HR a hint that this is not the thing.*[74]

Even popular organisers could find themselves at the centre of unpleasant gossip, and Mary Gawthorpe herself was not immune to its effects. Jennie Baines sniped at her during her early days in Manchester. When Annot Robinson was arrested during a local demonstration, Jennie wrote spitefully to Annot's husband, Sam: '[H]ow is it [Mary Gawthorpe] was not arrested instead? ... she thinks she is of to [*sic*] great a value to the Union to be locked behind prison bars'.[75] As a fellow-organiser, Jennie Baines knew the pressure to avoid arrest, and must have understood Mary's actions, but evidently resented the arrival of a popular new official on the Manchester suffrage scene.

With no forum where organisers could air their concerns, an amount of low-level sniping and muttering between disgruntled friends served as a useful safety valve. This changed in 1912 when the WSPU underwent a further shift in its internal structure. After the mass window-smashings in March, warrants were issued for the arrests of the Pethick Lawrences and Christabel Pankhurst. (Emmeline Pankhurst and Mabel Tuke were also summonsed, but were already in prison after the demonstration.) Christabel fled to France from where she attempted to direct the Union from exile.

The WSPU had functioned in effect as an autocracy up to this point, but the distance of its main strategist from day-to-day events was bound to make a difference. Christabel recalled Annie Kenney from her Bristol district and put her in charge of the Union in her absence, making what arrangements she could for clandestine visits to keep her abreast of events. Messages were passed between Paris and London by post and by word of mouth. In this climate gossip was viewed differently as it was essential for messages to spread effectively. There could be no room for misunderstanding or innuendo. Christabel was also fearful for her leadership, and warned Annie to be on her guard against intellectuals who would attempt to subvert her position as second in command. The warnings were justified when Annie discovered that she had 'just returned [from France] in time. Had I delayed, I should have found a small Committee, who were going to decide policy by separating those funds which were to be used for constitutional and for Militant work. A small sum only was to be set aside for Militancy'.[76]

Annie's report compounded a sense of frustration in Christabel, which was augmented by the feeling that she was rather out of things in France. She worried that others were gathering supporters around them to challenge her leadership, or to suggest alternative policies to those she had sanctioned. Shatteringly, her suspicions fell on the couple who had been her closest allies since 1906. Within six months of Christabel's departure to France, she and her mother had combined to oust Frederick and Emmeline Pethick Lawrence from the WSPU.

The reasons for this expulsion, which precipitated a further split in the ranks of the Union, have never been satisfactorily explained. Publicly, all four cited political differences, and issued a signed statement to the membership informing them that, 'at the first reunion of the leaders after the enforced holiday [i.e. the prison sentences and subsequent periods of recuperation] Mrs Pankhurst and Miss Christabel Pankhurst outlined a new militant policy which Mr and Mrs Pethick Lawrence found themselves altogether unable to approve'.[77] Their respective autobiographical accounts concurred. 'When Christabel lived with us', wrote Emmeline, she

> agreed that we had to advance in militancy by slow degrees in order to give the average person time to understand every move and to keep pace. But since her escape to Paris, Christabel had gone completely over to her mother's standpoint.[78]

Frederick agreed that, were more violent militancy to be pursued, vigorous educational work would have to precede it. The couple also suggested that Christabel should return to England and

> place the government in the awkward predicament of having to choose between repeating the conspiracy trial ... or of declining the challenge ... Whichever course they adopted would enhance her position and that of the WSPU.[79]

Things were more complex behind the scenes. The Pethick Lawrences had serious reservations about the wisdom of the WSPU's shift in targeting private instead of public property, but they were keen supporters of the move towards autocracy in 1907. Now, they were willing to go to any lengths to remain in the Union's leadership and obey the wishes of its supreme autocrats. When Mrs Pankhurst suggested that it might be better for the movement if they remained out of the way in Canada undertaking the 'great mission and role' of spreading 'the Movement ... throughout the Empire', they were quick to reassure her that they placed the Union's welfare above their own interests.[80] Emmeline's offer of the Canadian mission was made in a private letter, which explained a little more about her 'long and anxious thought' regarding her co-leaders. The decision of the authorities to pursue the Pethick Lawrences for costs in the conspiracy trial could 'weaken the movement'. Emmeline explained:

> So long as Mr Lawrence can be connected with militant acts ... they will make him pay ... they see Mr Lawrence as a potent weapon against the militant movement and they mean to use it ... they also intend, if they can, to divert our funds. If suffragists ... raised a fund to recoup Mr

Lawrence, it would mean that our members' money would go finally into the coffers of the enemy and the fighting fund would be depleted or ended. It would also reduce militancy to a farce for the damage we did with one hand would be repaired with another ...[81]

This was not entirely plausible. The WSPU had many wealthy supporters who might also have been targeted, none of whom received similar requests, although admittedly none was as close to the leadership as Frederick. June Purvis's biography of Emmeline Pankhurst suggests that her envy of Christabel's closeness to both Pethick Lawrences, and in particular Frederick's apparent infatuation with her, played some role.[82] Christabel, for her part, was much more preoccupied with the theoretical position underpinning the WSPU than with its day-to-day running, and had begun to find her treasurer's attitudes to finance rather wearing. In a rare illusion to the split, she confided to Harriet Kerr that Beatrice Sanders, now in charge of the finance department, was handling things better: 'She just gets things done quite as efficiently as in the old days and without a quarter of a rippling of the waters there used to be in connection with finance'.[83]

For whatever reason, Emmeline and Christabel 'now saw Frederick as a liability', although ultimately it was the break with his wife that proved more decisive.[84] Yet, whereas in the previous split of 1907, the antipathy that developed between Teresa Billington Grieg and her former friends had been mutual, this time feelings were less clear-cut. When Henry Nevinson, who was abroad at the time of the expulsion, met Frederick in November he found him still 'overcome in speaking of the breach'. Frederick was 'felt bitterly hurt', and was unable to discern 'the tangible causes of quarrel'.[85] Others were caught up in the sadness emanating from the leaders, which permeated the ranks of officials. 'I like them all too much', Elizabeth Robins wrote despairingly in her diary, although she ultimately resigned from the WSPU committee in support of the Pethick Lawrences.[86] Even Annie Kenney was confused, and, although she sided with Christabel, her 'life was far from happy at this point' as she too 'loved all of them'.[87]

Many members were similarly unsure where to position themselves, and the press seized on the uncertainty: 'Are you a Peth or a Pank?' *Punch* infamously demanded, but the deep affection of Annie Kenny was shared by other members and ultimately preserved the WSPU's organisation. Jessie Kenney concluded that 'after 1912 loyalties [were] even fiercer' in the Union.[88] The Pethick Lawrences kept control of *VFW* but resisted calls to set up an organisation in opposition to the WSPU.[89] Many other rank-and-file members with serious misgivings were still prepared to go along with the Union they had built up over the years. Their personal loyalty was so deep that Christabel hoped that at least some might 'find it possible to work for both parties'.[90] Meanwhile, Henry Nevinson summed up the feelings of many when he reported the following conversation with the new editor of the *Suffragette*, Rachel Barret, in January 1913: 'She said "the Lawrences are just the Lawrences but this is the movement" which is the tragic truth.'[91] It was more difficult for organisers, as they could not easily continue to work between two camps, and some valuable and experienced workers were lost. Not surprisingly Dorothy Pethick and Nelly Crocker, Emmeline's sister and cousin, resigned their organiser posts, although Nelly declared that she was still a member of the WSPU in 1913.[92] Mary Neal, who had worked with Emmeline Pethick Lawrence in the Espérance Club, also resigned from the WSPU committee. Nevertheless, enough women stayed, and the Union's organisation was restructured, overseen by Christabel from her Parisian base.

Despite her distance from London, Christabel's leadership remained hands-on. Jessie Kenney joined her in Paris to act as her secretary, while Annie Kenney, Grace Roe and other organisers made frequent visits. Rachel Barrett, Agnes Lake and Geraldine Lennox received regular letters concerning the content and layout of each edition of the *Suffragette*, as well as suggestions for potential advertisers. The office manager, Harriet Kerr, was bombarded daily with letters about arrangements for Lincolns Inn. No detail escaped Christabel – she even suggested to Miss Kerr that 'letting girls on each floor take trays to their respective floor' in their tea-breaks would save time and free up an extra room downstairs.[93] In many ways Christabel was happy in Paris: 'Imagine how one loves a place – delightful in any case – which has been one's haven' she confided to Constance Lytton.[94] The pace of life suited one who, on her own admission, preferred 'bed in the morning and work later'.[95] Jessie Kenney recalled her enjoying the leisurely continental breakfasts.[96] Sylvia found her sister 'serene', working extremely hard but also 'enjoying ... the shops and the Bois ... ready for sight-seeing ...'.[97] Public presentations of Christabel emphasised the frivolous aspects of Paris, with articles in the *Daily Sketch* and similar papers focusing on her costume and leisure activities, presenting an enviable picture of her new life.[98]

Less discernible was the strain that exile placed on Christabel. She was racked with worry about the effect of prison and persecution on the health of many of her members and of her mother. Jessie Kenney wondered 'how much longer we could have stood the strain of using other people's lives in the campaign'.[99] Christabel also became increasingly anxious about the loyalty of her colleagues, convinced that her position was about to be challenged or undermined. The police raid on Lincolns Inn House in April 1913 compounded her anxiety, as Rachel Barrett, Beatrice Sanders, Harriet Kerr, Geraldine Lennox and Agnes Lake, key figures in the restructured WSPU, were arrested and received heavy sentences.

Although all five women were released under the Cat and Mouse Act, they were no longer free to organise. Agnes Lake's health broke down completely.[100] On Harriet Kerr's release, the companion she lived with developed phlebites, and Harriet was torn: 'I cannot afford to kill my best friend and yet I will not turn my back on the Union', she wrote to Agnes Lake.[101] In the circumstances there was little that could be done, and, with her employers' approval, she gave the authorities an undertaking that she would refrain from further militancy, and left her post.[102] Miss Lennox, Miss Barrett and Miss Sanders went underground. The Union's increasingly clandestine operation affected its daily communications. The group who deputised for Christabel now continually shifted, adding to the confusion. Annie Kenney was in and out of prison under the Cat and Mouse Act, and so handed over much of her responsibility to Grace Roe. The prohibition on organisers being arrested was useless now that the Government was counting all suffragettes guilty by association, and Grace herself was arrested in June 1914, whereupon control was handed to Olive Bartels. Each arrest necessitated a new set of disguises and a further layer of secrecy. Rumour and counter-rumour held sway.

Even Christabel's devoted colleague Annie Kenny was suspected of disloyalty, and, after a meeting at which Annie was commanded to break her involvement with the theosophy movement if she wished to continue working for the WSPU, Christabel broke down in tears for the first time that anyone could recall.[103] Other organisers were not given the option of discussion. In August 1913, Mary Phillips, who had been a paid organiser for five years, was working in Plymouth, a difficult posting, as Mary explained in a letter to Lincolns Inn. Christabel's response was brutal:

> Apparently not much progress is being made in your district, but you seem to think that is inevitable. Under the circumstances I do not think that we are justified in having an official organiser. If local people will provide neither money nor work it is impossible for Headquarters to supply them with an organiser. We have been feeling this for a long time and have come to the conclusion that it would not be right to let matters drift any longer[104]

Mary was sent four weeks' salary in lieu of notice, with the express wish that she would continue to work for the WSPU in her 'leisure time'. Taking Christabel at her word, Mary explained to friends in the WSPU that she was no longer on its payroll because her district 'was not considered worth working'. When word of this reached Christabel, she sent Mary a list of her considered defects:

> I want to say that if we had thought you could have made a success of another district we would have asked you to take one … you are not effective as a district organiser … such was the view held at headquarters.
>
> As a shop secretary where you do not have so much responsibility for making things go you would I think probably be successful. That I shall say if my opinion is asked. But I cannot say that you would make a successful head of a district campaign because I do not think it.
>
> It is not possible the members shall have the impression that you have been unjustly dealt with in spite of your having been a fully competent organiser.[105]

Why Christabel, as chief organiser of the WSPU, would treat one of her longest-serving organisers in this way is difficult to fathom. She may have been concerned that Mary, who had idolised Mrs Pethick Lawrence at the time of her recruitment to the WSPU, was too conciliatory towards the Pethick Lawrences after their expulsion. Mary was not the only organiser to be treated in this way: Katharine Douglas Smith was dismissed soon after Mary. She had worked for some years at headquarters, had been imprisoned, and had also achieved a degree of notoriety when, as a publicity stunt, she and other WSPU suffragettes had dressed as firemen and driven around London. Like Mary Phillips she was stung by her dismissal and complained to Constance Lytton, who tackled Christabel directly about it. Christabel offered a rather dissembling reply, suggesting that Katharine's appointment was down to another 'head of a department' rather than herself, although in fact Christabel had suggested to Geraldine Lennox that Katharine would be 'just the right person' for a particular job the previous year.[106] Katharine, Christabel continued,

> has taken altogether too grim and tragic a view of the whole matter. As I said in my previous letter we need people at the office who are optimistic and philosophical and cheery. I do not consider that there was need for me to write to Miss D[ouglas] S[mith] a statement of her defects from the office point of view, but as soon as I realised that she wanted some statement from me I sent one. I am always ready to give the why and wherefore of things I do otherwise I should not be strong enough to do some of the hard things that have to be done. It is so much *easier* to give everybody their own way and one would probably be more liked. It is only a very clear vision of the necessity of certain actions that enables one to do them and hang the consequences.[107]

The reactions of many WSPU members to Christabel's decisions heightened her sense of concern for her position. As the pace of their own work speeded up, many felt moved to more public criticism. Mary Leigh had had a particularly difficult time organising in Ireland, where she had been sentenced to five years' penal servitude, along with her co-organiser Gladys Evans. Both women underwent a hunger-strike and were fed by force, before being released. Back in London, Mary, who continued active militancy and faced further arrest, was concerned by how she saw the campaign affecting other workers. She determined to tell Christabel the truth as she saw it:

> Some of our young women were on the run with no money, no food, no shelter. I saw two crouching in public phone booths ... I went [to Paris] with two other suffragettes. At the Gare du Nord, we drew lots, and I was made spokeswoman ... Christabel had changed. She was wearing elaborate Parisian clothes, had a small Pomeranian, seemed annoyed by our intrusion. She was almost flippant. We were wasting our time, she said. I said the militants were loyal, but they were sick of taking orders from young office girls while the leaders were in prison ... Had she nothing to say, no message to give? No she had not.[108]

Mary Leigh risked another visit, this time alone, in which she met with Christabel and Jessie Kenney, but felt that this time she was viewed as a 'crazy intruder' and quickly dismissed. She was not the only WSPU member to attempt to remonstrate with Christabel at this time. Beatrice Harraden, a well-known writer who was also on the committee of the Hampstead WSPU branch, wrote protesting at what she felt had become of the Union by January 1914. In her view, Christabel had been 'turning away deliberately or else alienating so many of our old and faithful comrades', and had 'shut the door in the faces of the finest, ablest and most devoted women' who had helped make 'the WSPU the very finest company of modern women in the world'. 'No proper care or forethought' was 'being given to the "mice"'. Beatrice painted a grim picture of the shifting hierarchies in the Union as she perceived them:

> Never a week passes but that some one has been slighted, rebuffed or dismissed. I see with my mind's eyes ... a long procession of the discarded, in fact, almost everyone one likes best and admires most is apparently outside the pale, if not outside what used to be the Union.[109]

Christabel had been more active than her accusers realised. She had paid close attention to Mary Leigh's own imprisonment, as it linked to the campaign in Ireland, which was essential if the WSPU was to put pressure on the Government from different sides, and a successful branch in Ireland could parallel the campaign being waged by Irish nationalists. Grace Roe had been spared from her work in London, despite the urgency of her situation there, to run a special campaign of agitation culminating in a huge demonstration in Phoenix Park. Christabel requested 'chapter and verse' from Beatrice to support the accusations of bad practice. Beatrice citied three cases: Olive Beamish; Lillian Lenton and her companions, who had been 'sent to some place to await money and instructions which never came; and, on their return to Headquarters, sent to Paddington Station and arrested there'; and 'the dismissal of Miss Lake'.[110]

Christabel repudiated the accusations. 'Nothing has occurred', she wrote, in the cases of the two "mice" Olive Beamish and Lillian Lenton, 'which is not perfectly correct and entirely credible' and she regarded the charge that nothing was being done for the mice 'with the greatest indignation'. As to Agnes Lake:

> The termination of the official relation between herself and the Union was a purely business matter. The circumstances under which her services were retained in a business sense had changed and to have continued to retain these services after the Union's need of them had ceased would have been most unjustifiable from the point of view of the Union and its subscribers. No organisation or business concern could possibly be carried on in the way in which by implication you suggest it ought to be. Suppose, for example, you yourself were to dispense with the services of your secretary, you would undoubtedly think it very extraordinary if third persons were to write to complain of your action. In connection with such matters as the termination of Miss Lake's engagement sentimentality is entirely out of place.[111]

Agnes Lake, whose health had been compromised during her hunger-strike, certainly made no public fuss about her 'dismissal'. Beatrice Harraden's letter contained other inaccuracies too. A list appended of those she claimed were no longer in the WSPU fold included Janie Allan, the Glasgow organiser who was very much involved until the outbreak of the First World War. Christabel began to despair of the atmosphere within the Union, although it had concerned her since she arrived in Paris: 'There is a plot-thickening feeling in the air, don't you think?' she wrote anxiously in a letter to Harriet Kerr.[112] The 'political flair' which had made her 'a match for the most subtle of minds' began to desert her, replaced by worrying signs of paranoia towards anyone she felt was seeking to establish an alternative suffrage court.[113] Her own sisters were next in line. Sylvia, who had never actually worked for the WSPU as an organiser, had been sent to run a campaign in the East End of London. Although this had begun under the auspices of the WSPU, her networks were increasingly divorced from any national campaign, and, in January 1914, she was summoned to a meeting in Paris and forced to leave the Union.

Less predictable was the rift with Adela, which happened during the same month. Christabel's youngest sister had been a paid organiser, but had given up work for the WSPU in the summer of 1912, overcome by nervous strain. For unspecified reasons, Christabel had long regarded her youngest sister as a direct threat, as Adela bitterly recounted to Helen Fraser:

> I didn't want a political career in the first place – but ... I could not help understanding political situations, probably all too well for my own good ... I knew ... that we were rapidly losing ground, I even tried to tell Christabel this was the case but unfortunately she took it amiss and was even persuaded I was about to found a counter organisation with myself as leader ...[114]

Christabel now feared that Adela might respond to an approach from Sylvia to join her in the East London Federation of Suffragettes. Sylvia *did* invite her but Adela rejected her offer immediately out of loyalty to her mother and Christabel.[115] Emmeline duly arranged a meeting with Adela, the result of which was that her youngest daughter was dispatched to Australia, an outcome which the young girl miserably felt was 'best for myself and all concerned'.[116]

It was undoubtedly more difficult to be a WSPU organiser in 1914 than it had been in 1908. The high-profile dismissals and expulsions of loyal workers carried the air of show trials. Nor were the leaders in an easy position. Christabel in particular was struggling to keep up with situations from a distance while being continually beset with complaints which she often felt to be misplaced or inaccurate. Yet for all these difficulties, the expulsions that opened the final year of the WSPU's campaign needs to be viewed in proportion. They did not prompt mass resignations from the branches. Even after the dismissal of the popular Emmeline Pethick Lawrence, most organisers remained within the ranks of the WSPU, whatever their private feelings might have been. This attitude towards internal problems suggests that much of the Union's structural strength derived from the loyalty of its most active workers and, in particular, its organisers.

While the pressures of their work undoubtedly encouraged among themselves a low-level culture of complaint, they remained in broad agreement with the Union's policy and tactics. Even when they disagreed, as in the case of the Pethick Lawrences, they were often willing to make quite significant compromises for the sake of overall unity. Few felt strongly enough to threaten the structure of the Union through seceding; neither of the large-scale splits involving organisers threatened the WSPU's existence at the local branch level. While they recognised that their employers were autocratic and somewhat capricious, most organisers evidently felt that the campaign was going in the right direction, and were willing to continue with their work, until it was interrupted by the war. Only then did any serious opposition emerge to the direction in which the Union was heading.

Notes

1 Christabel Pankhurst to Janie Allan, 26 May 1914, Acc 4498/3, Janie Allan Papers, National Library of Scotland.
2 E. Pankhurst, *My Own Story*, p. 59.
3 C. Pankhurst, *Unshackled*, p. 83.
4 See, for example, Cowman, *'Mrs Brown is a Man and a Brother!'*, ch. 5.
5 Crawford, 'Caroline Phillips', *Women's Suffrage Movement*, pp. 543–4.
6 Leneman, *A Guid Cause*, p. 71.
7 Ann McRobie to Caroline Phillips, 22 January 1909, quoted in *ibid.*, p. 71.
8 Caroline Phillips to Sylvia Pankhurst, n.d., quoted in *ibid.*, p. 72
9 *Ibid.*
10 *Ibid.*
11 Christabel Pankhurst to Janie Allan, 26 May 1914, Janie Allan Papers.
12 *Ibid.*
13 See C. L. Eustace, 'Daring to be free: the evolution of women's political identities in the Women's Freedom League, 1907–1930', DPhil thesis, University of York, 1993, p. 52.
14 Teresa Billington Grieg, autobiographical fragment, Box 397 A/6, TBG Papers.
15 Teresa Billington Grieg, fragment entitled 'Half century', Box 398 B/8/2, TBG Papers.
16 Teresa Billington Grieg, autobiographical fragment, Box 397 A/6, TBG Papers.
17 'Notes on the formation of the WFL', SFC.
18 *Ibid.*
19 *Ibid.*
20 E. S. Pankhurst, *The Suffragette Movement*, pp. 263, 265.
21 Emmeline Pankhurst to Sam Robinson, 22 June 1907, M220/1/2/4, Annot Robinson Papers.
22 Emmeline Pankhurst to Sylvia Pankhurst, 23 June 1907, 21/193, Sylvia Pankhurst Papers, International Institute for Social History.
23 Christabel Pankhurst to Sylvia Pankhurst, 19 June 1907 quoted in Mitchell, *Queen Christabel*, p. 104.
24 Christabel Pankhurst to Jennie Baines, 28 August 1907, Baines Papers.
25 E. Pethick Lawrence, *My Part*, p. 176.
26 Quoted by Purvis, *Emmeline Pankhurst*, p. 98.
27 Teresa Billington Grieg, 'The militant suffrage movement: emancipation in a hurry', in McPhee and FitzGerald (eds), *The Non-Violent Militant*, p. 160; on WSPU links with socialism see Leneman, *A Guid Cause*, p. 52, and Krista Cowman, '"Incipient Toryism?"

The Women's Social and Political Union and the Independent Labour Party, 1903–14', *History Workshop Journal*, 53 (2002), pp. 128–48.

28 C. Pankhurst, *Unshackled*, p. 81.

29 Huddersfield WSPU Minute Book, 18 September 1907, Key Papers, West Yorkshire Archive Service.

30 Edith How Martyn, 'The rise of the Women's Freedom League', *Vote*, 9 December 1909.

31 Leneman, *A Guid Cause*, p. 52.

32 Emmeline Pankhurst to Mary Phillips, 21 September 1907, Mary Phillips Papers, Camellia Collection.

33 Emmeline Pankhurst to Elizabeth Robins, 13 September 1907, quoted in Purvis, *Emmeline Pankhurst*, p. 97.

34 Rosen, *Rise Up Women!*, p. 92; see also Eustace, 'Daring to be free', p. 54, where it is said that a 'relatively small number' of WFL members came from the WSPU.

35 E. Pethick Lawrence, *My Part*, p. 178.

36 E. S. Pankhurst, *The Suffragette Movement*, p. 265.

37 Garner, *A Brave and Beautiful Spirit*, p. 22.

38 Mary Gawthorpe to 'Dearest Mammy Marsden', 2 April 1912, Dora Marsden Papers.

39 *VFW*, 17 and 24 December 1908.

40 Hilda Kean, *Deeds Not Words: The Lives of Suffragette Teachers* (London: Pluto Press, 1990), p. 13; Margaret Thompson also found that her employers dealt quite leniently with her after an arrest: M. and E. Thompson, *They Couldn't Stop Us! Experiences of Two (Usually) Law-Abiding Women in the Years 1909–1913* (Ipswich: W. E. Harrison & Sons, 1957), p. 32.

41 *VFW*, 1 March 1912; Miss Creaton was threatened with a fine, but her Union solicitor managed to have it overturned.

42 Notes on Elsa Myers, SFC.

43 *VFW*, 7 May 1909.

44 E. S. Pankhurst, *The Suffragette*, p. 367.

45 Emmeline Pethick Lawrence to Dora Marsden, 24 November 1909, Dora Marsden Papers.

46 *VFW*, 28 May 1909.

47 E. S. Pankhurst, *The Suffragette*, p. 446.

48 *Ibid.*, p. 447.

49 Christabel Pankhurst to Jennie Baines, 23 September 1909, Baines Papers.

50 Dora Marsden to Christabel Pankhurst, 28 November 1911, Baines Papers.

51 *Ibid.*

52 *Ibid.*

53 Emmeline Pethick Lawrence to Dora Marsden, 1 December 1909, Dora Marsden Papers.

54 *Ibid.*, 7 December 1909, Dora Marsden Papers.

55 Christabel Pankhurst to Dora Marsden, 25 June 1910, Dora Marsden Papers.

56 Emmeline Pethick Lawrence to Dora Marsden, 2 November 1910, Dora Marsden Papers.

57 Beatrice Sanders to Dora Marsden, 9 February 1910, Dora Marsden Papers.

58 Emmeline Pethick Lawrence to Dora Marsden, 25 February 1910, Dora Marsden Papers.

59 Christabel Pankhurst to Dora Marsden, 14 November 1910, Dora Marsden Papers.

60 Mary Gawthorpe to Dora Marsden, 13 November 1910, Dora Marsden Papers.

61 Emmeline Pethick Lawrence to Dora Marsden, 2 December 1910, Dora Marsden Papers.

62 Dora Marsden to Emmeline Pethick Lawrence, 9 January 1911, Dora Marsden Papers.

63 *Ibid.*

64 Mabel Tuke to Dora Marsden, 26 January 1911, Dora Marsden Papers.

65 Dora Marsden to Mrs Pankhurst, 27 January 1911; Mabel Tuke to Dora Marsden, 3 February 1911; Dora Marsden to Mabel Tuke, 5 February 1911, all Dora Marsden Papers.

66 Unsigned leter from Rona Robinson to Dora Marsden, 15 December 1910, Dora Marsden Papers.

67 Christabel Pankhurst to Dora Marsden, 27 January 1911, Dora Marsden Papers.

68 Hertha Ayrton to Mary Gawthorpe, 26 November 1911, Dora Marsden Papers.

69 Harold Smith, *The British Women's Suffrage Campaign, 1866–1928* (London: Longmans, 1998), p. 34.

70 *Egoist*, 15 June 1914.

71 *Ibid.*

72 Dora Marsden to Emmeline Pethick Lawrence, 9 January 1911, Dora Marsden Papers.

73 Theresa McGrath to Dora Marsden, 19 April 1912, Dora Marsden Papers.

74 Dora Marsden to Mary Gawthorpe, 14 October 1911, Dora Marsden Papers; see also Henrietta Lowy to Dora Marsden, 4 May 1911, Dora Marsden Papers.

75 Jennie Baines to Sam Robinson, n.d. (July 1908),718/19, Annot Robinson Papers.

76 Kenney, *Memories*, p. 176.

77 *VFW*, 18 October 1912.

78 E. Pethick Lawrence, *My Part*, p. 278.

79 F. Pethick Lawrence, *Fate*, p. 98.

80 Emmeline Pankhurst to Emmeline Pethick Lawrence, 8 September 1912, PL931, Pethick Lawrence Papers, Trinity College Cambridge; Emmeline Pethick Lawrence to Emmeline Pankhurst, 22 September 1912, PL 932, Pethick Lawrence Papers.

81 Emmeline Pankhurst to Emmeline Pethick Lawrence, 8 September 1912, PL 931, Pethick Lawrence Papers.

82 Purvis, *Emmeline Pankhurst*, p. 199.

83 Christabel Pankhurst to Harriet Kerr, n.d. (April 1913). TNA, DPP 1/19, Exhibit. 33.

84 June Balshaw, 'The Pethick Lawrences and Women's Suffrage', in Eustace and John (eds), *The Men's Share*, pp. 135–57, at p. 147. The two Emmelines never met again, and although Christabel corresponded with Emmeline Pethick Lawrence in the 1920s, it was not until after the latter's death that anything approaching a friendship was re-established with Frederick. He went on to deliver Christabel's memorial oration.

85 Henry Nevinson's diary, 28 November 1912.

86 Quoted in A. V. John, *Elizabeth Robins: Staging a Life* (London: Routledge, 1995), p. 169.

87 Kenney, *Memories*, p. 192.

88 Jessie Kenney, interview with David Mitchell, 24 March 1963, Mitchell Collection.

89 They finally helped set up the United Suffragists in 1914, but this was conceived as a bridge between many sections of the movement rather than an alternative to any single group: Cowman, '"A party between revolution and peaceful persuasion?"'.

90 Henry Nevinson's diary, 23 November 1912.

91 *Ibid.*, 28 January 1913.
92 A.J.R., *Women's Suffrage Annual*; it is likely that this is accurate, as the entries were self-penned and the same edition listed the WSPU committee without the Pethick Lawrences.
93 Christabel Pankhurst to 'My dear P' (Harriet Kerr) n.d. (April 1913), TNA, DPP 1/19, Exhibit 33.
94 Christabel Pankhurst to Constance Lytton, 14 May 1914, PL920, Pethick Lawrence Papers.
95 Christabel Pankhurst to 'My dear P', 9 April 1913, TNA, DPP 1/19, Exhibit 33.
96 Jessie Kenney, 'The flame and the flood', Book 4.
97 E. S. Pankhurst, *The Suffragette Movement*, pp. 383–4.
98 The *Daily Sketch* carried a picture feature on Christabel that was reproduced in *VFW*, 20 September 1912.
99 Jessie Kenney, interview with David Mitchell, 24 March 1964, Mitchell Collection.
100 Christabel Pankhurst to Agnes Lake, 28 September 1913, Agnes Lake Papers, Girton College, reproduced by kind permission of the Mistress and Fellows of Girton College, Cambridge.
101 Harriet Kerr to 'Dearest Pal and Fellow Convict', 23 September 1913, Agnes Lake Papers.
102 Harriet Kerr to Edith How Martyn, 22 January 1928, SFC.
103 Jessie Kenney, 'The flame and the flood', Book 6: 'The end of the movement.'
104 Christabel Pankhurst to Mary Phillips, 9 July 1913, Mary Phillips Papers.
105 *Ibid.*, 1 August 1913, Mary Phillips Papers.
106 Christabel Pankhurst to Constance Lytton, 14 January 1914, PL915, Pethick Lawrence Papers; Christabel Pankhurst to Geraldine Lennox, n.d. (March 1913), TNA, DPP 1/19, Exhibit 111.
107 Christabel Pankhurst to Constance Lytton, 14 January 1914, PL915 Pethick Lawrence Papers.
108 Mary Leigh interview with David Mitchell, 21 March 1965, MOL, Mitchell Collection.
109 Beatrice Haraden to Christabel Pankhurst, 13 January 1914, Janie Allan Papers.
110 *Ibid.*, n.d. (20 January 1914), Janie Allan Papers.
111 Christabel Pankhurst to Beatrice Harraden, 26 January 1914, Janie Allan Papers.
112 Christabel Pankhurst to Harriet Ker, n.d. (April 1913), TNA, DPP 1/19, Exhibit 33.
113 Frederick Pethick Lawrence, 'Preface' to C. Pankhurst, *Unshackled*, p. 12.
114 Adela Pankhurst to Helen Fraser, 11 February 1961, Mitchell Collection.
115 Purvis, *Emmeline Pankhurst*, p. 248.
116 Adela Pankhurst Walsh, 'My mother', quoted in Purvis, *Emmeline Pankhurst*, p. 249.

7

WSPU organisers and the war

W HEN WAR WAS DECLARED on 4 August 1914, the WSPU, in common with much of the British public, was taken by surprise. Readers of the *Suffragette* for 31 July and 7 August found little in its pages to suggest that the Union was on the brink of a major shift in direction. For suffragettes, it was very much business as usual. One of the main stories of July described the ingenious methods adopted by district organisers throughout the country, in response to the Government's attempt to impoverish the circulation of their paper by threatening to act against wholesale newsagents involved in its distribution. In Liverpool, Helen Jollie had organised her members to distribute the *Suffragette* direct to retailers themselves, although she reported that to date the local 'wholesale newsagents are still supplying us with our papers every week'. Margaret West, organiser in Leicester, had persuaded one member to lend the branch a pony cart which was used to ferry bundles of the newspaper around the city, and was confident that 'the circulation … will go up from this week onwards', now that the branch members were in charge of arranging it themselves.

All forms of militancy continued. There were reports of fires attributed to suffragettes in Bath, Birmingham, Dulwich and Hampstead, along with an attack on a pillar box in Belfast. One woman was arrested at Buckingham Palace where she had managed to dodge the duty policemen, and had 'thrown missiles of some heavy nature' at the upper windows. Fifteen suffragettes were in prison that week, with a handful more on remand as well as numbers of 'mice' in hiding at safe houses throughout the country. Other suffragettes carried out protests at theatres, handing out leaflets to the audience and delivering impromptu addresses in the intervals. Behind the scenes there was a sustained lobbying campaign among Bishops and senior clerics aimed at encouraging their intervention against forced feeding. Meanwhile, in the WSPU's London offices,

Gertrude Harding was co-ordinating volunteers and organisers in a national holiday campaign which the WSPU leaders hoped would further circumnavigate the authorities' attempts to dismantle their organisation.[1] The next issue of the *Suffragette* carried no hint either that it was to be the last for some time or that this was its final appearance as a suffrage paper. The paper's content was still overwhelmingly detached from international events. True, Christabel Pankhurst had contributed a page-long article, 'The War', but this reassured readers of the Union's continued priorities. It called on all 'Women of the WSPU' to 'protect our Union through everything' that was about to happen. There was still plenty of work to be done to acquire the vote.

Nowhere was there to be found a suggestion that the WSPU's organisation was facing some of its most serious challenges ever. Admittedly, the rank-and-file membership in provincial branches would have noticed very little difference in their day-to-day experience as suffragettes. In the branches work continued with the demands of meetings, paper sales, and fundraising in suffragette shops, local meeting-rooms and innumerable open-air locations. The optimistic tone of the *Suffragette* would have done little to disabuse the members of the notion that it was business as usual. Organisers, as officials of the Union, were in a slightly different position. Although they, too, were bound up in the minutiae of political work, they had noticed some changes since Christabel's departure in 1912.

The chain of command which she had set up to keep the Union running was beginning to fracture. Christabel herself had reportedly not left her Parisian apartment for two months, since the time of the last raid on Lincolns Inn, fearing that even in France she was no longer safe. Her mother, severely weakened by consecutive hunger-strikes, had been smuggled to St Malo to recuperate, where her old friend Ethel Smyth was horrified to witness 'the ghost of what had been Mrs Pankhurst' disembarking from the ferry, almost carried by two companions.[2] The organisers whom Christabel had left in charge in her absence were not faring much better: Annie Kenney was a 'mouse'; Grace Roe was in prison; and Olive Bartels, Grace's deputy, was attempting to direct operations from a series of secret addresses, posing as a widow. The costume alone was enough to depress Olive, who recalled the whole time as being 'dead black – black everything – the gloom – I almost began to think I was a widow'.[3] While organisers publicly remained upbeat about their ability to distribute the *Suffragette*, further government clampdowns were anything but welcome. The authorities were widening the range of their target, with the Post Office instructed to compile lists of all individuals who had the *Suffragette* delivered by the postal service.[4]

Life had become markedly more difficult for suffragette prisoners. Mary Richardson, who had just been released from Holloway with appendicitis, declared that the struggle currently going on inside the prison infirmary, where forced feeding had increased in brutality, was the 'worst fight on record'.[5] Although the authorities issued repeated denials, laboratory tests set up by Frank Moxon and Flora Murray, two doctors sympathetic to the WSPU, had confirmed that Mary herself, along with Phyllis Brady and Kitty Marion, had been unwillingly and unwittingly drugged with excessive doses of bromide when in prison, with the aim of curbing their resistance to forced feeding and dampening the complaints they were making to independent observers.[6] On top of this came worrying rumours that the Government was considering alternatives to prison in dealing with suffragette militants, which might include confinement in lunatic asylums. The emphasis of recent trials reminded all organisers that their work as officials of the Union put them in the front line for such punishments, regardless of their personal involvement in militancy. Grace Roe had been found guilty on a charge of conspiracy, while Flora Drummond had been jailed in May for using inciting language. As the remaining organisers struggled to keep an acceptable level of cohesion within the WSPU country-wide, they must have wondered which one of them would be the next to be arrested.

Fearful and exhausted, most of the WSPU's staff must have shared the sentiments of Elsie Bowerman, an intermittent organiser since her graduation from Girton in 1911, who received the final news of war 'almost with a sense of relief … as we knew that our militancy, which had reached an acute stage, could cease'.[7] Workers were called back from the field. Kitty Marion, who was out on licence, was in Leicester 'on danger duty' (a euphemism for setting fires) when 'a telegram arrived from Headquarters to stop all activity'.[8] Despite the individualism of the arson campaign, it was co-ordinated by organisers who knew how to get hold of the willing militants, to send them out where and whenever necessary or to call them back, as in this case.

Before all work could cease, there was still one important task for the Union to attend to, and their focus turned to the remaining suffragette prisoners. On 7 August, the Home Secretary Reginald McKenna offered to release any woman who would undertake not to commit further crimes, a promise which the Government hoped the WSPU's leaders would facilitate by suspending militancy permanently. The prison authorities pressured suffragettes to comply. In her Holloway cell, Grace Roe appreciated that there was a greater need to co-ordinate her members now than at any other time. Suffragettes would be particularly susceptible to any emergency powers that Parliament might introduce against the background of the national crisis. Fellow-prisoners called to Grace in her cell, giving her details of visits from 'officials ... trying to persuade each one to give an undertaking'. Grace 'climbed up to the window ... and ... said: give no undertakings, all will be done from outside'.[9] Her order spread rapidly from prisoner to prisoner in the courtyard below.

Unknown to Grace, some fellow-senior organisers were happier to accept the Government's terms. Other active militants refuted any idea of a compromise and sought nothing less than a full pardon. 'We are alright during the war, but after[?]' was one prisoner's anxious response when she heard that there might be a conditional surrender.[10] The French Government had released its political prisoners at the outbreak of the war, and many organisers, indignant even at this stage that WSPU prisoners were still not viewed as political offenders, began 'frantic private efforts' for more reassuring terms of release for their members.[11] Mrs Mansel was sent off to the Archbishop of Canterbury to explain that while the council of the WSPU (which in this instance comprised Christabel and Mrs Pankhurst, Mrs Tuke, Annie Kenney and Flora Drummond) 'honestly want to stop militancy just now ... they cannot get the more fanatical of the group to make in a public manner any promise beforehand, binding them to abstain from militancy'.[12] Archbishop Davidson agreed to intercede with the Home Secretary, although he wearily confessed to McKenna that he quite understood why the suffragettes' word might be doubted by politicians: 'They are absolutely hopeless persons to deal with on normal or reasonable lines. I feel the hopelessness every time I see any of them.' Despite these reservations, the Archbishop believed suffragettes' assurances 'that they will abstain from militancy at this time of National Crisis'. In support of this feeling, he appended a press release which the Union planned to send out as soon as its demands had been met, announcing its decision 'to suspend all hostilities and activities at once now that their loyal women political prisoners are released', adding that 'every member of the Union will loyally abide by this decision'.[13]

Three days later, on 10 August, the Home Secretary announced that all WSPU prisoners would be freed without condition, as would certain other prisoners who had been convicted during recent industrial disputes. The WFL ended its militant campaign the following day, but the WSPU's leaders remained cautious.[14] It was 12 August before Emmeline Pankhurst issued a circular letter to the membership explaining that the campaign was now suspended. 'Even the outbreak of war', she wrote, 'could not affect the action of the WSPU so long as our comrades were in prison.' Now that they were safely released, a new strategy could evolve.

Emmeline did not refute any of the recent developments in militancy, but felt that anything that the WSPU could achieve was bound to be 'rendered less effective by contrast with the infinitely greater violence of war'. There was no point in moving to different forms of suffrage propaganda, she felt, as 'such work [is] futile even under ordinary conditions' when not underpinned by militancy. The best policy for the WSPU at present was to 'economise the Union's energies and financial resources by a temporary cessation of activities'. The *Suffragette* would also halt publication with immediate effect. These moves would not only 'save much energy and a very large sum of money', but would have personal benefit, too, allowing space for 'those individual members who have been in the fighting line to recuperate after the tremendous strain and suffering of the past two years'.[15]

In anticipation that the war would soon be over, most suffragettes accepted this gratefully, while organisers continued ironing out the small ambiguities that required their immediate attention. Gertrude Harding was sent to Ireland to secure the release of Joan Wickham and Dorothy Evans. As they were in mid-trial, so not in prison or on remand, they did not come under the terms of the Home Office amnesty.[16] Back in London, the most urgent problem was the difficulty facing the 'mice' out on licence, whose position in terms of the amnesty was extremely uncertain. Although they were assured that they too were free, the lack of accompanying paperwork caused them difficulties. When one 'mouse', Mrs Crow, came out of hiding, she returned to her home in Newcastle, only to be re-arrested there by police who refused to believe that she no longer constituted a recognised threat to the State. The Home Secretary suggested that any suffragettes who fell into this category give themselves up at local police stations and return to prison where the necessary paperwork would be completed, leaving them free to go. Unsurprisingly the organisers mistrusted this assurance, and on 27 August Flora Drummond led a deputation to the Home Office to demand an immediate pardon for all mice. In what proved to be the last ever militant action of the suffrage campaign, Mrs Drummond, Mary Richardson, Norah Dacre Fox, Barbara Wylie and twelve other women were arrested, but released without charge.[17] Confusion reigned.

Rachel Barrett, then editor of the *Suffragette*, had been living in Edinburgh as Miss Ashworth, as the differences between Scottish and English newspaper law made her work much safer there.[18] As soon as war had been declared, she returned to London where she attempted to impose a degree of leadership on the situation, a task that proved difficult. The suspension of the *Suffragette* lessened the spread of reliable information, and the problems that this caused among the WSPU membership were compounded by difficulties in communicating with wartime France, where Christabel still remained. Nobody was sure of the best thing to do. Rachel tried to arrange another deputation the next day in support of an immediate amnesty for all mice, including Annie Kenney and Mrs Pankhurst, but found that for the first time members were unwilling to follow an organiser in a display of militancy. One of the mice, Kitty Marion, faced a particular dilemma as she was German by birth and was afraid that any arrest would be 'misconstructed into German Aggression … and seized upon as a weapon against the WSPU by our enemies'.[19] In a letter to Mrs Callender, her suffragette friend in Liverpool, Kitty explained her actions:

> A bit of rot was talked about the honour and dignity of the Union etc., and fighting for Mrs P[ankhurst], when I promptly pointed out that we were fighting for 'Votes for Women' and if we went we would … be no 'forwarder' fighting with the police and the crowds who would not know what we were there for and no paper to tell them the truth … Others spoke much in the same strain. We were quite willing to go if there had been the slightest chance of gaining anything, but there wasn't.[20]

Kitty Marion's letter neatly captured the disarray and disillusionment that engulfed many active militants at the very end of the WSPU's suffrage campaign. Other accounts constructed after the event offered a more ordered view of the WSPU's final days as a mass organisation. Mary Richardson chose to finish her autobiography with a different version of the Home Office protest which she concluded with a description of a final address from Mrs Pankhurst at 'Mouse Castle' in London the following day:

> She came down the stairs to bid each of us an individual farewell. As she took up her station near the front door, a voice chanted the first line of 'The March of the Women' … we sang it … as I think it had never been sung before. When we had finished, not an eye was dry.[21]

This romanticised version placed Emmeline Pankhust back in London a few days before her actual date of return, and provided a neat conclusion to the WSPU's work, but the reality was closer to the confusion described by Kitty Marion. Eunice Murray, an organiser for the WFL in Scotland, was horrified that the WSPU's employees were simply cast adrift on the outbreak of war. The organisation, she recorded in her diary, had 'dissolved and left all organisers unpaid, several applied to me for help to get them to their various homes'.[22] Olive Walton, Mary Allen and Laura

Underwood were possibly among those who went to Eunice for their train fares. Meanwhile in other districts, organisers began to dismantle the mechanisms that they had worked so hard to build and maintain. In Liverpool, Helen Jollie waited listlessly at the WSPU shop, gathering in the remainder of the money from the final paper sales and clearing the shelves.[23]

At the other end of the country, Mary Blathwayt watched the Bath branch withdraw from the shop she had helped to decorate, having decided it should 'shut ... until the war is over'.[24] With no further orders being received, many organisers had no idea what to do next. Janie Allan declared herself to be 'completely unsettled as to my future action about suffrage work' when Maude Arncliffe Sennett tried to enlist her for the Northern Men's Federation for Women's Suffrage, adding that she was 'completely tired out and [had received] orders to rest'.[25] Lettice Floyd, too, who had loyally followed Annie Williams to three different centres, had had quite enough of campaigning and also described herself as 'tired out'.[26] Kitty Marion noticed 'much dissatisfaction and withdrawal' on the part of members all around her.[27] Although some suffragettes were keen to keep working for the WSPU, it was entirely unclear how they might do this.

At the beginning of September, Christabel Pankhurst, recently returned to London, carried out a series of press interviews. 'Cheery and energetic as ever', according to the *Daily Telegraph*, she made it clear that her political energy was 'about to be launched in a direction which will have the approval and support of every patriotic Englishman and English woman, whatever their attitude in regard to the suffrage movement ...'.[28] Although much of her comment was directed at men who were able to fight, Christabel had not abandoned women completely. Her ardent Francophile disposition praised the 'love of country' evidenced by all French people, but 'particularly women', and she extended this observation to Belgium which, she informed the *Telegraph*, was a country that 'appeals very much to the women of the WSPU'.[29] To a reporter from the *Daily Star*, Christabel added that a German victory would be particularly disastrous for British women: 'The women in other parts of the world regard the position of the German women as extremely unsatisfactory. They have less liberty and less influence than English, French or American women ...'. This, she claimed, was 'a chief reason' for her return.[30]

A few days later, Christabel made her first speech in Britain for several years from the stage of the London Opera House. There, the enormity of what had happened to the WSPU in the space of a month became clear to its members. Christabel spoke of the need to defend Britain at all costs, and for the government to recognise the contribution that women might make. 'In France, from which country I have just come, the women … are able to keep the country going, to get in the harvest, to carry on the industries'.[31] In the absence of conscription, she appealed to all able-bodied men to volunteer for the armed forces. Working for the war effort and defeating Germany were to be the main points of her campaign from now on. When Victor Duval, founder of the Men's Political Union for Women's Enfranchisement, raised the old cheer of 'Votes for Women' at the end of her speech, she was dismissive, declaring that 'we can't discuss that now'.[32]

Emmeline and Christabel had always been adamant that their Union comprise only those women who were in agreement with their own leadership and aims. For the past decade they had struggled to retain a sense of unity among the membership, an aim which they had achieved for the most part, although with increasing difficulty with Christabel in France and Emmeline in and out of prison. Now, as the focus of the campaign altered, the Union's chief organiser and its treasurer had no real need for the old national structures. The Union was no longer fighting the Government, nor was it co-ordinating militancy country-wide. Gertrude Harding, who had been in charge of Mrs Pankhurst's bodyguard, remained on the payroll and saw how quickly the organisation fragmented. There was no one direction – Christabel 'advised everyone to follow their own feelings of duty to the country and act as individuals'. This new approach did not require an organisation the size of the WSPU: 'Most of the organisers were let go, and only a few were kept on.'[33] Lincolns Inn House was now quite empty. Olive Bartels, Grace Roe, Flora Drummond and Annie and Jessie Kenney, who had been at the heart of the work there since the dismissal of the Pethick Lawrences, were still there, but with no paper to publish and no campaign to organise there was very little to do, and the building was let go the following year.

The WSPU's leaders now began a series of meetings to put their new position across to an interested public. Emmeline addressed audiences throughout the country, while Christabel headed across the Atlantic to rally support for an American intervention in the war. Olive Bartels went with her, but soon realised that she had made a grave mistake: 'I hated it, because I hated her line on the war. I hated the whole thing.'[34] The final straw came when the New York State Women's Suffrage Party shunned Christabel's meetings in protest at her opposition to women pacifists.[35] Olive returned to England and severed her ties with the WSPU. Christabel replaced her with Gertrude Harding, and the pair decamped for Paris. Christabel claimed that the city was 'useful as a point of observation and information', but her continued absence did nothing to endear her to what remained of her membership.[36] Meanwhile, Gertrude found that this new job could not have been more different from her organiser's work before the war. During the militant campaign even secretarial staff had been caught up in the secrecy of the movement and inspired by its excitement to some degree. Now, Gertrude faced 'ten hour days, six days a week doing mainly desk work', a dull experience for a woman who, only months earlier, was drilling and deploying the armed bodyguard which surrounded Mrs Pankhurst.[37]

Administration had always formed a large part of the workload of WSPU organisers, but the few who were retained during the war now found themselves indistinguishable from secretaries. Moreover, they were so few in number that they had to return to the original tactics which had largely passed over to the rank-and-file membership in recent years. Before leaving for Paris, Gertrude Harding was sent to organise a meeting in Manchester where she 'walked the streets ... sold tickets, got newspaper publicity' and did a dozen other things.[38] These tasks would have been quite familiar to the Manchester members from a decade before, but they were less familiar to the WSPU's remaining leaders, many of whom had joined later in the campaign when there were more than enough volunteers for such tedious jobs. Although some of the earliest members, including Lillian Williamson, were still active in women's organisations in Manchester, they took no part in Gertrude's work. Nor was this attitude restricted to the provinces. Back in London, one of Olive Bartels's final tasks for the Union was to write a letter to Elsie Duval, informing her that 'General Drummond is speaking at Hampstead Heath on Thursday next ... We want this meeting thoroughly chalked in Hampstead on Wednesday evening. I am writing to ask if you could help ... will you let me have a card by return saying whether you can or not or will you ring me up[?]'[39] Without a network of regional branches and district organisers to set campaigns like this in motion, the few remaining women had to undertake all the work themselves. No longer regarded as leaders by a large rank-and-file membership, they had no choice but to get on with the drudgery and donkey-work of building up meetings from scratch.

The organisers who either decided to leave the WSPU in August 1914 or were not offered the option of staying on tried to utilise their talents in a variety of ways. Although most of them had worked closely together for a number of years, no standard response to the war situation emerged among them. Some found that their pre-war work initially militated against them, despite the *volte-face* of their most prominent leaders. Mary Leigh applied for war service, but was rejected at first 'because of her renown as a militant trouble-maker'. When she reverted to her maiden name of Brown, she was taken on and 'put thorough a special course of instruction as an ambulance driver by the RAC'. Mrs Leigh then went to the New Zealand Army Hospital in Walton on Thames where she drove patients in ambulances around London.[40] Olive Bartels joined the War Office, but believed that 'the authorities did not know [she had been] a suffragette. Votes for Women and all that were forgotten by 1915.' Olive later went into the Women's Army Auxiliary Corps and was sent to Tours where she became unit administrator for the American Central Record Office. Her final job, which demonstrated that she had lost none of the efficiency required of her as the WSPU's chief organiser, was overseeing the demobilisation branch of Queen Mary's Army Auxiliary Corps, for which she received an OBE.[41]

Although organisers felt the need to lose their suffragette identity once they embarked on war work, they could discover that they had not been as inconspicuous as they suspected. Helen Watts had been in jail, like Mary Leigh, and had then organised in Nottingham for a short while before taking up work as a nurse in Bath.[42] She continued nursing for a while during the war, and then went into the War Office. Helen was barely able to contain herself when one day 'news of the passing of the (limited) Votes for Women Bill reached her' at work. Overwhelmed, 'she scribbled a note to a woman colleague she barely knew. Back it silently came with the comment "bear up – I did 4 months!"'[43]

Some ex-organisers found the war experience so profound that it overshadowed any previous event in their lives, including their work for the WSPU. In this they were very much in step with the attitudes of Emmeline and Christabel Pankhurst, although they may well have disagreed with their former employers' newly honed political perspectives on the war. Theresa Garnett, a former worker at headquarters, went to nurse at the Front and was mentioned in dispatches for her heroism.[44] Her later reflections on her war efforts drew no parallels with her suffrage escapades, but positioned her new work as something quite separate. Such a sense of disconnection between pre-war suffrage militancy and the work done after war had been declared was not uncommon among former suffragettes. Teresa Garnett would have concurred with the sentiments expressed by Cicely Hamilton, WSPU activist and voluntary worker, on hearing that the vote had finally been granted. At the time Cicely was in northern France, working with the Scottish Women's Hospitals' Association. She wrote:

> I remember … receiving the official intimation that my name had been placed on the register of the Chelsea electorate. I was in Abbeville …

an enemy airplane was over taking photographs. I remember thinking as I read that notice of all that suffrage had meant for us a year or two before! How we had marched for the suffrage, and held meetings and been shouted at, and how friends of mine … had hurled themselves at policemen and broken windows and starved themselves in prison, and that now … what really interested me was not the thought of voting at the next election, but the puff of smoke that the Archies sent after the escaping plane [overhead]. Truth to tell, at that moment I didn't care a button for my vote; and rightly or wrongly I have always imagined that the Government gave it me in much the same mood as I received it.[45]

Others reacted quite differently to the end of the suffragettes' militant campaign. Rather than regarding it as a closed chapter, they desperately looked around for work that would match the satisfaction that they had found in political organising. Mary Allen certainly did not find the enormity of her war experiences sufficient to eclipse memories of her suffrage work. For her, it contrasted poorly with the excitement of working as an organiser in a militant society. Mary felt that war work was actually a step backwards, believing that for any of the many women 'who had been leaders and organisers in the tumultuous tide of the suffrage campaign, the ordinary channels of usefulness for the weaker sex in wartime – nursing, canteen work, sewing societies etc – made preciously little appeal'.[46] Mary consequently looked to the more flamboyant wartime initiative which saw women performing police duties and offered her the sort of experience she missed badly from her WSPU days. Not only did this attract similar levels of media attention, but Mary also hoped that it would offer her renewed opportunities to lead large numbers of volunteers rather than simply to take her place in the ranks of a larger organisation in which she would no longer be a leader in any sense.

A small number of ex-organisers tried to keep a suffrage campaign of sorts alive during the years of the war. While none of them went so far as to suggest a resumption or continuation of militancy, there were increasing levels of disquiet among the rank-and-file membership concerning the way that Emmeline and Christabel Pankhurst were presenting the WSPU's response to war. Admittedly, these were quite slow to materialise. The WSPU's immediate response of August 1914 was not noticeably out of step with those of other suffrage societies, and its decision to suspend militancy came slightly later than that of the WFL. It was only in the ensuing months that it became clear that the WSPU leadership was formulating a different concept of patriotism from that embraced by many other feminist groups. The reappearance of the *Suffragette*, with a largely altered content, in April 1915, and the decision to rename the paper the *Britannia* the following October, provoked anxiety among those who were not in total accord with the Union's direction since the outbreak of war.

Although a level of commitment to women's citizenship remained within the paper, it now spoke predominantly for 'King, Country and Freedom'.[47] Within its pages Christabel called for 'the military conscription of men and the industrial conscription of women', along with 'internment of all people of enemy race'.[48] When it became obvious that there was to be no return to the earlier work of the WSPU, the patience of members who sought a different campaign evaporated. Some attempted to challenge the Pankhursts directly about what they saw as the misappropriation of the WSPU's name and its funds. Mary Leigh, who had gone to Paris to confront Christabel over what she perceived as her lack of concern for militants during the height of the campaign, again challenged her former employers at one of the WSPU's regular meetings at the London Pavilion. When Mrs Pankhurst 'made remarks damaging to English women and in praise of the French', Mrs Leigh 'from the Gallery called "question, question".'[49] Mrs Pankhurst retorted: '[T]hat woman is pro German and should leave the Hall'.[50] When Mary repudiated this accusation, Mrs Pankhurst snapped out: 'I denounce you as a pro German and I wish to forget that such a person ever existed.'[51] The following week Mary Leigh called on fellow-suffragettes to protest and demand an apology, but Mrs Pankhurst refused calls from the gallery, declaring that if Mrs Leigh 'was not a pro-German, certainly her actions made it appear as if she were'.[52] Annie Bell, one of the WSPU's final prisoners, was thrown out and then denied admission to a further WSPU meeting, despite her continued membership. Annie reacted in traditional suffragette style, and was arrested for causing a disturbance outside the hall. She was jailed for a week, and immediately went on hunger-strike, her gestures offering an ironic counterpoint to the Pankhurst's current emphasis on co-operation with the authorities.[53]

Other suffragettes sought to redirect the WSPU by challenging its leaders in a more organised fashion. A group of disgruntled members, including some former organisers, began to criticise the Union publicly. Their action was unprecedented – even during the split of 1912 the Pethick Lawrences had refrained from any open discussion of the way they had been treated and kept their feelings to themselves. Now, some London members met 'informally ... to discuss the general situation and the possibility of continuing the struggle for peace and all which the vote entails'.[54] Elsie Duval and Miss F. Haughton were appointed the group's honorary organisers, and set to work 'to rally as many members of the WSPU as they could reach for a meeting of protest against the abandonment of suffrage work'.[55] Their job was made much more difficult by the legacy of the intense government pressure which had been brought to bear on the WSPU up to 1914.

After successive police raids on Clements Inn and Lincolns Inn, there were no coherent sets of records remaining that could be used to put activists in contact with one another. The *Suffragette* offered contact addresses for district organisers up to August 1914, but many of these were at offices no longer occupied by the Union. Most of its district organisers had been deployed away from their home towns and had no reason to stay in their new bases once the WSPU's formal work had ended. Some returned home and some 'joined other organisations or entered at best they could into national service of one kind or another', in Britain or abroad.[56] Those seeking to reactivate the campaign a year later faced an uphill struggle in simply finding their former colleagues and co-workers, who were now scattered throughout Britain, and sometimes beyond. The admirable infrastructure of the Union, which at its peak had surpassed those of most of its contemporary political organisations, no longer existed.

On 22 October, such sympathetic members as could be reached were invited to a meeting at Caxton Hall, a poignant location given its association with the Women's Parliaments. The audience was drawn mainly from around London, but some provincial members did manage to attend, while others, including the Liverpool Suffrage Club, sent messages of support to the project. The chair was taken by Rose Larmatine Yates, one of the most active members of Wimbledon WSPU. Recent accounts of Rose have placed her among the more difficult elements of the WSPU, who were 'open critics from within' and regarded with suspicion by the leadership; but while she'd had disagreements with elements of the campaign, Rose had nevertheless remained a constant member of the WSPU and had worked staunchly in its name, never moving against its structure.[57] Even now, as she chaired a meeting that commentators more hostile to the WSPU seized on as proof of a final split in its ranks, Rose's words were measured.[58] She had, she said, 'not the slightest desire … to criticise the merely personal opinions and actions of any official of the WSPU'. Rather, her protest was restricted to the way that the Union's 'name, its influence and its official paper had been autocratically deflected by those same officials into work of a non-suffrage character'.[59]

Dorothy Evans, a former WSPU organiser, was also present. Imprisoned in Ireland in 1914, she had been one of the final suffragette prisoners to be released, whereupon she had returned to England and managed to resume her teaching career despite worries that her record of militancy would militate against her. Dorothy was itching to get back to political work. She offered the meeting 'some practical suggestions as to the possibilities of future work', urging 'women of the Union ... [to] make up for lost time'.[60] A resolution was then passed and forwarded to Lincolns Inn that protested at the way the Union's 'name and its platform [were] no longer used for women's suffrage', and called for the publication of a balance sheet and a set of properly audited accounts. No reply was received.

At the next gathering, on 25 November, Eleanor Penn Gaskell presided over the drawing up of a manifesto. This made it clear that one of the most contentious issues was the way in which the Union's structure had been wasted, despite its comparative financial affluence at the outbreak of war. Those present condemned the fact that the Union, 'with its widespread organisation and network of local unions and branches throughout the country, might, undoubtedly, during the war, have done work of inestimable value to the nation'. 'The majority of the members', it was felt, 'would, if consulted, have been in favour of keeping the entire organisation ... alive and active' for 'national and patriotic purposes', including 'safeguarding the interests of women and children'. Instead, the Union had effectively been disbanded without consultation.[61] The manifesto was forwarded to Mrs Pankhurst, but again no reply was forthcoming. Consequently, on 4 December, Rose Larmatine Yates chaired another meeting at St George's Hall, Bloomsbury, to cement an organisational structure for the newly-united dissident members of the WSPU.

The dissenting meetings had attracted a level of publicity in the national press, where articles aired suffragettes' questions as to whether 'Mrs Pankhurst's ... present power over an organisation which she has no moral or possibly even legal right to control' could continue uncontested.[62] Not all members agreed with the dissenters. Several letters were sent to the second meeting in support of those suffragettes who were 'devoting [themselves] to war work' or 'recuperation' rather than 'maintaining and preaching our rights and citizenship'.[63] But enough felt sufficiently strongly for a new society to be initiated. Mary Leigh and Dorothy Evans were among the former organisers who attended. Gladys Evans and Dr Helena Jones were also involved. They came onto the new body's committee in March 1916, and Mary Richardson wrote some articles for its newspaper. The first meeting decided that the group should call itself the 'Suffragettes of the WSPU' (SWSPU) and be constituted 'on the same terms as the original membership cards'. Numerous resolutions were passed, including a pledge not to 'make any form of personal attack upon our late leaders of the WSPU', but to concentrate on 'working for Votes for Women'.[64] The *Suffragette News Sheet*, which became the SWSPU's paper, largely kept to this, although Helena Jones did comment that Mrs Pankhurst had 'gone over to the enemy' in an article written in September 1916.[65] The SWSPU continued to be active throughout the war. Its work replicated the early days of WSPU militancy, with public paper sales (co-ordinated by Annie Bell), public meetings in London parks (often with other suffrage societies) and regular 'At Homes' held in a room in the Emily Davison Lodge which was offered at 'a nominal rent'.[66] However, despite Dorothy Evans's commitment to an 'open declaration that we are ... made of the same stuff of which our pre-war fighting union was made', attacks on property did not feature.[67] Rather, the SWSPU gave suffragettes a space where they could meet together as suffragettes, despite the other pressures and commitments and attendant identities of wartime. It also enabled a small number of organisers to continue their political work, albeit on a much-reduced scale. Not all dissenters felt that this was enough. One woman wrote to Maude Arncliffe Sennet that the decisions passed on 22 October fell short of her expectations: 'I would have had the WSPU doing national work under its own flag and name and using at the same time every opportunity to advance our cause ...'.[68]

The SWSPU was not the only group to form from the remnants of the WSPU during the war. A further gathering on 21 March 1916 established the Independent Women's Social and Political Union (IWSPU). This new organisation, which embraced 'the old pledge card of the WSPU ... until such time as the members decide to frame a constitution for themselves', appealed to members who wished to 'work in the spirit of the old WSPU'.[69] The IWSPU succeeded in establishing a more robust national structure than the SWSPU's, although neither approached the size and scope of the original Union. Dorothy Evans, who left the SWSPU for the newer organisation, acted as its provincial organiser and addressed meetings across the country, while her former fellow-WSPU organiser Charlotte Marsh became the IWSPU's organising secretary. The historian Jacqueline de Vries has suggested that the IWSPU was attractive to women like Charlotte and Dorothy as it was 'more hostile to the Pankhursts' than was the SWSPU, although with so few copies of the former group's paper, the *Independent Suffragette*, surviving, it is difficult to offer any firm confirmation of this.[70] One thing that is clear is that the IWSPU was not confined to London. Although the *Suffragette News Sheet* offered some coverage of regional activities by supporters of the SWSPU, including those of one of the WSPU's earliest members, Lillian Forrester Williamson in Manchester, these reports were concerned largely with existing suffrage societies such as the Men's League for Women's Suffrage.[71] The IWSPU, by contrast, established proper branches in Preston (run by Edith

Rigby) and Glasgow. Zoe Procter, another WSPU member who went into the IWSPU by way of the SWSPU, recalled it as having 'members in a great many provincial towns', although neither she nor the *Independent Suffragette* provide a great deal of detail as to what these members actually did.[72]

For all the enthusiasm of some WSPU members to keep a campaign in public view during the First World War, conditions made this extremely difficult. Funds were almost impossible to raise. In February 1917, the IWSPU appealed to its supporters for a typewriter and a duplicator to help with propagandising. 'The price of the latter is 7s 6d', the paper announced, 'and the Treasurer is most anxious to acknowledge the receipt of that sum from a kind donor.'[73] This was a far cry from the thousands of pounds that the WSPU was once able to raise at a single meeting. With so many other things demanding people's time and attention, it was a struggle to keep the issue of suffrage prominent in the public eye. Why did some organisers bother to try to do this at all, given the other pressures on their lives in wartime, and the other directions for work that were available? Dora Marsden, who spent the First World War in literary rather than political work, unwittingly anticipated the response of those who would not leave the WSPU in a piece she wrote about Mary Leigh in August 1912. Women like Mrs Leigh, she explained, stayed in the WSPU, despite reservations about certain policies or tactics, out of a loyalty that had as much to do with themselves than with their view of the rights or wrongs of the WSPU's leaders:

> Her view of the WSPU is that of several others, to wit that it is her Union, an organisation which she has helped build up into a power by the passion of her own soul and the untellable hardships she has undergone. Therefore she refused to abandon it. When Mrs Pankhurst says if you do not like it, go, the retort is I don't like a good deal of it, but I shall not therefore go, and she remains jealous of its honour and political repute as in its earliest days of trial and sincerity.[74]

Not all organisers who wished to continue suffrage work felt that the WSPU could be saved, or even that there was still some point in trying to do so. Rather than attempt to redirect their work into newly formed subgroups, they managed to carry on their work during the war via existing suffrage societies. The United Suffragists, a group that formed in February 1914 to bridge an increasing gap between 'above ground … constitutional agitation' and the 'underground' militant wing of the suffrage movement, attracted a fair number of former WSPU workers after war had broken out.[75] At first the United Suffragists had made little headway in the provinces, but the decision of Emmeline and Frederick Pethick

Lawrence to make *VFW* the group's official newspaper helped spread awareness of its existence beyond London. The hand-over was set for August 1914, so co-incidentally the United Suffragists came into the provinces at exactly the same time that the WSPU's national organisation collapsed. Several WSPU branches made use of this fact. In Bolton, a small group, 'dismayed at the prospect of other suffrage societies laying down their arms ... decided to form a branch of the U[nited] S[uffragists]' out of their own WSPU branch.[76]

Organisers, too, benefited from the United Suffragists. Ada Flatman, Mary Richardson and Mary Phillips all found work therein during the war, although their jobs were less secure than they had been in the WSPU. With no militancy continuing and not much in the way of organisational structure, there was not a great deal of work for organisers to do. Many contented themselves with small gestures such as continuing to wear suffragette badges and holding social gatherings based around institutions like the Emily Davison Lodge in London and the suffrage club that met in Liverpool throughout the war.

Campaigns which were run, such as those aimed at securing better employment conditions for women involved in war work, were reactive and lacked the innovation that had characterised much of the militant campaign. The glamour had gone out of suffrage work, as previous investors realised: 'You must sigh over the depleted state of our advertising columns', wrote Evelyn Sharp, in March 1915, to Ada Flatman, who had seen the WSPU in its heyday. 'Our only consolation is that I do think we get more than most people but our finance is not our strong point at the present moment. The war gets more frightful every day. Prices go up, up, up: and incomes go down.'[77] Indeed, it was this lack of funding that seemed to finally end Mary Phillips's long association with suffrage work. In February 1916, Emmeline Pethick Lawrence wrote to Mary:

> Sorry that you are leaving the U[nited] S[uffragists] for I know your whole heart is in the women's movement. I am sorry to say that at present there is no possibility of paid work on the staff of the W[omen's] I[nternational] L[eague] and I cannot see any development of that kind ahead.[78]

The remnant of the WSPU, such as it now was, continued behind Emmeline and Christabel Pankhurst's jingoistic, anti-German offensive. Gigantic processions and parades for women's war work were organised in 1915 and 1916 which held echoes of the WSPU's monster demonstrations of the previous decade, except that they were now funded by the Liberal Government.[79] Flora Drummond again toured the country organising women workers, but this time her rallies aimed at directing them into munitions' factories rather than polling booths. As the WSPU's industrial campaign increased in pace, a few organisers who approved of its direction found themselves re-employed. Cynthia Maguire and Phyllis Ayrton, who had run the Clerks branch of the WSPU before the outbreak of war, were taken on and spent prolonged periods in provincial centres. Yet despite some continuity of personnel, the campaign bore little resemblance to their pre-war WSPU work. The organisation was a shadow of what it had been. Gertrude Harding recalled lengthy periods between salary checks, and sent desperate wires saying 'starving, no money' in the hope that this would rectify matters.[80] She feared that the WSPU was running out of money and, despite the broadly approbatory reception of its new campaign by the political establishment, gave up organising to work as a driver for a Kensington store. Cynthia Maguire and Phyllis Ayrton worked on, but found that in most places where they were sent, WSPU branches no longer functioned, and old, faithful workers could not be relied on to work. In most cases, they were drawing on a completely new base of women. The WSPU name was effectively redundant.

The WSPU's patriotic campaign was aimed entirely at the war effort, and not at building a large, autonomous, all-female organisation. Not that organisers who remained in more overtly feminist groups were faring much better. Even the most ardent opponents of the new direction of the WSPU baulked at resuming militancy during the war. Most suffrage societies returned to low-level propagandising activities; and in the majority of branches there were activists who by that time had considerable experience of such work and a co-ordinating district organiser was not necessary, even if one could be afforded. After the Representation of the People Bill had passed through the House of Lords in January 1918, suffrage organisers had no further role. A triumphant edition of *VFW* announced that success – and the simultaneous decision to wind up the United Suffragists – in March. The vote for women had been granted. The campaign was finally over.

Notes

1   All information from *Suffragette*, 31 July 1914.

2   Ethel Smyth, *Female Pipings in Eden* (London: Peter Davies, 1933), p. 235.

3   Raeburn, *Militant Suffragettes*, p. 235.

4   Confidential memo, 27 July 1914, TNA, HO 45 24665/253239/9.

5   *Suffragette*, 7 August 1914.

6   Raeburn, *Militant Suffragettes*, pp. 219–20; E. S. Pankhurst, *The Suffragette Movement*, pp. 557–61.

7 Elsie Bowerman, statement to David Mitchell, Mitchell Collection.
8 Kitty Marion typescript autobiography, SFC, p. 268.
9 Raeburn, *Militant Suffragettes*, p. 238.
10 'Auntie Maggie' (Kitty Marion) to Mrs Callender, 29 August 1914, SFC.
11 E. S. Pankhurst, *The Suffragette Movement*, p. 591.
12 TNA, HO 45 24665/253239/12.
13 *Ibid.*
14 *The Times*, 11 August 1914.
15 WSPU circular letter, 12 August 1914, Mary Phillips Papers.
16 Wilson, *With All Her Might*, p. 169; Dorothy Evans notes, SFC.
17 *The Times*, 28 August 1914; *VFW*, 4 September 1914; TNA, HO 45 253239/20.
18 Rachel Barret notes, SFC.
19 Kitty Marion, typescript autobiography, p. 271.
20 'Auntie Maggie' (Kitty Marion) to Mrs Callender, 29 August 1914, SFC.
21 Richardson, *Laugh a Defiance*, p. 191.
22 Eunice Murray's diary, October 1914, quoted in Leneman, *A Guid Cause*, p. 209.
23 Alice Ker's diary, September 1914, private collection.
24 Mary Blathwayt's diary, 15 August 1914, quoted by B. M. Willmot Dobie, *A Nest of Suffragettes in Somerset* (Bath: Ralph Allen Press, 1979), p. 50.
25 Janie Allan to Maude Arncliffe Sennett, 15 August 1914, Maude Arncliffe Sennett Collection.
26 Lettice Floyd to Edith How Martyn, 1 February 1931, SFC.
27 Kitty Marion, autobiography, p. 270, SFC.
28 *Daily Telegraph*, 4 September 1914.
29 *Ibid.*
30 *Daily Star*, 4 September 1914.
31 Christabel Pankhurst, 'The war: a speech delivered at the London Opera House on September 8th 1914', WSPU pamphlet, SFC.
32 David Mitchell, *Women on the Warpath: The Story of the Women of the First World War* (London: Jonathan Cape, 1966), p. 49.
33 Wilson, *With All Her Might*, p. 170.
34 Bartels to Harrison, Harrison Tapes.
35 Pugh, *The Pankhursts*, p. 305.
36 C. Pankhurst, *Unshackled*, p. 289.
37 Wilson, *With All Her Might*, p. 172.
38 *Ibid.*, pp. 170–1.
39 Olive Bartels to Elsie Duval, 24 May 1915, Duval Papers, Women's Library.
40 Mary Leigh to David Mitchell, 21 March 1965, Mitchell Collection.
41 Olive Bartels to David Mitchell, n.d., Mitchell Collection.
42 Emily Blathwayt's diary, 13 April 1911, Blathwayt Diaries.
43 *Calling All Women*, February 1967.
44 Obituary, *International Women's News*, 1967, Autobiographical Cuttings Files, Women's Library.
45 Cicely Hamilton, *Life Errant* (London: J. M. Dent, 1935), pp. 67–8.
46 Mary Allen, *The Pioneer Policewoman* (London: Chatto & Windus, 1925), p. 17.
47 *Britannia*, masthead by-line, October 1915–1918.
48 E. S. Pankhurst, *The Suffragette Movement*, p. 594.

49 Typescript, 'Particulars of a slander on Mary Leigh uttered by Mrs Pankhurst at the Pavilion on October 28th 1915', Maude Arncliffe Sennet Collection.

50 *Ibid.*

51 *Ibid.*

52 *Morning Advertiser*, 5 November 1915.

53 Mitchell, *Women on the Warpath*, p. 50.

54 *Suffragette News Sheet*, December 1915.

55 *Ibid.*

56 *Standard*, 27 November 1915.

57 Morley with Stanley, *The Life and Death of Emily Wilding Davison*, p. 176.

58 See, for example, the *Labour Leader*, 2 November 1915.

59 *Jus Suffragii*, 1 November 1915.

60 *Ibid.*

61 *Standard*, 27 November 1915.

62 *Daily News & Leader*, 17 November 1915.

63 *Suffragette News Sheet*, March 1916.

64 *Ibid.*, December 1915.

65 *Ibid.*, September 1916.

66 *Ibid.*, March 1916.

67 *Ibid.*, December 1915.

68 'Dulcie' to Maude, 25 October 1915, Maude Arncliffe Sennett Collection.

69 *Independent Suffragette*, May 1917.

70 Jaqueline de Vries, 'Gendering patriotism: Emmeline and Christabel Pankhurst and World War One', in Sybil Oldfield (ed.), *This Working Day World: Women's Lives and Cultures in Britain 1914–1945* (London: Taylor & Francis, 1994), pp. 75–88, at p. 79. There are two copies of the *Independent Suffragette* in the British Newspaper Library, for September 1916 and February 1917 (issue numbers 2 and 6); the Cavendish Bentick Collection at the Women's Library, London, holds further copies for June 1917 and June–July 1918 (issues 10, 22 and 23). No other copies have been traced.

71 *Suffragette News Sheet*, June 1916.

72 Zoe Procter, *Life and Yesterday* (London: Favil Press, 1960), p. 119.

73 *Independent Suffragette*, February 1917.

74 *Freewoman*, 22 August 1912.

75 *VFW*, 10 July 1914; for the United Suffragists, see Cowman, '"A party between revolution and peaceful persuasion?"'

76 *VFW*, 20 August 1915.

77 Evelyn Sharp to Ada Flatman, 3 March 1915, SFC.

78 Emmeline Pethick Lawrence to Mary Phillips, 8 February 1916, Mary Phillips Papers.

79 Nicolette F. Gullace, *The Blood of Our Sons: Men, Women and the Renegotiation of British Citizenship during the Great War* (Basingstoke: Macmillan, 2002), p. 126.

80 Wilson, *With All Her Might*, p. 185.

Conclusion

IT WAS THE OUTBREAK OF WAR in August 1914 rather than the final victory of their own campaign in January 1918 that made most of the WSPU's organisers redundant. The celebrations arranged by suffragettes to mark the gaining of the vote revealed what had become of the movement during the war. A modest victory dinner at the Lyceum bore no comparison with the monster demonstrations and militant skirmishes that had characterised the campaign in the preceding years, but was an anti-climatic finale to a movement, albeit one which had long ceased to function on a large scale.[1] At the time when Parliament approved a limited Women's Franchise Bill, most of the women who had been on the WSPU's payroll before 1914 had been scattered, by war, throughout Britain and beyond in a variety of jobs. Now, as the end of the war approached, these former organisers were unable to pick up their previous suffrage work but had to find something else to do. Women who had abandoned careers to work for the WSPU faced a choice between returning to their original paths or searching for new openings. Others who had not worked prior to their WSPU days also wondered whether their experiences might translate into permanent job opportunities.

While some organisers augmented their CVs with their recent war experiences, others were adamant that it was their WSPU work that had afforded their excellent grounding for future independent careers. In the 1960s, Elsie Bowerman told David Mitchell that the WSPU's 'habit of trusting young women with extremely responsible administration work' had been 'excellent training', while Olive Bartels was certain that it was in her work for the Union that she had developed the administrative skills she later used as organiser for the National Union of Women Teachers.[2] Yet, although suffrage-organising brought women experience they could transpose to many different fields, there was no single career trajectory for an ex-organiser. The importance of suffrage work in shaping women's

later careers may consequently have been underestimated, fueling interpretations of women's involvement in the militant campaign as a short-
lived pastime rather than a form of serious political activity that would
prepare them for careers.

Working for the WSPU offered women political work at a time when
the formal structures of Westminster remained closed to them, so it was
not surprising that some ex-organisers sought similar opportunities after
the war. Women were quick to test whether all political jobs now lay within
their reach. Now that they had the vote, might they also become MPs? To
test this, Nina Boyle of the WFL offered herself to the electorate of Keigh-
ley in the first by-election after the Representation of the People Act. Her
disqualification on technical grounds prompted a broader debate, and
further legislative change, confirming women's eligibility as parliamentary candidates. While suffragettes welcomed this new decision, its timing
was inauspicious, as only twenty-three days remained until the close of
nominations, posing a major hurdle for any woman hoping for a party
endorsement. The Labour, Liberal and Conservative Parties had each
identified suitable male candidates some time previously. Things were
not much easier for independent candidates: three-and-a-bit weeks was
barely long enough to get nomination papers together, let alone to work
up a new constituency without the help of an existing party machine.[3]

One ex-organiser, despite these obstacles, was determined to make
her way to Westminster. From its earliest days, the WSPU had nursed high
hopes for the political futures of its more prominent workers, and Teresa
Billington recalled excited conversations in the Manchester office before
the move to London when younger suffragettes eagerly 'prophesied a
Premiership for mother and Christabel on the Woolsack', tales which
'elder' members (including Teresa, then in her late twenties) heard with
humour, but not with incredulity.[4] Mrs Pankhurst was willing to stand
aside herself at this point, but she still cherished hopes of a political career
for her daughter. Christabel, too, retained her parliamentary ambitions,
and she, her mother and the WSPU's remaining organisers began to cast
around for an appropriate constituency, laying plans for the final fulfilment of early suffragette dreams.

Christabel's campaign challenged the gendering of British politics,
eschewing the 'men's party political machinery and traditions, which ...
leave so much to be desired' in favour of the WSPU's woman-centred
approach.[5] Sex, not class or party, would be the feature which determined
where on the ballot paper the newly enfranchised woman would place her
cross. To that end, in November 1917, the Women's Social and Political
Union renamed itself the Women's Party (WP), anticipating the final pass-

ing of the 1918 Act. The loyal Flora Drummond became its chief organiser and Annie Kenney stepped into the secretary's post; Mrs Pankhurst was the treasurer and Christabel edited *Britannia*. Cynthia Maguire and Phyllis Ayrton became WP organisers, and continued their district campaigns in industrial regions. Their programme, 'a strange amalgam of apparently conflicting ideas', mixed Christabel and Emmeline Pankhurst's new-found opposition to all things socialist or Bolshevik with schemes for social improvements such as communal housekeeping which could just as easily have been lifted from the rhetoric of the pre-war ILP.[6] Yet, despite the new party's potential to carry through many of the broader feminist concerns that had underpinned the WSPU's agitation, the divisions opened up by the Pankhursts' attitude towards suffrage work during the war remained raw, and few WSPU former members returned to the fold. Christabel was the WP's sole candidate. She stood at Smethwick in Staffordshire (after a brief flirtation with the Wiltshire constituency of Westbury) where the Unionist candidate, Major Thompson, stood down to increase her chances at the request of party leader Bonar Law. With her were a small number of WSPU ex-organisers, including Phyllis Ayrton, Barbara Wylie and Elsie Bowerman, the last of whom worked as Christabel's election agent. Their campaign echoed many that they had run for the WSPU before the war, only this time they fought to put their candidate in rather than to keep a Liberal out.

Despite their considerable electioneering experience, Christabel was defeated in a straight fight against J. E. Davison, the Labour nominee. This was an unworthy end to the election for which the WSPU had long worked, and the fact that Christabel persuaded over 8,000 of the electorate to vote for her was cold comfort against Davison's majority of a little over 700. There was irony, too, in the knowledge that Christabel had polled more votes than had any other woman standing in the election, including Constance Markiewiez ,who took St Patrick's ward in Dublin for Sinn Féin but refused to take her seat in accordance with her party's position. Had she not rejected Westbury, it seems entirely credible that Christabel would have been the first woman to sit in the British Parliament.[7]

Marginal or not, the defeat marked the end Christabel's attempts to capitalise on the 'perfect victory' of her organisation.[8] Disappointed and disillusioned, she withdrew from political life and threw her remaining energies into the Second Day Adventist movement. The failure of the WP experiment removed an obvious route into Parliament for many ex-organisers. One of the WSPU's more significant achievements had been its ability to unite large numbers of women behind its campaign, regardless of the other differences separating them. The WP had hoped to sustain this sex-based approach to political work by creating a party that would consistently elevate the needs and wants of a new female electorate. It believed that a 'sex-based party' was the only way to combat the fact that 'the subjects in which women [were] particularly interested, children, housing and the condition of female labour, [were] unlikely to receive proper legislative attention if the women's vote [were to be] absorbed by existing political parties'.[9] Once the WP collapsed, organisers who wished to remain in political life had no obvious platform. Some attempted to retain some form of feminist identity by standing as independent candidates: Norah Dacre Fox, who had stayed in the WSPU throughout the war, followed this route in her unsuccessful attempt on Parliament in Richmond, Surrey, in 1918. Others recognised that they would probably have to work within existing parties after all, although this divided them as a group and shattered the previous unity attained within the WSPU.

Emmeline Pethick Lawrence realised this immediately and returned to her political roots to stand unsuccessfully as a Labour candidate at Rusholme, Manchester, in 1918. By 1922, ex-organisers were seen on opposing sides, albeit contesting different seats. Mary Richardson and Barbara Ayrton Gould won Labour nominations while Mary Allen and Helen Fraser fought seats as Liberal and National Liberal candidates. None succeeded, women candidates proving too much of a novelty for many constituencies. More galling than failure for many former suffragettes was that the first woman MP, Nancy Astor, had no connection to their movement. Rather, as Adela Pankhurst grimly observed, she had 'got whatever benefit there was to be got from our campaign and never did a single thing to help it along'.[10] Few of those who had given up their lives, careers and leisure time to work for the vote managed to take their experiences into Westminster. It was not until 1945 that Barbara Ayrton Gould, elected for North Hendon as Labour Party candidate (her fifth attempt) became the first and only WSPU ex-organiser to sit in the House of Commons.

Although Parliament never housed a significant number of ex-organisers, electioneering did bring short-lived opportunities for some of them. In 1925 Emmeline Pankhurst returned to England after living variously in Canada and France, and was persuaded to accept the Conservative Party candidature for Whitechapel. Much has been said on the Left about the 'utterly amazing, infinitely sad' irony of the former member of the ILP's executive ending her political days among her earlier opponents, but the way in which Emmeline conducted her campaign displayed more continuity with her political roots than might be expected.[11] Despite her official candidacy, and her admiration for Stanley Baldwin, her relations with the party's Central Office were somewhat strained. June Purvis has suggested that in their eyes Emmeline, 'without money, property, landed family connections or even a motor car … was not true blue'.[12] Certainly her impoverished status did not ease her passage among the Tory elite, but nor did her continued determination to do things her own way. Emmeline gathered a small group of former suffragettes around her to organise a campaign that was directed towards women more than party. Kitty Marshall and Barbara Wylie helped her form a women's club in the constituency.[13] While avoiding much of the official Conservative machine, Emmeline hoped her new status as a party candidate could help WSPU former colleagues who were still searching for political work. Nellie Hall (now Mrs Humpherson), the daughter of Emmeline's old Manchester ILP colleagues Leonard and Pattie Hall, who had been one of the last organisers taken on by the WSPU in 1913, now heard from her:

> Would you like to come to me for say three months with the prospect of continuing with me or the Conservative Party afterwards … Even if I cannot raise funds to continue, it would be an introduction to the 'powers' of the party and would lead probably to something better … you could connect up with me and do the friendly human kind of work in connection with women generally.[14]

Nellie arrived in the constituency and worked hard, but her hopes for future work ended with her employer's death. Emmeline's predictions that her adopted party would recognise the potential of ex-suffrage workers was incorrect, and, once she had gone, her concerns for politicising the working women of her constituency were largely abandoned. The Conservative Party had no place for Nellie Hall. She contacted Christabel, who was equally unable to help but expressed surprise at the lack of openings for ex-organisers in political work, opining that she 'should have thought that the need of woman organisers would be very great'. Christabel advised Nellie to contact Cynthia Maguire and also to place a 'little notice in the personal column of the monthly post …'.[15] In the event, no work came, and Nellie and her family emigrated to Canada the following year, playing no further part in British politics.

While Emmeline Pankhurst's brief involvement with the Conservative Party did little to persuade its officials of the political value of ex-suffrage organisers, others from the ranks of her former employees had been building up their own political networks within existing parties that went beyond the parliamentary arena, in local government or as non-elected activists. For some, this was a return to previous affiliations and commitments which had lessened or been temporarily abandoned during their time as suffragettes. Others were new to party politics, but they regarded this shift as a natural progression from their suffragette work. As with those who stood as parliamentary candidates, there was no universal direction in terms of party affiliation. A small, but subsequently highly publicised, group of ex-organisers moved to the extreme right of the political spectrum in the inter-war years. In Australia Adela Pankhurst, who had been an ardent socialist and pacifist during the First World War, was interned for 'loose and generally pro-Japanese talk' from the platforms of Australia First, the nationalist organisation she had co-founded in 1941.[16]

At home, some ex-organisers were associated with the British Union of Fascists in the 1930s. Norah Dacre-Fox, who was then married to Dudley Elam, joined the BUF in 1934 and became the party's county women's officer for West Sussex.[17] Mary Richardson signed up to the BUF and was chief organiser of its women's section.[18] Mary Allen also actively supported the BUF, although she did not go so far as to take office.[19] Both Mary Richardson and Norah Elam used their suffragette experiences to explain their new political beliefs. For Mary, the Blackshirts 'stood for the same values of courage, loyalty and service as the Suffragettes had done', while Norah believed her new party to be concerned about the 'momentous issues raised by the militant women of a generation ago'.[20] The use that these two prominent ex-suffragette fascists made of their own political biographies when explaining their new beliefs has encouraged historians to search for 'some logic in their personal progress from the WSPU to the BUF'.[21] Indeed, Martin Pugh has gone so far as to suggest that Christabel Pankhurst was 'on the high road that leads to fascism' by 1917.[22] Yet although the attention that Mary Allen, Mary Richardson and Norah Elam have received implies that for ex-organisers looking for a continuity of political work fascism was the 'natural successor to militant suffragism', several of their former colleagues would have disputed the linearity.[23]

Rather than moving towards fascism, a clear majority of the WSPU's former workers who went into party politics found a more natural home on the left of the political spectrum. Hannah Mitchell, who had begun her political life as a socialist before joining the WSPU and then the WFL, returned to the ILP and socialist campaigning after the end of the war. Annot Robinson, who had worked with Hannah in Manchester, prefigured Hannah's move by organising for the WLL after she left the WSPU before the war. Other organisers who had remained in the WSPU for longer also took up socialist affiliations. Molly Murphy went on to work for the Communist Party after the war, together with her husband Jack. Mary Phillips, who had written a longstanding column for the Glasgow-based socialist newspaper *Forward* when working for the

WSPU, mentioned in a 1961 memorial pamphlet to her former organising colleague Charlotte Marsh that one of the strongest links between
them was 'a common interest in left-wing politics'.[24] Mary Gawthorpe,
who had given up organising for the WLL in favour of a WSPU post,
also returned to her political roots. She moved to America during the
war, and remained there after her marriage, working for a variety of left-
leaning causes including the Delaware Consumers' League and the Cook
County Labour Party in Chicago. Jennie Baines, who the WSPU helped
to emigrate to Australia in 1913 under the surname 'Evans' while she was
released from prison under the Cat and Mouse Act, joined the Victorian
Socialist Party, then the Communist Party, returning to the Labour Party
in Melbourne. Her final imprisonment was in March 1919 for flying the
Red Flag in defiance of local prohibitions. Mary Leigh, who had always
gone her own way within the WSPU, was 'still a socialist' at the end of
her life, and regularly took part in May Day demonstrations as well as the
Aldermaston Marches organised by the Campaign for Nuclear Disarma-
ment, always in her WSPU colours.[25]

The presence of ex-organisers at both ends of the political spectrum
suggests that there was no direct route from suffrage into any one particular political party, as well as reflecting the diversity of class and political
backgrounds among the women who worked for the WSPU during its
active campaign. Although socialist and fascist parties provided opportunities for suffragettes to continue to shape their political interests into
a meaningful career, others among their former colleagues felt that there
were too many compromises involved in developing party loyalties.

The woman-centred focus of the WSPU's political analysis provided
a unique structure, with complete reliance on women at every level of
the organisation, throughout its existence. All of its speakers, clerical
workers, volunteers and paid staff were female; male supporters could
not even become full members – indeed, excepting Frederick Pethick
Lawrence, who did editorial work, and the odd office boy, there was no
role for men within its ranks. After the war, many ex-organisers who had
learned their politics in this environment found it impossible to compromise and relocate to mixed-sex political parties. Consequently, several of
the women who had worked unceasingly for the vote prior to the war
eschewed parliamentary politics once it was granted and went on to find
work of some sort in the network of feminist organisations that spread
throughout Britain in the 1920s and the 1930s. Margaret Haig formed the
Six Point Group in 1921 to push for women's equality in the six areas of
politics, occupations, and the moral, social, economic and legal fields.
This pulled in many of her former WSPU colleagues, including the ex-

organisers Dorothy Evans, Helen Archdale, Geraldine Lennox, Charlotte Marsh, Theresa Garnett and Mary Phillips. Margaret Haig was involved in the Open Door Council, a pressure group formed in 1926 to push for equality of opportunity for women, particularly at work, and the ODC also offered some work to former suffragettes. Moreover, Margaret Haig's editorship of the feminist journal *Time and Tide* presented a forum for the ideas of the ODC and the Six Point Group, and allowed their support-ers to rehearse the journalist skills which they had practised in *VFW* and the *Suffragette*. Financing such work was a different matter, and although there were several ex-organisers committed to furthering feminist con-cerns in the 1920s and beyond, there were few full-time, paid opportuni-ties. The majority who worked for the Six Point Group and the ODC were volunteers, fitting their activism around full-time jobs, as some had done in the earliest days at Clements Inn. In the tight economic climate of inter-war Britain, full-time political work was something of a luxury. Local government was a little more accessible, and some ex-organisers did find a niche there, although this alternative provided elected office rather than a chosen career. Hannah Mitchell was an ILP member of Manchester City Council between 1924 and 1935. Dorothy Bowker, who had organ-ised in both Leicester and Hastings, served as a Borough Councillor at Lymington for several years as an independent, and was also elected as an alderman there in 1956.[26] Isabel Seymour was also a local councillor, serving on Hampshire County Council.

A very small number of ex-organisers managed to find congenial political work in other countries. Perhaps the best-known examples were Alice Paul and Lucy Burns, both of whom had worked as WSPU organ-isers duringtheir time in Britain. On their return to their native United States, they continued to work for the parliamentary vote there. Although Lucy Burns retired from public life once that campaign had ended, Alice Paul remained active in a variety of causes. She had followed the example of the WSPU in transforming her suffrage organisation into the National Women's Party, although her venture achieved much greater longevity. It did not, however, solve the problems of other ex-WSPU organisers still seeking political work. Ada Flatman, who was an organiser at the same time as Alice Paul, wrote to her ex-colleague asking if there were any paid opportunities in the National Women's Party at the end of the war, but received a disappointing reply.[27] The difficulties facing organisers who sought a continuity of employment evidently worked across national boundaries. In Canada, too, Nellie Hall returned to active political work for the Association of the Women Electors of Toronto, but again in a voluntary capacity. There were simply not enough political jobs to go around.

Party politics and feminist campaigning provided the most obvious career for WSPU ex-organisers, but these were not the only fields in which skills learned in the militant campaign could be usefully deployed. Some women took up careers that combined an interest in feminism with practical work. Different forms of public service or social work were popular. Phyllis Ayrton and Cynthia Maguire went to China – where Phyllis had lived for the first fifteen years of her life – in 1921. Cynthia returned to England the following year, but Phyllis remained in Hong Kong where she worked briefly in publishing before moving to the British Chamber of Commerce and then to the colony's Ministry of Information.[28] In England, Gabrielle Jefferey became a clerk for Middlesex County Council, where she specialised in maternity and child welfare, interests that echoed the rhetoric of the WSPU when it had called for votes for mothers.[29] Charlotte Marsh and Mary Phillips went into social work, although not necessarily as a first choice. Charlotte, who had trained as a sanitary inspector before joining the WSPU, had some time with the Women's International League for Peace and Freedom before going to the USA where she worked for the 'Community Chest' based in San Fransisco. The Overseas Settlement League then employed her, but that job finished when the organisation closed down. Charlotte then went to work for the Public Assistance Board, a civil service appointment which she tackled with some success, making lasting friendships among many of her clients.[30] Mary Phillips worked for the publications department of the National Council of Social Service, although her main paid employment was as editor of a daily news bulletin for the brewing industry. Cicely Hale, who had worked for many years in the WSPU's information department, trained as a health visitor and followed that career until after the Second World War, becoming a familiar name to many mothers through her column 'The Baby Circle', which appeared in *Woman's Own*.[31] Significant public work was undertaken by Jennie Baines, appointed children's court magistrate in Melbourne in 1928, a job she was still doing at the age of 81.[32]

Other ex-organisers used the skills that they had polished in the WSPU in quite different directions. During their suffragette days, many organisers had found themselves engaged in literary or artistic tasks in pursuit of the cause, writing plays and sketches, arranging local productions and musical entertainments in support of WSPU funds and compiling weekly reports for *VFM* and the *Suffragette*. Thus, Margaret Haig's editorship of *Time and Tide* built on the experience she gained at the *Western Mail*, which in turn had been prompted by a circular from WSPU headquarters instructing branch secretaries to supply regular reports of their activities to the local press.[33] She found that her experience on Wales' main daily paper afforded her an excellent foundation for her later editorial role. Evelyn Hambling, who had worked at headquarters, also went into journalism, and worked for both the *Vote* and *Time and Tide*, as well as publishing several plays before her death in 1955.[34] Vera Holme, who had been the WSPU's official chauffeur, became involved with the Pioneer Players during the First World War and continued to support local productions close to her home in Lochearnhead, as well as helping Edy Craig arrange the annual Ellen Terry Memorial performance which took place in Kent.[35] Other organisers, such as Mildred Mansell, the former organiser of the Bath WSPU, and Dorothy Shearwood, who had worked in Dundee, opted for administrative roles in the arts. Mrs Mansell, who remained in the West Country after the war, founded the Mid-Somerset Musical Competitive Festival which led to her later work as Honorary secretary of the British Confederation of the Arts.[36] Dorothy Shearwood (who became Dorothy Shearwood Stubbington) emigrated to Canada after the First World War, where she taught piano at the McGill Conservatory in Montreal and organised an annual music festival for a number of years.[37]

The quirky and fiercely independent qualities that made many women useful workers for the WSPU led some of them into unusual fields after the suffrage campaign ended. A number found that religion offered them a sense of purpose akin to what they had experienced when campaigning for the WSPU's cause. Christabel Pankhurst's public advocacy of Second Day Adventism took up much of the remainder of her life, making it the longer of her two public careers. Clara Codd, whose time in the WSPU had been briefer, worked for the theosophical movement as an itinerant evangelist. Annie Kenney, who trained Clara as a WSPU organiser, also became involved with theosophy and the Rosicrucian Order, although she took no great part on its behalf in public. Edith Rigby, the founder and long-serving honorary organiser of Preston WSPU, became interested in the work of Rudolph Steiner.[38] For other women, independence and equality were the most motivating concerns. Jessie Kenney became the first woman to qualify as a ships' radio officer, although the regulations at the time precluded her from getting a job in this field, so she worked as a steward instead before becoming a school secretary. Elsie Bowerman became one of the first women to be called to the Bar in 1924.

Although most ex-organisers were now forming new alliances, there were still causes to be fought and important victories to be won. Even those who appeared to have retired from public life found it hard to let go of their former affiliations and beliefs. Clara Giveen married Phillip

Brewster, the brother of the Midlands suffragette Bertha, in 1914. After the war, the Brewsters lived in Peaslake, Surrey, where Clara (now known as Betty) settled into village life and became known for her work with the Women's Institute and other village affairs. Those who knew her were mindful of an occasion when a local woman admitted in Betty's hearing that she was not intending to vote at the next General Election. 'Betty Brewster flared up "People have died to get you the right to vote" with a forcefulness that lived on in the memory forty years.'[39]

The variety of the work that ex-organisers felt equipped to undertake stands as testimony to the complexity of the WSPU's campaign. Although it is often presented as examplifying single-issue politics, most of the Union's supporters would not have recognised this description. The deceptively simple slogan of 'Votes for Women' served to unite women in the Union's ranks, but was never intended to restrict their activity. Suffragettes who had undergone imprisonment used their experiences to press for prison reform while the WSPU's campaign was still ongoing. Organisers and activists also campaigned consistently against the sexual double standard. While this was most obvious in their promotion of Christabel Pankhurst's *The Great Scourge* in 1913, the Union had a longstanding interest in the issue. Suffragettes had prepared a high profile petition calling for clemency in the case of Daisy Lord, a young woman sentenced to death for killing her illegitimate child following an affair with her employer in 1908. Long before their final incarnation as *Britannia* would run campaigns for conscription and industrial peace, the WSPU's publications *Suffragette* and *VFW* were calling attention to society's issues: the poor conditions of women industrial workers in Britain; the progress of feminism in other countries; the work being done by women in the fields of local government and education. Those who worked full-time for the WSPU developed real expertise in a several areas.

Once the vote had been won, there was no obvious single avenue for the skills acquired in campaigning for it, as the examples sketched above illustrate. The WSPU's organisers dispersed and were no longer as visible as a single group. Some of them joined the Suffragette Fellowship, an organisation that welcomed into its ranks also former members of the WFL and the relatives of active suffragettes, and consequently offered no separate 'old girls' club' restricted to organisers and workers alone. Such equality is admirable feminist practice, but carried unfortunate consequences for the status historians have awarded to organisers. While the Fellowship was busily compiling information for its 'Book of Suffragette Prisoners', no similar attempts were made to record the specific contributions of the WSPU's workers to their campaign. Even when organisers' work was recognised, it was frequently not described. 'Formerly organiser of the WSPU' was how the *Daily Telegraph* referred to Rachel Barrett when it announced her death in 1953, but it was only in the less widely read feminist periodical *Women's Bulletin* that her fellow-organiser Mary Phillips sketched out a few details of Rachel's career.[40] The Fellowship's own magazine *Calling All Women*, which appeared annually from 1936 (when it was known as the newsletter) until 1977, often carried death notices acknowledging women who had served as organisers, but offered no obituaries elaborating on their work.[41] The deaths of others passed unnoticed, the Suffragette Fellowship never having quite managed to re-unite the numerous women loyal to the WSPU before the war whose contact details had been lost so many years before.

The absence of a discrete group of records describing the work of suffrage organisers either contemporaneously with the WSPU's campaign or as part of a historical retrospective has contributed to their neglect within the historiography of the suffragette movement. Early accounts took their cue from the Suffragette Fellowship's shaping of a WSPU narrative that privileged certain acts of militancy over other forms of activism. The historian Laura E. Nym Mayhall has noted that as early as the 1920s such a focus had 'fetishised militancy at the expense of the political rationale' behind it.[42] Sandra Holton's consideration of the development of suffrage historiography observed how 'the action' in subsequent historical accounts 'tends not to occur in the committee room ... but on the street corner, at the hustings, and, above all, in the prison cell'.[43] Historians concerned with exploring local dimensions of WSPU organisation have also observed that despite the symbolic importance of London as the site of political power, most suffragettes 'gained their political experience' in their own towns.[44] And although local studies have recognised the contributions of particular organisers within their own branches, no attempt has yet been made to compare those accounts systematically. They are both present within yet absent from the historical record, referred to as 'volunteers', 'activists' and even simply 'members', or they are afforded the title 'organiser' with no interrogation of what that might mean.[45]

Collective consideration of its paid organisers reclaims the WSPU as a *political* organisation with a functioning national network, not a haphazard collection of sympathetic freelance militants. This is possibly closer to how many WSPU members viewed their organisation in its own time, but it is a perspective that has been eclipsed. The focus on organisers also suggests that a far wider variety of individuals were involved in the suffrage movement as militant activists rather than as occasional sympathisers than has hitherto been supposed. Women from many different backgrounds worked full-time for the WSPU. Some left careers to do so, while others found that WSPU work offered them the perfect route out of a repressive domesticity. Their political and religious affiliations were equally mixed, as were their personal circumstances. Several were young women, though age was no barrier, and older organisers were also welcome. The majority were single, but a few needed all the support their husbands could offer as they struggled to combine political organising with familial responsibilities. These differences were subsumed while women were working together for the suffragette cause, but they did not vanish altogether, despite the efforts of several feminists, but re-emerged in the political realignment that followed the WSPU's collapse.

Despite the relative anonymity of most of their number, it is no exaggeration to say that without the efforts of its full-time organisers the WSPU could not have built or sustained a national campaign. It was the organisers who did the recruitment, who built up the branches and organised the paper sales. The responsibility which the Union placed on them was considerable, reflecting the trust in which they were invested. And although there were some notable exceptions, for the most part this trust was not misplaced. For many provincial women, the local organisers *were* the Union, as trips to London were rare and even the most indefatigable speaker could not visit every single part of Britain. In the final assessment of their achievements, the last word fittingly goes to Christabel Pankhurst, the WSPU's chief organiser for many years. Although she was by no means uncritical of many of her employees during the suffrage campaign, Christabel's version of the WSPU's history recognised them as a group and her reappraisal of them was generous. Recalling their work, she declared:

> Our organisers must have their tribute … They were willing to sacrifice all, and attempt all, for the cause. Sent, it might be, to some outpost in North, South, East or West of the country, they would plant the flag, take an office, interview the Press, call upon the leading women of the place … address meetings, enrol members, arrange more meetings … and in addition to all, raise the money for their own campaign and have a balance to send to the central treasury. Their political understanding made them equal to every occasion … Scorning delights, they lived laborious days and joyed in doing it, finding their happiness in present service and future victory.[46]

Of course, not every organiser would have agreed. The many descriptions of exhaustion, both mental and physical, that have been retrieved from the archives while researching this book do not sit comfortably alongside Christabel's claims that her workers were consistently to be found glorying in the self-sacrifice demanded of them. Nevertheless, it was clear that organisers drew a tremendous sense of fulfilment from their work, and it is perhaps this feeling that Christabel was attempting to recapture or acknowledge, in her rather puritanical way. Without the organisers, the WSPU could not have functioned as it did. Accordingly, any appraisal of the WSPU's structure and of its struggles must award a central importance to the contributions they made, both in London and throughout the country.

Notes

1   For details, see *Vote*, 1 February 1918.
2   Statement from Elsie Bowerman, n.d., Mitchell Papers; Bartels to Harrison, Harrison Tapes.
3   See Cheryl Law, *Suffrage and Power: The Women's Movement 1918–1928* (London: I. B. Tauris, 1997), p. 116.
4   Teresa Billington Grieg, 'Autobiographical writing', TBG Papers Box 397, A6.
5   Women's Party statement, 1917, quoted in Purvis, *Emmeline Pankhurst*, p. 302.
6   Rosen, *Rise Up Women!*, p. 267.
7   This is certainly the view of her less-than-sympathetic biographer Martin Pugh: Pugh, *The Pankhursts*, p. 350.
8   Christabel Pankhurst, *Unshackled*, p. 295.
9   Article from *Daily Express*, reprinted in *Britannia*, 9 November 1917.
10 Adela Pankhurst Walsh to Helen Fraser Moyes, 22 January 1960, Museum of London.
11 E. Sylvia Pankhurst, *The Life of Emmeline Pankhurst*, p. 172.
12 Purvis, *Emmeline Pankhurst*, p. 347.
13 *Ibid.*, p 346.
14 Emmeline Pankhurst to Nellie Hall, 13 November 1927, Nellie Hall Papers.
15 Christabel Pankhurst to Nellie Hall, 2 July 1928, Nellie Hall Papers
16 See Coleman, *Adela Pankhurst*, pp. 156–64.
17 Julie V. Gotlieb, *Feminine Fascism: Women in Britain's Fascist Movement, 1923–1945* (London: I.B. Tauris, 2000), p. 301.
18 *Ibid.*, p. 336.
19 *Ibid.*, pp. 278–80.
20 Richardson (writing in *Blackshirt*) and Elam (*Fascist Quarterly*) quoted by Martin Durham, 'Gender and the British Union of Fascists', *Journal of Contemporary History*, 27, 3 (1992), pp. 513–29, at p. 520.
21 Gottlieb, *Feminine Fascism*, p. 148.
22 Pugh, *The Pankhursts*, p. 342.
23 *Ibid.*
24 Marion Lawson, 'Memories of Charlotte Marsh' a Suffragette Fellowship pamphlet, 1961.
25 Anon., 'Mary Leigh, still a militant', Mitchell Papers, Museum of London.
26 *New Milton Advertiser*, 4 August 1973.
27 Alice Paul to Ada Flatman, June 1921, SFC.

28 Notes given to Jessie Kenney by Cynthia Maguire about Phyllis Ayrton, July 15 1964, Mitchell Papers.
29 Obituary, *The Times*, 26 March 1946.
30 Obituary, *The Times*, reprinted in Lawson, 'Memories of Charlotte Marsh'.
31 See Hale, *A Good Long Time*.
32 Undated press cutting, Autobiographical Cuttings File, Women's Library.
33 Haig, *This Was My World*, pp. 30, 31.
34 *Women's Bulletin*, 16 September 1955.
35 Crawford, *Women's Suffrage Movement: A Reference Guide, 1866–1928*, p. 290.
36 *Ibid.*, p. 374.
37 Grace Roe to Nellie Hall, 28 February 1959, Nellie Hall Papers.
38 Hesketh, *My Aunt Edith*, p. 100.
39 Overton and Mant, *A Suffragette Nest: Peaslake, 1910*, p. 43.
40 See 'Rachel Barret', Autobiographical Cuttings File, Women's Library.
41 See, for instance, notices of the deaths of 'Miss Violet Hughes, WSPU organiser' and 'Nell Kenney, organiser', *Calling All Women*, February 1954.
42 Mayhall, *The Militant Suffrage Movement*, p. 135.
43 Sandra Stanley Holton, 'The making of suffrage history', in Holton and Purvis (eds), *Votes for Women*, pp. 13–33, p. 21.
44 J. Hannam, '"I had not been to London" : women's suffrage – a view from the regions', in Purvis and Holton (eds), *Votes for Women*, pp. 226–45, at p. 226.
45 Antonia Raeburn, for example, interviewed several ex-organisers as part of her research for *The Militant Suffrage Movement*, a book that offers much detail of their work at Clements Inn, but less about provincial deployments, and lacks a thorough consideration of what an organiser's role was within the WSPU.
46 C. Pankhurst, *Unshackled*, p. 126.

Biographical appendix

Sources

The women listed below were identified as organisers in *VFW*, the *Suffragette* and *Women's Franchise*; the list includes a small number mentioned in *Calling All Women* and those identified at the trial of Harriet Kerr and other suffragette leaders in 1913 (TNA, DPP 1/19). The locations of the main biographical data for each subject reproduced here do not exhaust the sources of relevant information. Some personal details have been taken from the 1891 and 1901 census returns and the Family Records Centre, London.

* Denotes an individual arrested and imprisonment in the course of WSPU activities.

ABBREVIATIONS

CAW	*Calling All Women*
DLB	*Dictionary of Labour Biography*, 12 vols (Basingstoke: Palgrave Macmillan, 1970–2004)
NDNB	*New Dictionary of National Biography* (online: http://www.oup.com/oxforddnb)
SA	A.J.R. (ed.), *The Suffrage Annual and Women's Who's Who*
VFW	*Votes for Women* (periodical)
WSM	Crawford, *The Women's Suffrage Movement*

Shortened titles are used for those publications detailed in the Select bibliography

*Miss Laura Ainsworth (1885–1958)   Born Blything, Northumberland, daughter of John Ainsworth, a school inspector, and Eliza Ainsworth. Laura worked as a governess and a teacher but resigned in 1909 to work as an organiser. Assistant organiser in Birmingham in June 1909, then worked in Leicester (1909), the midlands (1909), Battersea and district (1910), Rochester (1910), North Kent (1911), Saltburn and Redcar (1911), and Newcastle (1911). Resigned from the WSPU in 1912 supporting the Pethick Lawrences. Later worked for the British Legion and had some contact with the Suffragette Fellowship.
Sources: *CAW*; *VFW*; *WSM*.

*Miss Janie Allan (1868–1968)   Daughter of Alexander Allan, owner of Allan Shipping Line. Joined WSPU in 1907 from constitutional society. Became organiser in Glasgow in 1912 and remained until outbreak of war when she refused to commit to any other suffrage society. Later in the war she was involved with the Scottish Council for Women's Trades. Kept in touch with some suffragette friends but was not very interested in the Suffragette Fellowship.
Sources: *WSM*; Janie Allan Collection, National Library of Scotland; Arncliffe Sennett Collection; Pethick Lawrence Papers; Leneman, *A Guid Cause*; *Scottish Suffragettes*.

*Miss Margaret (Greta) Allen   Born Cork, daughter of T. Allen, B.Sc, and Margaret Allen, née Dowden. A hospital nurse, she gave lectures on sanitary matters to county councils, and published health and hygiene advice pamphlets. Organised in Brighton from February 1911.
Sources: *SA*; *VFW*.

*Miss Mary Sophia Allen, OBE (1878–1964)   Born Glamorgan, daughter of Thomas Isaac Allen, superintendent of the Great Western Railway, and Margaret Allen. Educated at Princess Helena College, Ealing. Joined WSPU in 1909. Offered organising post by Emmeline Pankhurst after forcible feeding compromised her health. Worked in Bexhill (Feb 1912), Edinburgh (Oct 1913), then variously in Hastings and Aberdeen. Joined Women Police Volunteers during First World War succeeding founder Margaret Damer Dawson as commandant of Women's Auxilliary Service in 1920. Also founded and edited *Policewoman's Review*. Stood unsuccessfully as Independent Parliamentary candidate in 1922, later joined the British Union of Fascists (1939) and converted to Roman Catholicism (1953).
Sources: *SA*; *WSM*; *NDNB*; Obituary, *The Times*; autobiographical writings: M. S. Allen, *Lady in Blue* (London: Stanley Paul, 1936); M. S. Allen with J. H. Heyneman, *The Pioneer Policewoman* (London: Chatto & Windus, 1925); M. S. Allen and J. H. Heyneman, *Woman at the Crossroads*.

*Mrs Helen Archdale (1876–1949)   Daughter of Alexander Russel and Helen De Lacy Evans Russel née Carter. Educated St Leonard's School, St Andrews, then University of St Andrews. Married Theodore Montgomery Archdale, army officer, in 1901, three children, Nicholas, Alec and, Helen Elizabeth (Betty). Spent time in India, became involved in suffrage on return to England, going to Scotland to deflect objections from her husband's Colonel. Also organised in Sheffield with Adela Pankhurst then moved to London as Prisoners' Secretary, with Jennie Kenney as governess to her children. During First World War worked for *Britannia*, on the land, for the WAAC and in the Women's Department of the Ministry of National Service. Edited *Time and Tide* until 1926. Later involved in Open Door Council, Equal Rights International and the Women's Political and Industrial League, and catalogued many early donations to the Suffragette Fellowship's Reading Room. Her marriage effectively ended during the suffrage campaign although the Archdales did not divorce; Theodore was killed on leave in First World War.
Sources: *WSM*; *NDNB*;TNA DPP 1/19; Kenney Papers; Haig, *This Was My World*; McPherson, *The Suffragette's Daughter*.

*Miss Barbara Bodichon Ayrton (later Gould; 1886–1950)   Daughter of William Edward Ayton, engineer and physicist, and Pheobe Sarah (Hertha) Ayrton, née Marks, also a physicist. Educated at Notting Hill High School and University College London, joining WSPU in 1906 and giving up postgraduate study to organise. Married Gerald Gould in 1910 but continued suffrage activity, escaped to France to avoid arrest disguised as a schoolgirl in 1913. Joined United Suffragists and became its first secretary, working for suffrage throughout First World War. Later joined socialist movement working for *Daily Herald* as publicity manager and briefly editing *Labour Woman*. Elected to Parliament in 1945, represented Hendon North for five years. Also involved in the Women's International League and other feminist organisations.

Sources: *WSM; DLB; NDNB*; Sharp, *Hertha Ayrton: A Memoir*.

Miss Phyllis Ayrton (1884–1975)   Born Wnechow, China, daughter of William Ayrton, British Consul. Returned to England c. 1899 on death of mother. Joined WSPU in 1909 and founded Clerks' WSPU with Cynthia Maguire. Went to Birmingham as organiser in May 1914. During First World War worked for Dr Flora Murray then for WSPU as Woman's Party organiser. Later returned to China and worked in publishing and for the Ministry of Information in Hong Kong. Spent 4 years in a prison camp in World War Two.

Sources: *SA; WSM*; Mitchell Collection.

*Mrs Sarah Jane (Jennie) Baines (1866–1951)   Born Birmingham, daughter of James Edward Hunt, gun maker, and Sarah Ann Baines. Started factory work aged 11. Involved in Salvation Army as evangelist to an independent working men's mission in Bolton. Married George Baines, bootmaker and had five children, three of whom survived. Involved in temperance and the ILP, joined WSPU in 1905. Appointed paid organiser in 1908, was deployed as an itinerant organiser throughout North West and Midlands and sometimes further afield. Several arrests including as 'Lizzie Baker' in Dublin. Escaped with family to Australia as 'mouse.' In Melbourne joined the Victoria Socialist Party and the Women's Political Association. Involved in pacifist movements in First World War and campaigned against conscription. Later involved in Communist Party but was expelled in 1925 and returned to the Labor Party. Appointed Children's Court Magistrate in Melbourne in 1928, worked into her eighties.

Sources: *VFW; WSM; NDNB*; Baines Papers; Smart, 'Jennie Baines: an Australian connection'.

*Mrs Lucy Minnie Baldock (c. 1864–1964)   Worked in shirt factory then married a fitter and West Ham councillor. The couple joined ILP. She was one of the WSPU's earliest London members; appointed organiser by 1906, involved mainly in itinerant campaigning. Developed cancer in 1911 and stopped active work, retaining membership of the WSPU and the Church League for Women's Suffrage. Carried a banner at Mrs Pankhurst's funeral and was involved in the Suffragette Fellowship (SF).

Sources: *CAW; WSM*; Lucy M. Baldock Papers, Suffragette Fellowship Collection (SFC).

Miss Barbar   Co-organised in Retford, December 1910. No further information traced.

*Miss Rachel Barrett (1874–1953)   Born Carmarthen, daughter of Rees Barrett, land and road surveyor, and Anne Barrett, neé Jones. Educated at private boarding school in Stroud, then (with a scholarship) Aberystwyth College, gaining a London B.Sc via extension studies. Taught in Welsh country schools and joined the WSPU in 1906. Enrolled for D.Sc at the London School of Economics, stopped February 1908 to become organiser. Worked at Devon by-election and held a district post in North Wales then moved to the National Office. Chief sub-editor of the *Suffragette* but took over much of the day-to-day organisation of the WSPU when Christabel Pankhurst was in Paris. Sentenced for a month for conspiracy to damage property in April 1913 but released under the Cat and Mouse Act. Produced *Suffragette* from Scotland because of different publishing laws. Later worked to raise funds for Mrs Pankhurst's statue and was a member of the Suffragette Fellowship.

Sources: *VFW*; *WSM*; *NDNB*; SFC; Obituary, *Women's Bulletin*; Agnes Lake Papers.

Miss Olive Bartels, OBE (1889–1978)   Born Surrey, daughter of an army contractor, her mother, Marion, was one of first Irish women to receive a degree. Olive attended Streatham High School then went to art college, leaving to work for the WSPU. Worked as a district organiser with Grace Roe then at headquarters. During First World War went to America with Christabel Pankhurst but dissented from her line on war so returned to England and left WSPU. Worked at War Office then in Tours as administrator for the Women's Army Auxiliary Corps, awarded OBE. Later ran a small holding in Gurnsey, organised for the NUWT and worked for Land Settlement Association. Worked for Women's Voluntary Service in WW2.

Sources: Harrison Tapes; *WSM*.

Miss G Bentley   Organised in Tunbridge Wells, January 1914. No further information traced.

Miss Billing   Organised in Maidstone, then north and west Kent, 1911. No further information traced.

*****Miss Teresa Billington (later Billington Grieg; 1876–1964)**   Born Preston, daughter of William Billington, an engineer turned shopkeeper, and Ellen Billington. Educated at the Convent of Notre Dame, Blackburn, forced to leave at 13 to add to family income. Father considered mill work, mother attempted to apprentice her to a milliner, so Teresa left home to live with relatives in Manchester, trained as a pupil teacher and took a BA through extension studies. Joined WSPU in its earliest days. Stopped teaching in 1905 to organise for ILP, leaving in 1906 for WSPU post. Worked at headquarters then Scotland where she met and married Frederick Grieg. Disagreements with WSPU culminated in formation of Women's Freedom League in October 1907 for which she worked until resigning in 1910. During First World War she helped at husband's billiard works, later established the Women's Billiards Association. Rejoined WFL in 1937, also involved in Six Point Group.

Sources: *SA*; *WSM*; *NDNB*; *DLB*; Billington Grieg Papers.

Miss Pearl Birch (later Lady Dickens; c. 1890–1970)   Born in India, daughter of Colonel William Birch and Flora Birch. Joined WSPU in 1912 and worked at headquarters mainly involved in propaganda and fundraising. Married Gerald Dickens before the First World War.
Sources: CAW; Wilson, *With All Her Might.*

Miss Ethel Birnstingl   Worked at headquarters c. 1910–11, mainly in the banner department. Cancelled early subscription to *Freewoman* due to its attitude to WSPU.
Sources: *VFW*; SFC; Dora Marsden Papers.

Miss K. S. Birnstingl was Ethel's sister. She became a volunteer organiser in Bournemouth and Southampton 1909; also cancelled subscription to *Freewoman.*
Sources: *VFW*; Dora Marsden Papers.

Miss Mary Blathwayt ('Bay') (1879–1961) Daughter of Colonel Linley Blathwayt and Emily Blathwayt, née Rose. Family moved to Eagle House, Batheaston, when Linley Blathwayt retired from the army. Mary attended Bath High School. Joined constitutional suffrage society, then the WSPU, becoming treasurer of the Bath branch in 1908. Worked as itinerant organiser throughout west country under Annie Kenney. Parents were active supporters, offering hospitality to itinerant speakers and exhausted prisoners. Their garden contained a 'suffragette arbour' planted by WSPU visitors. Emily left the WSPU in 1909, concerned over mounting levels of violence, but continued to welcome suffragettes to her home. Mary had health problems and cut down on propaganda work but ran WSPU shop in Bath. Resigned from WSPU in May 1913 but retained an interest in its local activities. During First World War she worked with the Red Cross in Bath. Took no further part in public life but kept some personal contact with former suffrage friends until her death.
Sources: *WSM*; *NDNB*; Blathwayt Diaries; B. M. W. Dobie, *A Nest of Suffragettes in Somerset: Eagle House, Batheaston* (Bath: Batheaston Society, 1979); Hannam, 'Suffragettes are splendid for any work'.

Miss Theodora Ellen Bonwick (1876–1928)   Born London, daughter of William Priessnitz Bonwick, schoolteacher, and Sarah, née Beddow. Educated at Stockwell College, and subsequently taught in London elementary schools. Joined WSPU in 1905 and spoke at Hyde Park demonstration in June 1908. Retained her teaching post but organised in Islington during election campaign, January 1910. President of Women Teachers' Franchise Union and active in the Association for Moral and Social Hygiene, as well as in the National Union of Women Teachers after First World War.
Sources: *SA*; *VFW*; *NDNB*; H. Kean, *Deeds Not Words: The Lives of Suffragette Teachers* (London: Pluto Press, 1990).

Miss Helen Boswell   Organised in Wolverhampton, September 1909; no further information traced.

*Mrs Euginia Anna Bouvier (1865–c. 1935)   Born St Petersburg, daughter of George and Amelia Weber. Married P. E. Bouvier, French master, City of London School, to whom she bore a daughter. Founded Lewisham WSPU, of which she was secretary, 1907–11, then acting-secretary for Men's Political Union for Women's Enfranchisment. Organised in Newcastle, February 1909, and for other itinerant campaigns. Later returned to Russia.
Sources: *SA*; *CAW*; *VFW*.

Miss Elsie Bowerman (1889–1973)   Born Tunbridge Wells, daughter of William Bowerman (d. 1895), who owned drapers' shops, and Edith Bowerman (later Mrs Chibnall). Educated at Wycombe Abbey School and Girton College, Cambridge. Joined WSPU with her mother in 1909 and organised a branch at college. Organised in St Leonards after graduation. Elsie and Edith survived the sinking of the *Titanic* in April 1912. Worked with Dr Elsie Inglis in Scottish Women's Hospitals' Unit in Serbia and Russia during First World War. Next worked for WSPU's industrial peace campaign, then as Christabel Pankhurst's election agent in Smethwick. Later involved in the Women's Guild of Empire with Flora Drummond. Took up law and was one of the first woman barristers. In 1934 helped Lady Reading form the Women's Voluntary Service. Worked for the Ministry of Information in the Second World War, then for the United Nations in New York as head of its Status of Women section.
Sources: *WSM*; *NDNB*; Elsie Bowerman Papers.

*Miss Dorothy Bowker (1886–1973)   Initially an anti-militant, but was converted by Mrs Pankhurst and joined the WSPU in 1908, working with Mrs Haverfield in Paddington. She then worked with Dorothy Pethick, thereafter going to Hastings and St Leonards as district organiser. Joined Women's Land Army in First World War, then spent some time in Canada and the USA. Returned to England, elected to Lymington Borough Council as an Independent in 1934; served for nineteen years, becoming an alderman.
Sources: *WSM*; *CAW*; Obituary, *New Milton Advertiser*.

*Miss Georgina Brackenbury (1865–1949)   Born Woolwich, daughter of General Charles Brackenbury and Hilda Brackenbury. Trained at the Slade and became a portrait painter. Joined WSPU in 1907 – her mother and her sister Marie (a landscape painter) were both keen WSPU members. Undertook speaking campaigns for the WSPU and deputed for Mary Gawthorpe in Manchester in the autumn of 1910. The Brackenbury family's house was known as 'Mouse Castle' as it regularly housed suffragettes out of prison on licence under the 'Cat and Mouse' Act. Georgina Brackenbury's portrait of Mrs Pankhurst hangs in the National Portrait Gallery and she was a pallbearer at the latter's funeral.
Sources: *SA*; *WSM*.

Miss Brewer   Organised in Derby, June 1910. No further information traced.

*Miss (Evelyn) Hilda Burkett (later Mrs Mitchener; 1876–1955)   Born Wolverhampton, daughter of Reuben Launcelot Burkett. Worked as a secretary and ran

publicity campaigns for WSPU in the Midlands from 1908, then several itinerant militant campaigns.
Sources: *SA*; *CAW*; *WSM*.

*Miss Lucy Burns (1879–1966) Born Brooklyn. Educated at Vasar College, Yale University and Universities of Berlin and Bonn, and Oxford University. Joined WSPU in 1909 on visit to London. Organised in Scotland, including holding a district post in Edinburgh. Returned to USA in 1912, where she co-founded the Congressional Union for Women's Suffrage, later the Women's Party. Retired from public work after US women won vote.
Sources: *SA*; Leneman, *A Guid Cause.*

Miss Margaret Cameron Born West Highlands, daughter of Reverend Donld Cameron, Kilmonivaig, Invernesshire. Educated almost entirely at home. Was secretary for the London Women's Suffrage Society before joining the WSPU. Organised in Glasgow, then London.
Source: *VFW*.

Mrs Mary Clarke (?1863–1910) Younger sister of Mrs Pankhurst, born in Salford. Unhappily married and left her husband early in twentieth century. Became WSPU organiser in 1907 and worked mainly in Brighton. Died suddenly on Christmas Day 1910.
Sources: *VFW*; *WSM*.

*Miss Clara Codd (1876–1971) Born Barnstaple, Devon, daughter of Henry Frederick Codd, a school inspector, and Clara Virginia Codd. Educated at home, but to a standard sufficient to allow her to work as a governess herself when her family moved to Geneva on her father's death. Returned to England in 1903, where she joined the Theosophy Society and the Social Democratic Federation. Joined the WSPU in 1907 and worked with Annie Kenney as an apprentice organiser in Bristol. Declined full-time organiser's post in favour of the Theosophical Society, for which she worked for most of her life.
Sources: *WSM*; *NDNB*; Clara Codd, *So Rich a Life*; Lily Darby, 'Clara Codd: off the platform', *Theosophist*, October 1976.

*Miss Gertrude Conolan (1872–?) Born New Ferry, Cheshire, grand-daughter of Sir Oswald Mosley, MP, and of Major Chetwynd, MP. Educated at St Margaret's Convent, East Grinestead, then trained as a teacher at the Kindergarten Training College and in Paris. Ran co-educational school in Hampstead, studied at the Sorbonne, then worked at Highbury and Islington GPDST High School. Joined WSPU in 1906. Appointed organiser March 1908, and worked in Glasgow. Arrested as 'Mary Lane' in 1908 and 1910. Succeeded Joan Dugdale as secretary of the Actresses' Franchise League in 1911, and from 1912 was honourary secretary of the Federated Council of Suffrage Societies.
Sources: *VFW*; *WSM*; TNA, DPP 1/19.

Miss Cooke Worker at headquarters 1913. No further information traced.

Miss A. D. Corson   Influenced by her mother's interest in women's higher education before she joining WSPU; worked as assistant organiser to Miss Keevil in Wolverhapton, then went to work in London. Helped organise in Sheffield and Manchester.
Source: *VFW*.

*Miss Helen Millar Craggs (later McCombie, then Lady Pethick Lawrence; 1888–1969)   Born London, daughter of Sir John Craggs, accountant, and Helen, née Millar. Educated at Rodean, and returned as staff member. Joined WSPU at 19 and worked as volunteer for 1908 Manchester by-election. Left home when father disapproved of her WSPU involvement, taking up Mrs Pankhurst's offer of a paid post. Hunger-strike in 1912 rendered her unfit, so trained as a midwife. Married a GP, Alexander McCombie, and worked as a dispenser in his East End practice; also made jigsaws commercially. Spent some time in USA and Canada after the Second World War, then returned to England. Married Frederick Pethick Lawrence in 1957, and was active in the Suffragette Fellowship until her death.
Sources: *SA*; *WSM*; Nellie Hall Papers; S. Walker, 'Helen Pethick Lawrence'; Raeburn (ed.), *The Militant Suffragettes*.

*Mrs Annie Rhonda Craig   Born in Gravesend, daughter of Henry and Anne Jane Walker. Referred to herself as both the 'first militant suffragette in Scotland' and the 'first woman member of Dumbartonshire ILP'. School board member, Old Kilpatrick Parish, Dumbartonshire. WSPU organiser for Glasgow in 1909.
Sources: *SA*; *VFW*.

*Miss Ellen (Nellie) Crocker (1872–1962)   Born Stogumber, Somerset, daughter of Jonathan Crocker, MRCS. Resigned from Women's Liberal Association in 1907 and joined WSPU; appointed organiser in 1908. A cousin of Emmeline Pethick Lawrence, her association with the WSPU ended when the Pethick Lawrences were expelled.
Sources: *SA*; *WSM*; autobiographical typescript, Girton College, Cambridge.

Miss Fanny Crocker   Organised Devon by-election in 1908. No further information.

*Miss Alice Davies (c. 1870–?)   Born Liverpool. Joined the Carl Rosa Company at 18, but later trained as a nurse and worked as head of a private surgical home. Liverpool District Organiser, 1911–12. Returned to nursing in First World War.
Sources: *VFW*; Liddle Collection, University of Leeds; Cowman, *'Mrs Brown is a Man and a Brother!'*

*Miss Emily Wilding Davison (1872–1913)   Born Blackheath; educated at Kensington High School and Holloway College. Worked as governess on death of her father to fund completion of her degree. Taught until c. 1909. Joined WSPU in 1906; carried out itinerant protests in Newcastle and Manchester; also worked in WSPU's Information Department. Initiated pillar-box firing in 1911. Died 4 June 1913 while participating in a protest at the Epsom Derby. Her spectacular funeral, arranged by Grace Roe, is one of the enduring images of the WSPU campaign.

Sources: *WSM*; *NDNB*; Colmore, *The Life of Emily Davison*; Stanley with Morley, *The Life and Death of Emily Wilding Davison.*

Miss Dawson   Organised in Coventry 1909. No further information traced.

Miss Dallas   Organised at headquarters 1909. No further information traced.

***Mrs Flora Drummond** (1878–1949)   Born Manchester, daughter of Francis Gibson, a tailor, and Sarah Drummond. Family returned to Isle of Arran; Flora studied there and at service school in Glasgow. Qualified as postmistress but was considered below the regulation height for the job. Married Joseph Percival Drummond, a journeyman upholsterer. Returned to Manchester, and became involved in ILP and joined WSPU late 1905; appointed organiser December 1906. In charge of all local unions, she arranged many of the WSPU's demonstrations and pageants, and ran campaigns aimed at recruiting working women into the WSPU. Adopted a 'uniform' of cap, sash and epaulettes in WSPU colours, and was often known as 'the General'. Complications in her second pregnancy (her first child died in infancy) led to an early prison release. Organised throughout Scotland in 1909, then returned to London. Remained with WSPU in First World War, and helped during Christabel Pankhurst's election campaign. Founded the Women's Guild of Empire, for which she worked for many years. Divorced in 1922; married Alan Simpson, a marine engineer.
Sources: *SA*; *WSM*; *NDNB*; obituaries in *The Times, New York Times, Daily Herald.*

***Miss Una Dugdale** (later Mrs Dugdale Duval; 1880–1975) and **Miss Joan Stratford Dugdale** (later Mrs Cruikshank)   Daughters of Commander Edward Stratford Dugdale. Both educated at Cheltenham Ladies' College and joined WSPU in 1907. Una was active in several by-elections, while Joan assisted in the Worcester by-election in February 1908. During her wedding to Victor Duval of the Men's Political Union for Women's Enfranchisement, Una omitted 'obey' from her wedding vows; subsequently published 'Love and Honour but not Obey', a pamphlet defending her actions. Ran husband's business during First World War, then worked as treasurer of the Suffragette Fellowship. Joan Duval was secretary of the Actresses' Franchise League 1910–1911 and was the author of several published short stories.
Sources: *SA*; *WSM*; *NDNB*; Harrison Tapes.

***Mrs Louise Eates** (1877–1944)   Born Louise Peters, Richmond, Yorkshire; educated Edinburgh Ladies' College. Her GP husband converted her to suffrage after their marriage in 1901. Worked for Women's Industrial Council, joining the WSPU in 1907. Worked mainly with Kensington branch (secretary 1906–10); also involved in Hull by-election. From 1910 to 1912 she and her husband lived abroad, returning to Britain in 1913. Stepped back from public life following birth of daughter. Joined United Suffragists, and became involved with the St Johns Wood Infant Welfare Centre and Day Nursery during First World War. Later lectured for the WEA; secretary of WI branch in Kent and honourary secretary, then president, of Acton Women's Citizens Association.
Source: *WSM*; SFC.

Miss Elliott   Banner secretary, 1913. No further information traced.

*Miss Dorothy Evans (1888–1944)   Born London; daughter of Edward Evans, a builder turned commercial clerk, and Marian Evans. Educated North London Collegiate School, then trained as a PE teacher. Joined WSPU in 1907, and gave up teaching to become an organiser in 1909. Organised in Birmingham 1910–12, worked at headquarters, then in Ireland, in 1913. One of last suffragettes released under amnesty of August 1914. Converted to pacifism in First World War; attempted to attend International Women's Congress in the Hague. Joined the Independent WSPU. Later involved with the Married Women's Association, Women's International League for Peace and Freedom (WILPF), Standing Joint Committee on Industrial Women's Organisations and (as chairman) Six Point Group. Unmarried, Dorothy had a daughter with Emil Davies, a London county councillor.
Sources: *SA*; *WSM*; *NDNB*; M. Whatley, *Dorothy Evans and the Six Point Group* (London: Six Point Group, 1946); Harrison Tapes.

*Miss Caprina Fahey (later Mrs Knight; 1883–?)   Born Capri, daughter of Albert Gilbert, RA, a sculptor. Married Alfred Fahey, an artist, who died leaving her with a young son. Worked as a masseuse and joined WSPU at Hyde Park demonstration in June 1908. Involved as organiser in Middlesex during the January 1910 election campaign, as well as in holiday campaigns. Arrested as Charlotte Hay.
Sources: *VFW*; *WSM*.

Miss Stella Fife   Organised in Reading, March 1911. No further information traced.

*Miss (Susan) Ada Flatman (1876–1952)   Born Suffolk. Heard about the WSPU while travelling abroad, and joined on her return to London late 1907–early 1908. Appointed organiser, working in by-elections, then briefly in Bristol and Aberdeen, then Liverpool (1909–11), Cheltenham and Hereford. Resigned for unspecified reasons in July 1912, but kept links with the suffrage movement. Worked for an American suffrage paper and published in British suffrage press in First World War. Later unsuccessfully sought work with National Women's Party. Worked in Poland with Russian refugees, and attempted to start a suffrage society in South Africa in the 1920s. Tried to establish Women's Peace Party during Second World War, again without success.
Sources: *SA*; *WSM*; SFC; Cowman, *'Mrs Brown'*.

*Miss Lettice Floyd (1865–1934)   Born Berkswell, Warwickshire. Worked as a hospital nurse in childrens' hospital and for some time as under-matron at Bedales School. Joined WSPU in 1908. Met Annie Williams through her early organising work in Bristol, and the two women became companions, organising together in Newcastle, then in Halifax, Huddersfield and Wales. Later involved with the National Council of Women, the WI and the Women's International League; also some contact with Suffragette Fellowship.
Sources: *SA*; *WSM*; *VFW*; SFC.

Mrs Joan Dacre Fox (later Mrs Elam)   Organiser for local unions in 1913. Worked for various government commissions during First World War, then stood unsuccessfully as an Independent in the 1918 election. Joined the BUF in 1934 with her husband and became county women's officer for West Sussex. Interned during the Second World War.
Source: Gottlieb, *Feminine Fascism*.

*Miss Helen Fraser (1881–1979)   Born Leeds, daughter of James Fraser, a tailor's cutter, and Christiana Fraser. Family returned to Scotland, where James established a wholesale clothing firm. Attended Higher Grade School, Glasgow, then worked as an artist. Joined WSPU in 1906. Helped in Huddersfield by-election, and then sent to Scotland as organiser. Resigned Summer 1908, having found her committee difficult to work with. Employed by NUWSS until First World War. Supported Mrs Fawcett's view of the war and worked for the National War Savings Committee and the Board of Agriculture, before undertaking a speaking tour in the USA which inspired her book *Women and War Work*. Later promoted the need for women MPs and stood unsuccessfully as a National Liberal three times. Married and emigrated to Australia, where she remained in touch with several ex-suffragettes.
Sources: *WSM*; SFC; *NDNB*; Helen Fraser Moyes, *A Woman in a Man's World*.

Miss Fraser Smith   Organised in Dundee, November 1910. No further information traced.

*Miss Violet Friedlaender (c. 1879–1950)   Joined WSPU in 1908 and helped organise a holiday campaign in Lowestoft in the summer of 1909. A published novelist and poet after First World War.
Source: *WSM*.

*Miss Theresa Garnett (1888–1966)   Born Leeds, daughter of Joshua Garnett, an iron planer, and Frances Theresa Garnett. Educated at a convent school, and spent some time as a teacher. Joined the WSPU in 1906–7 and worked as an organiser in itinerant militant protests and as district organiser in Camberwell. Trained as nurse at London hospital in 1912; nursed at the Front with the Civil Hospital Reserve in First World War, and was mentioned in dispatches 'for gallant and distinguished services in the field' in 1916. Later involved with the International Alliance of Women for Suffrage and Equal Citizenship, the Six Point Group and the Suffragette Fellowship. Edited the Women's Freedom League's *Bulletin*.
Sources: *WSM*; *CAW*; *NDNB*; Obituary, *International Women's News*.

Miss Olive Garrett   Organised in Reading and Leeds. No further information traced.

Mrs Eleanor Penn Gaskell (née Lindsay; c. 1861–1973)   Involved in social work and with the RSPCA. Joined WSPU in 1908 and organised in Middlesex in the January 1910 election campaign; was involved with the Suffragettes of the WSPU during First World War.
Source: *WSM*.

*Miss Mary Gawthorpe (later Mrs Sanders; 1881–1973)   Born Leeds, daughter of John Gawthorpe, a leather worker, and Annie, née Mountain. Pupil teacher, took university degree as extension student. Joined ILP and Leeds Suffrage Society, and became organiser for Women's Labour League, resigning in 1906 to work for the WSPU. Was on the WSPU national committee, and organised its Lancashire campaign, also undertaking much itinerant work. Resigned 1911 following prolonged illness; briefly co-edited *Freewoman* but disagreed with direction of paper. Attempted to organise independent mass hunger strike of women to secure vote. Went on family visit to USA in First World War and recommended suffrage work for New York State Women's Suffrage Party. Later worked with Cook County Labour Party, Illinois, National Consumers' League, League of Mutual Aid and Amalgamated Clothing Workers of America. Married an American, John Sanders, in 1921. Ceased most active political work but continued to support many radical causes. In 1930s worked actively to promote Sylvia Pankhurst's *The Suffragette Movement* and became involved with the Suffragette Fellowship.
Sources: *SA*; *WSM*; *DLB*; *NDNB*; Dora Marsden Papers; SFC; Mary Gawthorpe Papers; Gawthorpe, *Uphill to Holloway*; Holton, *Suffrage Days*.

*Miss Clara Giveen (later Mrs Betty Brewster; 1887–1967)   Born Cooldargh, Coleraine; daughter of Captain B. M. Giveen and Alice Giveen. Clara joined the WSPU in November 1910, incensed at the treatment of women on Black Friday. Organised in Norwich, Bexhill and Hastings, and also for itinerant militant protests. Married Philip Brewster, sister of suffragette Bertha Brewster in 1914. Later involved in Peaslake Women's Institute.
Sources: *SA*; TNA; Overton and Mant, *A Suffragette Nest*.

Miss Eleanor Glidewell (c. 1889–1966)   Born London, daughter of Arthur Glidewell, a tobacco packer. She missed the first Albert Hall meeting because she was taking exams, but volunteered for the next deputation. Organiser in Leeds, 1913. Had some later contact with former suffragette friends.
Sources: *VFW*; *CAW*.

Miss B Goldingham   Organised in Eastbourne, March 1914. No further information traced.

Miss Grant   Organised in Dundee, October 1913. No further information traced.

Miss Green   Organised in Leicester, January 1914. No further information traced.

Miss Elizabeth Grew (later Elizabeth Grew Bacon;?–1959?)   Organised in Birmingham, Stafford, then Barrow and Whitehaven, and arranged first commemorations for Emily Wilding Davison before First World War. Later emigrated to America, and remained in touch with Grace Roe.
Sources: *VFW*; Harrison Tapes; Nellie Hall Humpherson Papers.

*Mrs Elsa Gye (1881–1943)   Born London, educated Croydon High School and Guildhall. Joined WSPU in 1907, and organised political and election campaigns in Nottingham, Devon, Derby, Camberwell and Peckham. Married Will Bullock

(later Gye), a doctor she met when organising in Nottingham, and they had three sons. Later secretary of the Suffragette Fellowship.
Sources: *WSM; VFW;* SFC.

*Miss Florence Haig (1856–1952)   Daughter of James Haig, a Scottish barrister. Worked as an artist but took time out to organise for the WSPU in Chelsea during the January 1910 election campaign. Attended founding meeting of the East London Federation of Suffragettes (ELFS) but remained with the official WSPU as secretary until at least 1916. Was pallbearer at Emmeline Pankhurst's funeral. Bequeathed suffrage material to the Suffragette Fellowship.
Sources: *WSM;* Florence Haig Papers, SFC.

Miss Cicely Hale (1884–1981)   Born London, daughter of a GP. Educated at home, trained as a secretary then joined the WSPU and went to work for the information department at Clements Inn. Typesetter for *Britannia* in First World War, left in 1916 uncertain about its views on the war. Trained as a health visitor and wrote the 'Baby Circle' for *Woman's Own*. Worked for Girl Guides' Association, 1947–68.
Sources: *WSM; CAW; NDNB,* Hale, *A Good Long Time.*

*Miss Nellie Hall (later Mrs Humpherson; 1895–?)   Born Manchester, daughter of Leonard Hall and Martha (Pattie) Hall. Her parents were ILP activists, and Pattie was one of the WSPU's founder members. Joined WSPU as a schoolgirl, and helped at the Birmingham office then at headquarters as prisoners' secretary. Worked for the Post Office and as a welfare officer in a munitions plant in First World War. She was Emmeline Pankhurst's agent during her 1928 election campaign and carried a flag at her funeral. Later emigrated to Canada and was on the Board of the Joint Committee for Penal Reform for Women (Ontario) and the Association of the Women Electors of Toronto.
Sources: *WSM; CAW;* Mitchell Collection; Nellie Hall Humpherson Papers.

Miss A Hambling   Worked at headquarters, often organised large-scale militancy such as window-smashing.
Sources: *VFW;* Janie Allan Papers.

*Miss Evelyn Hambling (?–1955)   A college graduate, organised in Coventry then Belfast (as Edwardina Carson) with Dorothy Evans. Took up journalism during First World War and wrote for *Time and Tide,* as well working as assistant editor of the *Vote;* also wrote plays. Bedridden for last eight years of life, but continued writing.
Sources: *CAW;* Obituary, *Women's Bulletin.*

Nurse Harmar   Co-organiser in Retford in 1910. No further information traced.

Miss V Hartley   Organiser in Tunbridge Wells, February 1914. No further information traced.

*Mrs Alice Hawkins (1863–1947)   Born Stafford, daughter of Henry Riley. Married Alfred Hawkins, who became active in MLWS, with whom she had 7 children (5 survived). Worked for ILP and Women's Labour League; became secretary of Leicester WSPU and was effectively local organiser; was also president of the Women Boot and Shoe Makers' Union.
Sources: SA; VFW; WSM.

*Miss Gladys Hazel (1880–1959)   Born Sheerness, daughter of James Hazel, a naval officer, and Katherine Hazel. District organiser in Birmingham, Leicester and Bristol. Some contact with the Suffragette Fellowship.
Source: CAW.

Miss Margaret Hewitt   Worked on election and itinerant campaigns, Bermondsy, Weymouth, and Burnley 1909. No further information traced.

Miss Mary Home   Ran the information department at WSPU headquarters, 1908–13. No further information traced.

*Miss Elsie Howey (1884–1963)   Born Finningley Rectory, Nottinghamshire daughter of Reverend Thomas Howey and Emily Howey. Joined WSPU with (widowed) mother and her sister, Marie, in December 1907; organised in Plymouth, then the west of England.
Sources: SA; WSM; NDNB.

Miss Violet Hughes (c. 1894–1954)   Born Altrincham, daughter of William Hughes, fire insurance clerk, and Eliza Hughes. Pupil teacher; organised in Lancashire, 1911.

Miss Jarvis   Organised for elections in Fulham, Surrey and Putney. No further information traced.

Miss Gabrielle Jeffrey (1886–1940)   Born Devon, educated at the Convent of the Religious of the Cross, Hampshire. Joined WSPU in 1909 and organised in Newport. Founded the Catholic Women's Suffrage Society (later the St Joan's Social and Political Alliance) in 1911. Worked for clerk to Middlesex County Council in First World War, then in maternity and child welfare work for the remainder of her working life.
Sources: WSM; Obituary, The Times.

*Miss Maud Joachim (1869–1947)   Daughter of a wool merchant, educated Girton College, Cambridge. Joined WSPU in 1907. Organised for Worcester by-election and was assistant organiser in Bedford (1910) and Aberdeen (1912), and worked in press department at headquarters. Joined ELFS in First World War and helped with Sylvia Pankhurst's anti-fascist campaigns in the 1930s.
Sources: WSM; VFW

*Miss Helen Jollie   Organised in Kingston, February 1912, moving to Aberdeen, then Liverpool, 1913–14. No further information traced.

Miss Violet Key Jones (c. 1883–?)   Born County Kildare; daughter of Hariet Jones. Family moved to York where Violet became WSPU organiser, working there and in Doncaster.
Sources: *VFW*; Seymour Pearson Scrapbook.

Dr Helena Jones (c. 1870–?)   Born Conway, entered Church of England sister-hood at 18. Worked in prison mission and left to study medicine in London, 1895, graduating in 1901. Medical officer in a lunatic asylum, then Greenwich Infirmary, and subsequently Medical Officer King's Norton Education Board. Honorary organiser in Halifax from 1912. Later involved in Votes for Women Fellowship and Suffragettes of the WSPU.
Sources: *VFW*; *Suffragette News Sheet*.

Miss Elizabeth Jordan (?–1960)   Worked in WSPU offices. No further information traced.

*Miss Gladice Keevil (later Mrs Rickford; 1884–1959)   Born London, educated at Frances Mary Buss School and Lambeth Art College. Worked in France and USA as governess, then joined WSPU in 1907 and was appointed organiser spring 1908. Organised in Rossendale Valley and Hull by-elections, then appointed district organiser for Midlands, 1908–9. Undertook further itinerant campaigns, then suffered health breakdown. Married in 1913.
Sources: *VFW*; *WSM*.

*Miss Annie Kenney (later Mrs Taylor; 1879–1953)   Born Lancashire, one of the daughters of Horatio Nelson Kenney, a cotton minder, and Ann Kenney. Began mill work at 10, becoming involved in socialism, trade union work and then suf-frage. Appointed organiser c.1905; worked full-time for WSPU in Lancashire and Yorkshire, in Bristol 1907–12, and at headquarters, effectively taking charge during Christabel Pankhurst's exile. Remained with WSPU during First World War. Later studied theosophy. Married James Taylor, an engineer, in 1920.
Sources: *SA*; *WSM*; *NDNB*; Kenney Papers; F. Pethick Lawrence, *Annie Kenney: A Character Sketch*; Kenney, *Memories of a Militant*.

*Miss Nell Kenney (1880–1953)   Sister of Annie and Jessie, she began work in a factory but left due to ill-health and found work in a shop. Appointed organiser in 1907 and worked in north-east England, Midlands and Plymouth.
Sources: *CAW*; Kenney Papers.

Miss Jessie Kenney (1887–1985)   Sister of Annie and Nell, she began work in a cotton mill, but qualified as typist through part-time study. Appointed Mrs Pethick Lawrence's secretary at the age of 19, then became WSPU organiser, charged with arranging publicity and militancy from London. A lung infection forced her to take time out and she visited Switzerland in 1913, moving to live with Christabel Pankhurst in Paris and travelling incognito with messages to the *Suffragette*'s printers in Scotland. Remained with Pankhursts throughout First World War and visited Russia with Mrs Pankhurst in 1917. She became secretary of the Women's Party then went to Paris, working for the American Red Cross.

Became first woman to qualify as a ship's radio officer but her sex precluded an appointment, so she worked as a ship's steward instead, then as secretary of one of the first comprehensive schools.

Sources: *WSM*; Kenney, 'The flame and the flood'.

*Miss Harriet Roberta Kerr (1859–1940)   Born Sussex, daughter of an architect. Ran her own typing and secretarial business which she gave up to manage the WSPU's general office. Never actively militant but was arrested along with department heads in 1913. Mrs Pankhurst permitted her to secure her release from prison by agreeing to keep the peace so that she might nurse a sick friend. Took no further part in the campaign but raised money for the impoverished Mrs Pankhurst just before the latter's death.

Sources: *WSM*; SFC; Agnes Lake Papers.

Miss Esther Knowles (?–fl. 1961)   Friend of the Pethick Lawrences. Passed the civil service exams but took a job at Clements Inn instead. Worked in the office until the outbreak of war. Was Emmeline Pethick Lawrence's election worker in 1918.

Source: *CAW*.

*Miss Agnes Lake (Mrs Whatmough)   Wife of Dr William Whatmough. Worked at headquarters, charged largely with selling advertising space.

Sources: Agnes Lake Papers; TNA, DPP/1/19.

*Miss Aeta Lamb (c. 1887–1928)   Born Demerara, British Guiana, daughter of a botanist in the Government Secretariat and granddaughter of General Henry Nicoll. Returned to England on her father's death and spent a short time at Notting Hill High School. Qualified as a teacher, but was unhappy in the work. Joined WSPU in 1906. Organised in west of England then went to headquarters where she remained until 1914 working in the information department. Worked in various war depots during First World War, then underwent cookery training, but failed to find congenial work. Died of cancer in 1928.

Sources: *WSM*; 'Aeta Lamb', tyspescript biography, SFC.

Miss Aimee Law   Organised in Droitwich election campaign, January 1910. No further information traced.

*Mrs Mary Leigh (née Brown; 1885–fl. 1978)   Born Manchester. Worked as a teacher before her marriage to a builder. Joined WSPU c. 1906–7 and became full-time organiser, engaged mainly in itinerant militant work. She and Edith New were first suffragette stone-thrower. Organised in Dublin 1912, where she was sentenced to five years in prison for firing a theatre, but was released on licence. Critical of WSPU leaders and moved towards the ELFS. Thrown out of a WSPU meeting for heckling during First World War. Also worked as ambulance driver. Later involved in socialist and pacifist groups, and would make annual pilgrimage to Emily Wilding Davison's grave.

Sources: *WSM*; *NDNB*; *VFW*; Arncliffe Sennett Collection; Mitchell Collection.

*Miss Geraldine Lennox (1883–1958)   Born Cork, daughter of Edward Dawson

Lennox. Educated at Trinity Church School, Cork, joining WSPU in 1909. Worked at headquarters and was sub-editor of the *Suffragette*, then returned to Cork in 1914 as organiser. Worked with a hospital unit in France in First World War. Later ran a secretarial bureau and was involved with the Women's Pioneer Housing Association, the Six Point Group, the Women's Auxilliary Service and the SF.
Sources: *SA*; *WSM*; SFC; *CAW*.

Miss Gwenllian Lewis Organised in Bournemouth. No further information traced.

*Lady Constance Lytton (1869–1923) Born Vienna, daughter of Edward, first Earl of Lytton, and Edith, Lady Lytton. Joined WSPU in 1909, took salaried post. Famously imprisoned disguised as working-class suffragette Jane Warton, and forcibly fed despite a heart condition. She suffered strokes between 1911 and 1912 and wrote most of her book *Prisons and Prisoners* with her left hand, remaining a semi-invalid until her death.
Sources: *SA*; *WSM*; *NDNB*; Lytton, *Prisons and Prisoners*; Balfour Papers; *Letters of Constance Lytton*, ed. B. Balfour.

Miss Florence Macaulay (1862–1945) Book-seller's daughter who went to Somerville College, Oxford, on a scholarship but had to leave when her father died. Taught in various schools and in an orphanage, then returned to Somerville, but again left through lack of funds and returned to teaching. Joined WSPU in 1907 and organised in Edinburgh in1909, and Thanet and Canterbury in 1910.
Sources: *VFW*; *WSM*.

Miss MacLean Organised in Dundee, 1909, No further information traced.

*Miss Elsie Mackenzie A civil engineer's daughter, was employed as a hospital nurse then as a worker in the slums, before becoming an organiser in Cardiff 1909, Monmouthshire 1909 and Lewisham (election) 1910.
Source: *VFW*.

Miss Cynthia Maguire (1889–1966) Born London, daughter of Sidney Maguire, stockbroker, and Helen Maguire. Co-organised Clerks WSPU with Phyllis Ayrton. Remained close to the Pankhursts and organised for the Women's Party during First World War.
Sources: *SA*; *WSM*.

*Mrs Mildred Ella Mansel (1868–1942) Born Roehampton, daughter of Arthur E. Guest and Adeline Mary Guest (later Mrs Chapman). Married Colonel J. D. Mansell of Smedmore in 1888, with whom she had three children. Founded the Mid-Somerset Competitive Festival which she ran until 1910. Joined WSPU 1909 and organised in Bath 1910. Rented a 'safe flat' in London during Christabel Pankhurst's exile and carried messages from London to Paris. Later secretary of the British Confederation of the Arts.
Sources: *SA*; *WSM*.

*Miss Catherine Margesson   Daughter of Sir Mortimer Margesson and WSPU member Lady Isabel Margesson. Graduated from Newnham College, Cambridge. Joined WSPU 1909, and organised in Reigate and Reading.

*Miss Charlotte Malcolm Lester Markwick (1886–?)   Born Karachi, India. Joined WSPU in 1909. Appointed organiser 1911; worked in Wandsworth and Dulwich then Warwickshire and Shropshire.
Sources: *SA*.

*Miss Dora Marsden (1882–1960)   Born Marsden, Yorkshire, daughter of Fred Marsden, woollen-waste manufacturer, and Hannah Marsden. Father went to work in USA, leaving family impoverished. Dora was a pupil teacher, then won a scholarship to Owen's College, Manchester, where she joined the WSPU, giving up teaching for organising in 1909. Worked in Manchester and north-west Lancashire, then as district organiser in Southport, resigning January 1911. Briefly worked for WFL, then founded the *Freewoman*, the *New Freewoman* and then the *Egoist*. Later devoted herself to philosophical writing and lived as a semi-recluse at 'Seldom Seen' in the Lake District. Admitted to Crichton Hospital, Dumfries after a breakdown in 1935, remaining there until her death.
Sources: *WSM*; *NDNB*; Les Garner, *A Brave and Beautiful Spirit: Dora Marsden, 1882–1960* (Avebury: Gower Publishing, 1990); Dora Marsden Papers, Princeton University.

*Miss Charlotte Marsh (1887–1961)   Born Northumberland, daughter of Arthur Hardwick Marsh, watercolourist, and Ellen Marsh. Educated St Margaret's School, Newcastle upon Tyne, and Roseneath, Wrexham, then spent a year in Bordeaux. One of the first women to train as a sanitary inspector, but took up WSPU organising instead, working in Nottingham, Yorkshire, Oxford and Portsmouth. Was a motor mechanic, Land Girl and Lloyd George's chauffeuse during First World War. Disagreed with WSPU line on the war and was involved with the Independent Suffragettes. Later worked for the WILPF and did social work in San Francisco. Returned to England and worked for the Public Assistance Department of London County Council and with the Six Point Group.
Sources: *SA*; *WSM*; *NDNB*; Lawson, *Memories of Charlotte Marsh*; Obituary, *The Times*.

*Mrs Nellie Martel (?1885–1940)   Born Cornwall. Family emigrated to Australia where she became involved with the Labour movement and the Australian suffrage movement; stood unsuccessfully for the Australian Parliament. Came to England in 1904 and became involved in WSPU. Organised itinerant campaigns throughout Britain c. 1906–8. Appears to have left WSPU late 1908. Was in UK for a celebratory dinner in 1920.
Sources: *VFW*; *WSM*.

*Mrs Rosamund Massy (1870–1947)   Daughter of Lady Knyvett and Colonel Massy of the Dragoon Guards. Took part in various itinerant and election campaigns c. 1908–14. Helped Mrs Pankhurst's election campaign in 1928.
Sources: *SA*; *WSM*; *VFW*; SFC.

*Miss Winifred Mayo (later Winifred Monk-Mason; c. 1870–1967)   Born India. Educated privately then at Italia Conti Dramatic School. An actress, she worked at WSPU headquarters and served on the executive committee of Actresses' Franchise League and, during First World War, the committee of the British Women's Hospital. Later involved with the Six Point Group, Open Door Council, Equal Rights International and the SF.
Sources: *SA, WSM.*

*Mrs Hannah Mitchell (1872–1956)   Born Derbyshire. Worked as dressmaker before marriage to Gibbon Mitchell, a shop assistant. Became involved in the socialist movement and was an early member of the WSPU; organiser in 1906. Left WSPU after suffering a nervous breakdown in 1907, then joined the WFL and worked as an organiser again. Worked for the No-Conscription Fellowship and the WFL in First World War. ILP councillor in Manchester 1924–35 and as magistrate 1926–46. Some involvement in SF.
Sources: *WSM: NDNB*; Mitchell Papers; Mitchell, *The Hard Way Up.*

*Miss Lilias Mitchell (1884–1940)   Born Edinburgh, daughter of a timber merchant. Joined WSPU 1907–8. Organised in Edinburgh then in Newcastle 1911–12 and Birmingham 1913. Later secretary of the Edinburgh and South YWCA and a member of the local Women Citizen's Association.
Sources: *SA; WSM;* Leneman, *A Guid Cause;* memoir, private collection.

*Miss Edith Bessie New (1877–?)   Born Swindon, Wiltshire, daughter of James Frederick New and Isabella New. Trained as a pupil teacher and gained certificate from Stockwell College, then taught in East Greenwich and Deptford. Joined WSPU in 1906. She and Mary Leigh were the first suffragette 'window-smashers'. Appointed organiser 1908, district organiser in Newcastle and also in Leicester.
Sources: *SA; WSM.*

Miss Nourse   Organiser in Marylebone during January 1910 election. No further information traced.

*Miss Adela Pankhurst (later Mrs Walsh; 1885–1961)   Daughter of Richard and Emmeline Pankhurst. Trained as a pupil teacher, then worked in an elementary school. Began organising in summer 1906 and worked in Leeds, Yorkshire, Aberdeen, Scarborough and Sheffield. Gave up organising through ill-health in 1912, then trained as gardener before emigrating to Australia to work for the Women's Political Association (later Women's Peace Army). After First World War was involved in socialist politics, then the Australian Communist Party. Thereafter moved to the right politically, helping to found the Australian Woman's Guild of Empire. Interned during Second World War for her pro-Japanese views.
Sources: *WSM; NDNB*; Mitchell Papers; Pankhurst Walsh Papers; Harrison Tapes; V. Coleman, *Adela Pankhurst: The Wayward Suffragette 1885–1961* (Melbourne: Melbourne University Press, 1996).

*Miss (later Dame) Christabel Pankhurst (1880–1958)   Born Manchester, daughter of Emmeline and Richard Pankhurst. Educated Southport High School

for Girls, Manchester High School for Girls, then studied law at University of Manchester. Was chief organiser for WSPU throughout its existence. Stood unsuccessfully as Women's Party candidate at Smethwick by-election after the First World War, but then withdrew from politics and spent much of remainder of her life in America working as a Second-Day Adventist.
Sources: *SA; WSM; NDNB;* C. Pankhurst, *Unshackled;* S. Pankhurst, *The Suffragette Movement.*

*Mrs Emmeline Pankhurst (1858–1928)   Born Manchester, daughter of Robert Goulden, a cotton printer, and Jane Goulden. Married radical barrister Richard Pankhurst and had long involvement in radical and socialist politics before founding WSPU in 1903. Worked continually as itinerant speaker–organiser for WSPU until end of First World War. Parliamentary candidate for Conservative Party in Whitechapel in 1928.
Sources: *SA; WSM; NDNB;* E. Pankhurst, *My Own Story;* E. S. Pankhurst, *The Suffragette Movement;* Sylvia Pankhurst Papers.

*Miss Frances Mary Parker (1875–1924)   Born New Zealand, daughter of Frances Kitchener and Harry Rainy Parker. Educated Newnham College, Cambridge, then taught in France and Aukland. Joined WSPU on return to England in 1908. Appointed organiser in 1912 and worked in Glasgow, then in Dundee. In First World War worked for the WFL, then the Women's Army Auxiliary Corps, for her service to which she received an OBE. Died in Archacon, France.
Sources: *SA; WSM; NDNB.*

*Mrs Jane Pascoe   A Cornish woman, Falmouth organiser 1912.

*Miss Alice Paul (1885–1977)   Born New Jersey. Educated at Swarthmore College, New York School of Philanthropy, University of Pennysylvania and in England at University of Birmingham. Moved to London to do settlement work and study at the London School of Economics. Joined WSPU in 1908 and worked as itinerant organiser. Left for USA in 1912 and continued suffrage work there, being one of the founders of the National Women's Party.
Sources: *SA; WSM; VFW;* Mitchell Papers.

*Miss Dorothy Pethick (1881–1970)   Born Somerset, sister of Emmeline Pethick Lawrence,. Educated at Cheltenham Ladies' College and trained in social work at a university settlement, thereafter becoming superintendent of a girls' club in Nottingham. Attended WSPU meetings from 1906 and became an organiser 1907. Left when her sister was expelled, and joined women's police patrols during First World War and also United Suffragists. Later secretary for the Rudolf Steiner School in Hampstead.
Sources: *VFW; WSM.*

*Mrs Emmeline Pethick Lawrence (1867–1954)   Born Bristol, daughter of Henry Pethick, a businessman. Educated at a boarding school in Devizes then a dayschool in Weston Super Mare where her family then lived. Worked for Methodist mission in London then founded Espérance Girls' Club with Mary Neal. Married

Frederick Lawrence, editor of the *Labour Record* and a friend of Keir Hardie, who introduced her to Emmeline Pankhurst. She joined the WSPU in 1906 becoming treasurer and co-editor of its paper. Expelled in 1912. Formed Votes for Women Fellowship and then became involved with the United Suffragists. Converted to pacifism in First World War and was involved with the WILPF. Stood unsuccessfully as a Labour candidate in Rusholme, Manchester, in 1918, then returned to feminist politics. Involved with the Open Door Council, Six Point Group, National Union of Societies for Equal Citizenship and the WFL.
Sources: *SA*; *WSM*; *NDNB*; E. Pethick Lawrence, *My Part*.

*Miss Mary Phillips (1880–1969)   Born Hampshire, daughter of Dr W. Fleming Phillips, MB CM, and Elizabeth Louisa Phillips. Raised in Glasgow. Joined WSPU in March 1907; became organiser June 1908, and undertook itinerant work before becoming district organiser in Liverpool, Cornwall, Yorkshire, Bradford and Plymouth. Sacked by Christabel Pankhurst in 1913, then worked for the ELFS and for the United Suffragists during First World War. Later worked for the WILPF and the Save the Children Fund, as well as editing a daily news service for the brewing trade 1928–55. Worked in publications department of the National Council of Social Service after retirement, also involved in the Six Point Group.
Sources: *SA*; *WSM*; *NDNB*; Mary Phillips Papers, private collection; M. Phillips, *The Militant Suffrage Campaign in Perspective* (London: Edward O. Beck, 1957)

Miss Pridden   Organised in Bristol 1912 and Edinburgh 1913. No further information traced.

*'Miss Catherine Reid' (Arabella Scott, later Mrs Colville-Reeves; 1886–fl. 1946)   Born Argyllshire, daughter of Captain William Scott of Indian Army. Joined WFL c.1908, then became increasingly involved in militancy. While on the run under the 'Cat and Mouse' Act organised for WSPU in Brighton as Catherine Reid. Later emigrated to Australia and was involved in the Australian Suffragette Fellowship.
Sources: *SA*; *WSM*.

Miss Richards   Organised in Oxford, May 1910. No further information traced.

*Miss Mary Richardson (1882/3–1961)   Born in Britain, but raised by her Canadian mother in Belleville, Ontario, where her grandfather was a bank manager. Returned to Britain, and studied art and did some freelance journalism. Joined WSPU after Black Friday and went to work at headquarters, also undertaking clandestine itinerant campaigns. Worked with ELFS in First World War. Published a novel, *Matilda and Marcus*, and two volumes of poetry, and edited the Young Women's Christian Association's magazine. Later tried unsuccessfully to get into Parliament as a Labour candidate in 1922, 1924 and 1931. Joined Oswald Mosley's New Party, then the British Union of Fascists, working for the latter 1934–35.
Sources: *NDNB*; *WSM*; Richardson, *Laugh a Defiance!*; Gottlieb, *Feminine Fascists*; Kean, 'Some problems of constructing and reconstructing a suffragette's life'.

*Mrs Edith Rigby (1872–1950)   Born Preston, daughter of Alexander Clement Rayner, a surgeon, and Mary Rayner. Educated at Preston High School and Penrhos College, north Wales. Married Charles Rigby, a doctor, in 1893. Prior to joining WSPU was involved in a textile workers' recreation club, a ladies' public health society, the ILP, and the WLL (she resigned from its national executive committee in 1907). Never an official organiser but undertook much itinerant militancy, including placing a bomb in the Liverpool Stock Exchange. Involved in the Women's Land Army and the Independent WSPU during First World War. Later interested in environmental concerns and in the works of Rudolph Steiner.
Sources: *SA*; *WSM*; *NDNB*; Mary Gawthorpe Papers; Hesketh, *My Aunt Edith*.

*Miss Gladys Roberts (1888–?)   Born Bradford. Joined WSPU in 1907, appointed organiser in 1908, working mainly in Nottingham until 1912.
Source: *SA*.

*Miss Grace Roe (1885–1979)   Born London. Educated at co-educational boarding school, going on to art school. Joined WSPU in 1908 and began organising in 1909; was 'third in command', running the Union during Annie Kenney's imprisonment, when Christabel Pankhurst left for Paris. Remained working for WSPU in the war, then studied theosophy with Annie Kenney. In 1921 she travelled to Canada, then the USA, with Christabel Pankhurst and helped her with her Second-Day Adventist work, also doing some social work, then running a bookshop and library in Santa Barbara. She remained close to Christabel Pankhurst and helped publish *Unshackled* after her death.
Sources: *WSM*; *CAW*; Harrison Tapes.

*Mrs Annot Robinson (née Wilkie; 1874–1925)   Born Scotland, the daughter of a draper. Attended Montrose Academy, then worked as a pupil teacher after taking external courses at University of St Andrews. Joined the WSPU in 1906. Also involved in ILP and married its Manchester secretary Sam Robinson in 1908; appointed WSPU organiser shortly afterwards. Left WSPU and worked as part-time organiser for WLL from 1910, returning to suffrage work for the NUWSS after the election fighting fund had been set up. Became a pacifist during First World War and from 1918 was organiser for the WILPF. Later separated from husband and returned to teaching.
Sources: *WSM*; Annot Robinson Papers, Manchester Central Library; C. Collette, *For Labour and for Women: The Women's Labour League, 1906–1918* (Manchester: Manchester University Press, 1989); Harrison Tapes.

*Miss Rona Robinson (c. 1885–fl. 1931)   Daughter of Jessie Robinson. Attended University of Manchester on a Dora Muir Scholarship, where she took first-class honours in chemistry, then taught at the secondary school and pupil teacher centre, Altrincham, taking an MSC through evening study in 1907. Appointed organiser 1909, stopping shortly after her friend Dora Marsden. Did some work with the *Freewoman*, then applied for a postgraduate course in home economics in London. Later returned to Manchester and kept in touch with WSPU friends.
Sources: *VFW*; Gawthorpe Papers; Garner, *A Brave and Beautiful Spirit*.

*Miss Bertha Ryland (1882–fl. 1963)   Joined WSPU in 1908, becoming honorary assistant organiser in Birmingham in 1909, then worked in Stoke on Trent in 1911. Some involvement with old suffragette friends in 1930s and 1940s.
Source: *WSM*.

*Mrs Beatrice Helen Sanders (née Martin; c. 1874–1932)   Married to a London County Council alderman who was also involved with the ILP and the Fabian Society. Joined the WSPU in 1907 and worked at headquarters, becoming financial secretary by 1913.
Sources: SFC; *WSM*.

Miss Isabel Seymour (1882–fl. 1973)   Born Middlesex, daughter of Philip Seymour, who became collector for borough hospital in Birkenhead, and Mary Seymour. Joined WSPU in 1906, working as hospitality secretary at headquarters. Undertook speaking tours of Germany, Austria, Belgium and Canada for the WSPU. She was a friend of the Pethick Lawrences, but remained with the WSPU until at least 1913. Later spent some time in Canada then returned to England and was elected to Hampshire County Council.
Sources: SA; *WSM*; SFC; Raeburn, *The Militant Suffragettes*.

*Miss Evelyn Sharp (later Nevinson; 1869–1955)   Born London, daughter of John James Sharp, slate merchant, and Jane Sharp, sister of Cecil Sharp, the folk-song expert. Schooled in London and Paris. Published short stories and novels and was a well-known journalist by the time she joined the WSPU in 1906. Undertook several itinerant speaking engagements and worked at WSPU headquarters. After the Pethick Lawrences' expulsion she continued with them and edited *Votes for Women*. Involved with the WILPF and the United Suffragists during First World War.
Sources: *WSM*; Sharp, *Unfinished Adventure*.

Miss Dorothy Shearwood (later Mrs Shearwood Shibbington)   Organised in Dundee in March 1914. Later lived in Canada and founded a music festival in Montreal.
Sources: *VFW*; Nellie Hall Humpherson Papers.

*Miss Marguerite Sidley (1886–?)   Born Nottingham, daughter of John Sidley, a cotton manufacturer's agent, and Lillian Sidley. Came to London in 1888, and was educated at Camden School for Girls then learned typing and shorthand, taking first place in the country in the Royal Society of Arts exam. Worked as office typist and joined WSPU, becoming an organiser in 1907, but poor health forced her to work on itinerant outdoor campaigns until 1908 when, with her mother, she left the WSPU for the WFL, for which she worked until 1916.
Sources: *WSM*; SFC.

*Miss Katharine Douglas Smith   Daughter of Henry Smith, Professor of Surgery, Kings College, London; orphaned at 15. Studied music in Dresden, then followed a musical career before joining the WSPU in 1907. She spoke in Hyde Park in June 1908 and engaged in high-level publicity, driving a bus and a fire

engine around London to advertise the WSPU. Organised in Leicester, October 1909, and Bedford, October 1910, then went to help in the WSPU's press department in 1913, but was dismissed by Christabel Pankhurst for unspecified reasons.
Sources: *SA*; *VFW*.

Miss Olive Smith   Was prisoners' secretary prior to Joan Wickham. No further information traced.

Miss H. Sprott   Organised in Southampton 1913. No further information traced.

*Miss Jessie Stephenson (1873–1966)   Born Lincolnshire. Spent some time in Germany and France teaching English, then worked as secretary to Josephine Butler. Joined WSPU in 1907; appointed organiser when she lost her job in a legal office following arrest. Went to Manchester as district organiser in 1911, but suffered a breakdown and withdrew from public work. Family ostracised her for her suffrage work at the time, but requested that the SF send purple, white and green flowers to her funeral.
Sources: *WSM*; SFC; *CAW*.

Miss C. A. Stuart   Organised in Nottingham 1914. No further information traced.

Miss F. C. Tristram   Organised in Hastings 1914. No further information traced.

*Mrs Mabel Tuke (1871–1962)   Born Plumstead, Kent, daughter of Richard Lear, clerk of works at Woolwich Arsenal, and Emma Lear. Married, briefly, to James Braidwood, a gas engineer, then, in South Africa, to George Tuke, a captain in the South African Constabulary. On his death in 1905 she returned to England, meeting the Pethick Lawrences on the voyage. Joined the WSPU in 1906 and was its official honorary secretary, based at headquarters. Later helped Emmeline and Christabel Pankhurst run tea-rooms in Juan-les-Pins.
Sources: *WSM*; *NDNB*; *CAW*.

*Miss Leonora Tyson (c. 1884–1959)   Daughter of Helen Tyson, organised in Lambeth 1910.
Source: *WSM*

Miss L. M. Underwood   Organised in Glasgow, September 1912. No further information traced.

Miss Vibert   Organised at WSPU headquarters, 1913. No further information traced.

*Miss Olive Walton (1886–1937)   Daughter of Charles Walton, retired wine merchant, and his second wife who had been a missionary. Educated at a small private school and in Germany, at home, by her family. Attended cookery classes, thereafter returning to London to do social work. Joined NUWSS in 1908 and WSPU in 1911, and was appointed organiser, first in Tunbridge Wells, then in

Aberdeen. Joined Women Police Volunteers in First World War and worked with the Royal Irish Constabulary. Later involved with Christian Science and worked as an almoner in a London hospital.
Sources: *SA*; *WSM*; Harrison Tapes.

*Miss Florence Ward (1859 –?)   Born Stapleton, near Bristol. Did social work for Christian organisations for eight years. Joined WSPU in 1908, taking over position as honorary organiser in Walsall in 1912.
Source: *SA*.

Miss A. M. Waters   Was temporary organiser in Bristol 1913. No further information traced.

*Miss Helen Watts (1881–fl. 1965)   Born Sunderland, daughter of the Rev Alan Watts and Ethelinda Watts. Joined WSPU in 1907 and worked as assistant organiser in her home city of Nottingham. Left area in 1911 to nurse in the West Country. Worked for WFL, organising a campaign in Poplar in 1914. Continued nursing, then worked for War Office during First World War. Later emigrated to Canada.
Sources: *SA*; *WSM*; Watts Papers.

*Miss Vera Wentworth (born Jessie Spinks; 1890–1957)   Born London. Worked as shop assistant, joining WSPU in 1908 for which she was an organiser (mainly itinerant work) for three years, leaving to study at University of St Andrews. Published some plays and newspaper articles. Became a committed Christian and joined the Air-Raid Precaution service in Second World War.
Sources: *SA*; *WSM*.

*Miss Margaret West (1884–?)   Born London, daughter of James Ross West. Joined WSPU in 1908, and organised in Norwich, Newcastle and Leicester.
Source: *SA*.

Miss Joan Wickham (later Mrs Joan Hodgson; d. 1966)   Irish origin. Became WSPU prisoners secretary 1913 and organiser in Dublin 1914. No further information traced.
Sources: *CAW*; Wilson, *With All Her Might*.

*Mrs Lillian Dove Wilcox (later Mrs Buckley; 1875–1963)   Born Lilian Dugdale in Bristol to suffragist mother. Joined WSPU c. 1908, a widow,, and took over Annie Kenney's work in 1911. Supported ELFS during First World War; later involved with the SF.
Source: *WSM*.

*Mrs Adeline Redfern Wilde   Born in Hanley, daughter of Frederick and Elizabeth Redfern. Her sisters Emily and Elizabeth were also suffragettes. Joined the WSPU in Birmingham in 1908 and worked in various local campaigns, acting as organiser for her home district of Stoke-on-Trent.
Source: *SA*.

***Miss Annie Williams** (c. 1860–1943)   Born Cornwall, taught in Council schools before joining the WSPU. Gave up post as headmistress to work as organiser and was deployed to Newcastle, Halifax, Huddersfield and Wales. Stayed in the WSPU until the outbreak of war, then took no further part in public life.
Sources: *SA; WSM; VFW.*

Mrs Edith Williams   Relative of Annie Williams, was WSPU organiser for Cornwall 1913.
Source: *VFW.*

***Miss Barbara Wylie** (1862–1954)   Organiser in Glasgow, then worked at headquarters. Later involved in the Women's Party.
Sources: *WSM;* Mitchell Collection.

Select bibliography

Archival collections

Janie Allan Papers, National Library of Scotland
Autograph Letter Collection, Women's Library, London
Jennie Baines Papers, Fryer Library, University of Queensland
Balfour Papers, National Archives of Scotland
Rosa May Billinghurst Papers, Women's Library, London
Teresa Billington Grieg Papers, Women's Library, London
Blathwayt Diaries, Gloucester Record Office
Camellia Collection, Linton Park
Mary Gawthorpe Papers, Tamiment Library, New York
Nellie Hall Humpherson Papers, Birmingham Art Gallery
Henry Devenish Harben Papers, British Library
Brian Harrison, Taped Interviews, The Women's Library, London
Edith Key Papers, West Yorkshire Archives Service
Kenney Papers, University of East Anglia
Dora Marsden Papers, Princeton University
David Mitchell Collection, Museum of London
Hannah Mitchell Papers, Manchester Central Library
The National Archives: Home Office Papers, HO45: Metropolitan Police Papers,
    MEPOL 2; Director of Public Prosecutions Papers, DPP 1/19
Henry Nevinson Papers, Bodleian Library, Oxford
Mrs Seymour Pearson Suffragette Scrapbook, Camellia Collection
Pethick Lawrence Papers, Trinity Hall, Cambridge University
Mary Phillips Papers, Camellia Collection
Annot Robinson Papers, Manchester Central Library
Maude Arncliffe Sennet Collection, British Library
Suffragette Fellowship Collection, Museum of London
Helen Watts Papers, Nottingham Record Office

Newspapers and periodicals

Calling All Women
Clarion
Daily Chronicle
Daily Mail
Daily Mirror
Daily News
Daily Telegraph
Freewoman
Labour Record and Review

Liverpool Daily Post
Manchester Guardian
Radio Times
Spare Rib
Standard
Suffragette
Sunday Times
The Times
Times Higher Educational Supplement
Vote
Votes for Women
Women and Progress
Women's Bulletin
Women's Franchise
Worker

Books

A. J. R. (ed.) *The Suffrage Annual and Women's Who's Who* (London: Stanley Paul, 1913).

Allen, M. S. and Heyneman, J. H. *Woman at the Crossroads (Reminiscences of Mary S. Allen)* (London: Unicorn Press, 1934).

Angerman, A., Binnerman, G., Keunen, A., Poels, V. and Zirkzee, J. (eds) *Current Issues in Women's History* (London: Routledge, 1989).

Bartley, P. *Emmeline Pankhurst* (London: Routledge, 2002).

Campbell, B. *The Iron Ladies: Why Women Vote Tory* (London: Virago, 1987).

Cazalet-Kier, T. *I Knew Mrs Pankhurst* (London: Suffragette Fellowship Collection, n.d.).

Codd, C. *So Rich a Life* (Pretoria: Institute for Theosophical Publicity, 1951).

Colmore, G. *Suffragette Sally* (London: Stanley Paul, 1911).

Colmore, G. *The Life of Emily Davison* (London: Women's Press, 1913).

Cowman, K. *'Mrs Brown Is a Man and a Brother!' Women in Merseyside's Political Organisations, 1890–1920* (Liverpool: Liverpool University Press, 2004)

Crawford, E. *The Women's Suffrage Movement: A Reference Guide 1866–1928* (London: UCL Press, 1999).

Eustance, C., Ryan, J. and Ugolini, L. (eds) *A Suffrage Reader: Charting New Directions in British Suffrage History* (London: Leicester University Press, 2000).

Fulford, R. *Votes for Women* (London: Faber & Faber, 1957).

Gawthorpe, M. *Uphill to Holloway* (Penobscot, Maine: Traversity Press, 1962).

Gullace, N. *The Blood of Our Sons: Men, Women and the Renegotiation of Citizenship during the Great War* (Basingstoke: Macmillan, 2002).

Joannou, M. and Purvis, J. (eds) *The Women's Suffrage Movement: New Feminist Perspectives* (Manchester: Manchester University Press, 1998).

Haig, M. *This Was My World* (London: Macmillan, 1933).

Hale, C. *A Good Long Time* (London: Regency Press, 1973).

Hamilton, C. *Life Errant* (London: J. M. Dent, 1935).

Hannam, J. and Hunt, K. *Socialist Women: Britain, 1890s to 1920s* (London: Routledge, 2002).

Harrison, B. *Peaceable Kingdom: Stability and Change in Modern Britain* (Oxford: Clarendon Press, 1982).

Hesketh, P. *My Aunt Edith* (Preston: Lancashire County Books, 1996 [1992]).

Kenney, A. *Memories of a Militant* (London: Edward Arnold, 1924).

Lawson, M. *Memories of Charlotte Marsh* (London: Suffragette Fellowship, 1961).

Leneman, L. *Martyrs in Our Midst: Dundee, Perth and the Forcible Feeding of Suffragettes* (Dundee: Abertay Historical Society, 1993).

Leneman, L. *A Guid Cause: The Women's Suffrage Movement in Scotland* (Edinburgh: Mercat Press, 1995).

Leneman, L. *The Scottish Suffragettes* (Edinburgh: National Museums of Scotland, 2000).

Lytton, C. with Warton, J. *Prisons and Prisoners: Some Personal Experiences* (London: Heineman, 1914).

McPhee, C. and Fitzgerald, A. (eds) *The Non-Violent Militant: Selected Writings of Teresa Billington Grieg* (London: Women's Source Library, 1987).

McPherson, D. *The Suffragette's Daughter: Betty Archdale, Her Life of Feminism, Cricket, War and Education* (Dural Delivery Centre, New South Wales: Rosenberg Press, 2002).

Mayhall, L. E. N. *The Militant Suffrage Movement: Citizenship and Resistance in Britain, 1860–1930* (Oxford: Oxford University Press, 2003).

Mitchell, D. *The Fighting Pankhursts: A Study in Tenacity* (London: Cape, 1967).

Mitchell, D. *Queen Christabel: A Biography of Christabel Pankhurst* (London: Macdonald & Janes, 1977).

Mitchell, H. *The Hard Way Up* (London: Virago, 1977).

Montefiore, D. B. *From a Victorian to a Modern* (London: E. Archer, 1927).

Morley, A. with Stanley, L. *The Life and Death of Emily Wilding Davison* (London: Women's Press, 1987).

Morrell, C. *Black Friday: Violence Against Women in the Suffrage Movement* (London: Women's Research and Resources Centre Publications, 1981).

Moyes, H. F. *A Woman in a Man's World* (Sydney: Alpha Books, 1971).

Overton, J. and Mant, J. *A Suffragette Nest: Peaslake 1910 and After* (Surrey: Hazeltree Publishing, 1998).

Pankhurst, C. *Unshackled: The Story of How We Won the Vote* (London: Cresset Library, 1987 [1959]).

Pankhurst, E. *My Own Story* (London: Eveleigh Nash, 1914).

Pankhurst, E. S. *The Suffragette* (London: Gay & Hancock, 1911).

Pankhurst, E. S. *The Suffragette Movement* (London: Virago, 1977 [1931]).

Pankhurst, E. S. *The Life of Emmeline Pankhurst: The Suffragette Struggle for Women's Citizenship* (London: T. Werner Laurie, 1935).

Pethick Lawrence, E. *My Part in a Changing World* (London: Gollancz, 1938).

Pethick Lawrence, F. *Annie Kenney: A Character Sketch* (London: Labour Record and Review Pamphlets, n.d. (1907)).

Pethick Lawrence, F. *Fate Has Been Kind* (London: Hutchinson, 1943).

Pugh, M. *The March of the Women: A Revisionist Analysis of the Campaign for Women's Suffrage 1866–1914* (Oxford: Oxford University Press, 2000).

Pugh, M. *The Pankhursts* (London: Penguin, 2001).

Purvis, J. *Emmeline Pankhurst: A Biography* (London: Routledge, 2002).

Purvis, J. and Stanley Holton, S. (eds) *Votes for Women!* (London: Routledge, 2000).

Raeburn, A. (ed.), *The Militant Suffragettes* (London: Michael Joseph, 1973).

Richardson, M. *Laugh a Defiance!* (London: Wiedenfeld & Nicholson, 1953).

Rosen, A. *Rise Up Women! The Militant Campaign of the Women's Social and Political Union, 1903–14* (London: Routledge & Kegan Paul, 1974).

Rover, C. *Women's Suffrage and Party Politics in Britain* (London: Routledge & Kegan Paul, 1967).

Sharp, E. *Hertha Ayrton 1854–1923: A Memoir* (London: Edward Arnold & Co., 1926).

Sharp, E. *Unfinished Adventure* (London: Allan Lane, 1933).

Smith, A. K. *Suffrage Discourse in Britain during the First World War* (Aldershot: Ashgate, 2005).

Stanley Holton, S. *Suffrage Days: Stories from the Women's Suffrage Movement* (London: Routledge, 1996).

Van Wingerden, S. *The Women's Suffrage Movement in Britain 1866–1928* (Basingstoke: Macmillan, 1999).

Wilson. G. *With All Her Might: The Life of Gertrude Harding, Militant Suffragette* (New York: Holmes & Meier, 1998).

Articles and chapters in books

Cowman, K. "'A party between revolution and peaceful persuasion": a fresh look at the United Suffragists', in M. Joannou and J. Purvis (eds) *The Women's Suffrage Movement: New Feminist Perspectives* (Manchester: Manchester University Press, 1998), pp. 77–88.

Cowman, K. "'Crossing the great divide": inter-organisational suffrage relationships on Merseyside, 1895–1914', in C. Eustance, J. Ryan and L. Ugolini (eds) *A Suffrage Reader: Charting Directions in British Suffrage History* (London: Leicester University Press, 2000), pp. 37–52.

Cowman, K., "'Incipient toryism?" The Women's Social and Political Union and the Independent Labour Party, 1903–14', *History Workshop Journal*, 53 (2002), pp. 128–48.

Cowman, K. "'The stonethrowing has been forced upon us": the function of militancy within the Liverpool Women's Social and Political Union, 1906–14', *Transactions of the Historical Society of Lancashire and Cheshire*, 145 (1995). pp. 171–92.

Darby, L. 'Clara Codd: off the platform', *Theosophist*, October 1976.

Hannam, J. "'I had not been to London:" women's suffrage – a view from the regions', in J. Purvis and S. S. Holton (eds) *Votes for Women* (London: Routledge, 2002), pp. 226–45.

Hannam, J. "'Suffragettes are splendid for any work!" The Blathwayt diaries as a source for suffrage history', in C. Eustance, J. Ryan and L. Ugolini (eds) *A Suffrage Reader: Charting New Directions in Suffrage History* (London: Leicester University Press, 2000), pp. 53–68.

Harrison, B. 'The act of militancy: violence and the suffragettes, 1904–14', in B. Harrison, *Peaceable Kingdom: Stability and Change in Modern Britain* (Oxford: Clarendon Press, 1982), pp. 26–81.

Kean, H. 'Some problems of constructing and reconstructing a suffragette's life: Mary Richardson, suffragette, socialist and fascist', *Women's History Review*, 7:4 (1998), pp. 475–93.

Lawrence, J. 'Contesting the male polity: suffragettes and the politics of disruption in Edwardian Britain', in A. Vickery (ed.) *Women, Privilege and Power: British Politics 1750 to the Present* (Stanford, California: Stanford University Press, 2001), pp. 2001–26.

Park, J. 'The British suffrage activists of 1913: an analysis', *Past and Present*, 120 (1988), pp. 147–62.

Smart, M. 'Jennie Baines: suffrage and an Australian connection', in J. Purvis and S. S. Holton (eds) *Votes for Women!* (London: Routledge, 2000), pp. 246–66.

Unpublished typescripts

Anon. 'Aeta Lamb', Museum of London.

Kenney, J. 'The Flame and the Flood', Kenney Papers, University of East Anglia.

McNeill, L. K. Manuscript, National Library of Scotland.

Marshall, E. K. W. 'Suffragette Escapes and Adventures', Museum of London.

Murphy, M. Autobiographical manuscript, People's History Museum, Manchester.

Stephenson, S. J. 'No Other Way', Museum of London.

Walker, S. 'Helen Pethick Lawrence: A Memoir', Women's Library.

Index